THE SOCIAL DYNAMICS OF INFORMATION AND COMMUNICATION TECHNOLOGY

The Social Dynamics of Information and Communication Technology

Edited by

EUGENE LOOS
Utrecht School of Governance, The Netherlands

LESLIE HADDON
London School of Economics, UK

ENID MANTE-MEIJER
Utrecht School of Governance, The Netherlands

Routledge
Taylor & Francis Group

LONDON AND NEW YORK

First published 2008 by Ashgate Publishing

Published 2016 by Routledge
2 Park Square, Milton Park, Abingdon, Oxon OX14 4RN
711 Third Avenue, New York, NY 10017, USA

Routledge is an imprint of the Taylor & Francis Group, an informa business

British Library Cataloguing in Publication Data
The social dynamics of information and communication
technology
    1. Information technology - Social aspects
    2. Telecommunication - Social aspects
    I. Loos, Eugene II. Mante-Meijer, Enid III. Haddon, Leslie
    303.4'83

Library of Congress Cataloging-in-Publication Data
The social dynamics of information and communication technology / [edited by] Eugène Loos, Leslie Haddon and Enid Mante-Meijer.
    p. cm.
    Includes bibliographical references and index.
    ISBN 978-0-7546-7082-7
    1. Communication--Technological innovations. 2. Information technology--Social aspects.
I. Loos, Eugène, 1963- II. Haddon, Leslie. III. Mante-Meijer, E.A., 1939-

    HM851.S633 2008
    303.48'33--dc22

               2008002526

ISBN 13: 978-0-7546-7082-7 (hbk)

Contents

**PART I   DISCIPLINARY INSIGHTS INTO THE SOCIAL
DYNAMICS OF INNOVATION AND DOMESTICATION**

**PART II   THE INTERNET AS A TOOL TO ENABLE USERS TO
ORGANISE EVERYDAY LIFE**

List of Figures

List of Tables

Notes on Editors and Contributors

Editors

Eugène Loos holds a PhD in International Business Communication from Utrecht University in the Netherlands. He is currently a Senior Lecturer in the Utrecht School of Governance at the same university. As a linguist he has conducted research and written several books and articles in the field of organisational (intercultural) communication. Currently his research focuses on the role of digital media related to accessible service delivery for the elderly.

Leslie Haddon teaches part-time at the London School of Economics, where he is currently involved in the project *EUKidsOnline*. He is also a Visiting Research Associate the University of Essex and a Research Associate at the Oxford Internet Institute. For over two decades he has worked chiefly on the social shaping and consumption of information and communication technologies. This has covered computers, games, telecoms, telework, intelligent homes, cable TV and mobile telephony and Internet use. His international projects have led him to develop his current interest in cross-cultural analysis. Haddon has published numerous journal articles and book chapters and has authored, co-authored and co-edited several books.

Enid Mante-Meijer is currently an Emeritus Professor in the Utrecht School of Governance at Utrecht University in the Netherlands. As an (organisational) sociologist, she taught Methods and Techniques of Social Research at Leiden University, and was, until 2003, Senior Researcher at the Dutch Telecom research department, KPN Research. She is also part of the European network COST 298. In 1999–2002 she was project leader of a large European research project, sponsored by Eurescom, on Information and Communication Technology and Users. Since 2005 her main field of research has been on consumers of ICT, both in an individual and institutional context.

Contributors

Hermina Anghelescu earned her MA in Foreign Languages and Literatures (French and English) from the University of Bucharest (Romania) and her MLIS and PhD from the Graduate School of Library and Information Science, University of Texas at Austin (USA). Currently she is an Associate Professor at the Library and Information Science Program, Wayne State University, Detroit, Michigan, USA.

Her publications include co-edited books on library history published by the Center for the Book of the Library of Congress, back-of-the-book and cumulative indexes, and bibliographies. She has published research articles, chapters, dictionary and encyclopedia entries and translations, as well as some fifty book reviews. She is a member of the editorial board of several international periodical publications.

Boldur Bărbat obtained his MSc in Electronic Engineering, as a postgraduate specialised in Programming and has a PhD in Digital Computers ('Politehnica' University Bucharest). Currently he is working as a full Professor at 'Lucian Blaga' University of Sibiu, Romania, Faculty of Sciences, Department of Computer Science and Business Informatics. He is also working at 'Politehnica' University Timişoara, Faculty of Automation and Computers, where he is also advisor for doctoral studies in Computer Science. He has written a variety of books, articles and papers in the field of Artificial Intelligence and Software Engineering and related fields.

John Beckers holds a PhD in Psychology from the Erasmus University of Rotterdam, a Master's degree in Psychology from the University of Amsterdam and an MBA from the University of Oregon, USA. He is also a graduate from the Dutch international business school Nijenrode. He is currently working as a knowledge manager at the Central Office of Maastricht University in the Netherlands. Most of his professional life he has worked in the media industry (newspapers, telecommunication, Internet), more specifically as a manager and consultant in the fields of communication, marketing, training and more recently, e-learning and knowledge creation. He is very interested in the interaction between users and new media and how to support users in innovative ways. As a researcher he has conducted various studies with respect to the psychological dimensions of using e-products and services, in particular looking at the phenomenon of computer anxiety.

Fanny Carmagnat is currently working as a sociologist at France Télécom research centre. She has published studies of the uses of telecommunications devices and services such as public phones, the Internet and mobile phones, as well as on the uses of new means of communications by political activists, by families and by Wifi pioneers.

Alberta Contarello is a Professor of Social Psychology at the University of Padova in Italy. Currently her publications focus on the social construction of knowledge – including with regard to new technologies – social psychology and qualitative research, and social psychology and literary texts.

Julie Deville holds a PhD in Sociology. She is currently teaching at University Paris 8 and in social work schools. Her main research subjects are education, youth, gender and social work.

Leopoldina Fortunati teaches the Sociology of Communication at the Faculty of Education of the University of Udine. She has conducted several research projects in the field of gender studies, cultural processes and communication and information technologies. She is the author of several books and articles. Very active at European level, she has organised several international workshops and conferences. Her works have been published in eleven languages: Bulgarian, Chinese, English, French, German, Italian, Japanese, Korean, Russian, Slovenian and Spanish.

Lieve Gies studied media and cultural studies and law in Belgium and the UK. She obtained her PhD from Keele University in 2001. Currently Lieve is a Lecturer in the School of Law at Keele University (UK). She coordinates the law and culture research of the AHRC Centre for Law, Gender and Sexuality.

Keith Gladstone carried out most of his research while he was Head of Technical Research at the RNIB (Royal National Institute of Blind People). The various projects, mostly funded by the EU Commission, focused on a number of specific issues around improving access to information by visually impaired people. Although the topics varied widely, from robotics and automated speech to braille and audio transformation, they all involved ways of capturing, storing, indexing and processing information. Members of the research team had skills in psychology, ergonomics and languages as well as in software and systems engineering. He is now Head of Product Development and Evaluation at RNID (Royal National Institute for Deaf People).

Pedro Gomez Fernandez obtained an MA in Pedagogy and Psychology and a PhD in Mass Communication and Journalism. He is a Communication and Journalism Studies Scholar in the Department of Sociology at the Complutense University of Madrid. He teaches Public Opinion and Political Communication. He is also working in the Spanish Public Broadcasting Corporation, where he was the director of the project to introduce information technologies into the newsroom services. He also coordinated the organisational analysis of the implementation of the new technologies in the aforementioned corporation. His research and most important publications are focused on new technologies in journalism and political communication.

Raija Halonen obtained her PhD from the Department of Information Processing Science at the University of Oulu in Finland. She is currently working in the Department of Information Processing Science at the same university and in the Oulu University of Applied Sciences. She is interested in and publishes on social dynamics and the role of people in the implementation of information systems.

Marianne Jensen obtained her Cand. Polit. degree in Media and Communication from the University of Oslo in 1992. Since 1994 she has worked at Telenor Research and Innovation, the research department of the Norwegian owned international telecommunication operator, studying ICT usage in different domains such as in the home and in learning processes. She contributed to the report from the ISTAG Working Group on *Experience and Application Research Involving Users in the Development of Ambient Intelligence* (2004). Her current research has moved in the direction of mobile communication and internationalisation.

Arjan de Jong studied Business Economy at the Erasmus University in Rotterdam, the Netherlands, and is currently working as the leader of a small team of strategy and management consultants for housing associations. Previously he worked as a researcher and a teacher in the Utrecht School of Governance at Utrecht University where he taught courses on governance, public administration and project management. His main field of research is societal entrepreneurship. He has a specific interest in how the flexibilisation of labour can improve efficiency and effectiveness in organisations.

Eugène Loos See editor

Enid Mante-Meijer See editor

Aurélia Mardon has a PhD in sociology. Her main research subjects are socialisation, youth, the body and gender.

Andrei Moiceanu graduated from the 'Lucian Blaga' University of Sibiu, Faculty of Sciences, Mathematics and Informatics, in 2006. Since 2005 he has been working as a programmer. He is currently a PhD student at the 'Politehnica' University of Timişoara, Faculty of Automation and Computers in Romania under the guidance of Prof. Bărbat, with the thesis 'Self-Awareness in Agent-Based Systems'.

Isabella Maria Palombini is an electronic engineer. Having worked for many years as a researcher with Fondazione Ugo Bordoni, since 2006 she has been an officer at the Italian Ministry of Communications, where she collaborates directly with the Diplomatic Councillor.

Jo Pierson is Senior Researcher at SMIT (Studies on Media, Information and Telecommunication) – a member of IBBT (Interdisciplinary Institute for BroadBand Technology) – and holds a PhD in Social Science (Communication Studies). In the past he has worked as researcher-advisor for the Dutch knowledge institute TNO in Delft. He now lectures on Bachelors' and Masters' courses on socio-economic issues of the information society and on qualitative research methods at the Vrije Universiteit Brussel in the department of Communication Studies (Faculty of Arts and Philosophy). His research is situated in the field of innovation strategic research on the meaning and use of fixed and mobile media technologies at home, at work and in public settings. In this domain he is managing a range of projects. In addition he is conducting research involving users in the technological development process based on an ethnographic study and Living Lab research. He has published several articles and papers on user-centred innovation strategies and on the adoption and use of ICT by small businesses (SMEs and micro-enterprises).

Niina Rintala is a work psychologist and Project Manager at the Helsinki University of Technology in Finland. She has conducted numerous research and development projects mainly in the area of job design, competence development, knowledge management and work-related well-being. She is especially interested in carrying out research and practical interventions that help knowledge workers to manage their work stress, develop their competencies and share tacit knowledge about their work. She has over 30 publications with some of the most recent ones appearing in the *International Journal of Nuclear Knowledge Management*.

Heidi Rognskog Mella was educated as an artist (MA) at the Norwegian School of Art and Design (1991) and the Kunstakademie in Dusseldörf in Germany (1995). She has been working at the research department at Telenor since 1997. Her main research has been within concept development, user experience, prototyping, and innovation. In 2006 she was the inventor of a patented service that combined mobile network and screen technology in public spaces.

Bartolomeo Sapio is an electronic engineer and a researcher with Fondazione Ugo Bordoni. He is also Chairman of COST (COoperation in the field of Scientific and Technical Research) Action 298 'Participation in the Broadband Society', a field in which he has written a variety of publications.

Henk Schmidt is a Professor of Psychology at Erasmus University's Faculty of Social Sciences and founding Dean of its problem-based psychology curriculum. Presently, he is the Dean of the Faculty of Social Sciences, Erasmus University, Rotterdam, in the Netherlands. Previously, Schmidt held academic positions as Professor of Cognitive Psychology, Faculty of Psychology, Maastricht University, and as Professor of Health Professions' Education at the same university. His administrative positions include the Deanship of the Faculty of Health Sciences of Maastricht University. In 1999, he was a speaker at the Nobel Forum, upon invitation by the Nobel Prize Committee, Karolinska Institutet, Stockholm, Sweden. His research areas of interest are learning and memory, and he has published on problem-based learning, long-term memory and the development of expertise in medicine. Schmidt is among the most cited Dutch psychologists; in 2005 the Royal Dutch Academy of Sciences (KNAW) selected him as one of the top 200 Dutch scientists.

Maria Sourbati obtained a BA Political Science (Athens), MA Communication Policy (City, London), and PhD (Brunel, London). She teaches as Senior Lecturer in the School of CMIS, Division of Information and Media Studies, the University of Brighton, UK. Her research interests are in the areas of media regulation, communications policy and social policy. She focuses especially on matters of end-user access to public electronic communications services. Her earlier work has been on content diversity in broadcasting markets. Recent research includes digital television, online connectivity and electronic service delivery and older people, internet access, and public service provision.

Kristin Thrane obtained her Cand. Philol. degree in ethnology from the University of Oslo in 1999. She has worked in Telenor Research and Innovation since 2000. Thrane has focused on the domestic usage of information and communication technology. Her work has focused on ICT use in family settings. In this field, she contributed to the COST 269 program, where she examined different ICT capabilities.

During the last two years her research has centred on the impact of mobile telephony in relation to youth culture. This research has been carried out through comparative qualitative and quantitative studies in Telenor's European and Asian markets.

Tomaž Turk is an economist and has a PhD in Information Sciences. He is Assistant Professor and researcher at the University of Ljubljana, Faculty of Economics. He teaches the Development of Information Systems, Economics of Information Technology, Economics of Tele-communications, and Business Simulations. Currently, his research work includes themes from communication networks management, Internet society issues and the economics of information systems.

Olga Vershinskaya has a PhD in Economics. As a professor, she is the head of the department of Social Problems of Information Society Development in the Russian Academy of Sciences. She conducts research and has published on the topic of the social impact of ICT dissemination since the beginning of 1990s.

Daniel Volovici obtained a degree in 1983 from the Politechnical University of Bucharest in Electronics Engineering and Telecommunications, a degree in 2000 from 'Lucian Blaga' University of Sibiu in Psychology and a PhD in Electronics Engineering and Telecommunications in 1994 from the Politechnical University of Bucharest. He is currently a full professor in the Department of Computer Science and Automatic Control at the 'Hermann Oberth' Faculty of Engineering of 'Lucian Blaga' University of Sibiu, Director of the Center for Research in Interdisciplinary and Border Fields. He is also an expert evaluator for scientific programmes. He teaches Systems Reliability, Fundamentals of Artificial Intelligence, Artificial Neural Networks, Machine Learning and Cognitive Psychology and he has published several books and scientific papers.

Jelte Wicherts is an Assistant Professor at the Psychological Methods Department of the University of Amsterdam in the Netherlands. The research for his Masters' thesis (cum laude) was concerned with the equivalence of psychological tests and questionnaires that were either administered in a paper and pencil format or in a computerised format. In 2007, he successfully defended his PhD thesis on the psychometric meaning of intelligence test scores (cum laude). In the same year, he was awarded a prestigious Post-Doctoral grant from the Netherlands Organisation for Scientific Research, with a project aimed at measurement problems in psychological experiments. He specialises in Structural Equation Modelling and is interested in measurement of psychological traits, particularly moods and intelligence.

Introduction

Leslie Haddon, Enid Mante-Meijer and Eugène Loos

Social Dynamics

Both governments and the European Commission have great expectations regarding the extent to which democratic society can be furthered and the role of the citizen in the co-construction of that society. They see Information and Communication Technologies (ICTs) as providing Europe with the boost to enable it to play a central role in the world of tomorrow. The ambition is that Europe will be the main economic power in the world in 2010. There will be a completely transparent government for all people concerned. The use of ICTs will enable people and states to create a society in which equality of opportunity and the empowerment of citizens will be realised. These visions are largely promoted by the designers and producers of ICTs.

Although the speed with which ICTs in the form of the PC, the mobile phone and the Internet have found their way within modern society is remarkable, there is still a good deal of debate on many issues concerning their adoption and use. First of all there are the characteristics of ICTs themselves, often not very easy to use, especially for non-technically minded people. Ubiquitous access, seamless connections and invisible interfaces are still, at best if at all, years away. Moreover, ICTs can only be tools to enhance user experiences or to provide solutions to particular problems if they are perceived as such. They need to fit into the everyday lives of the user and, if the above visions are to be realised, their use will have to be expanded in various ways from its current level.

We have used the term 'social dynamics' in the title of our book because technology push in itself will not bring about an 'ideal' society. It is the social dynamics at work between potential users and those in their social environment (their household, their social networks), as well as between users and other stakeholders such as engineers and designers, producers, policy makers and managers, that shape which ICTs will be used, how they will be used and what type of society will emerge. If we translate that into more academic frameworks, then the perspective informing this book is that of a 'social constructivist' approach, whereby the development, adoption and use of ICTs is viewed as a socio-technological innovation process in which design and appropriation of ICTs mutually shape each other, within a specific socio-economic context. This is allied to a 'domestication' perspective that considers the social dynamics surrounding the adoption and use of ICTs as people try to find a place for new technologies in their everyday lives.

Origins and Questions

For some years there has been a network of European researchers from telecommunication departments, universities and operators, together with independent consultants, that has at different points in time collaborated as successive COST actions – originally COST 248, then COST 269[1] and at the time of writing COST 298.[2] These cross-disciplinary groups have been analysing the social dimensions of people's relationships to ICTs using the frameworks outlined above, and others. In September 2003, COST 269 organised a conference at the University of Art and Design in Helsinki entitled *The Good, the Bad and the Irrelevant: The User and the Future of Information and Communication Technologies*.[3] This conference was unique in the degree to which it was an international and interdisciplinary event addressing a broad range of ICTs. Its broad remit to consider the social context of ICTs is shown in the titles of the conference strands: 'the extended human', 'users as innovators', 'dealing with diversity' and 'the reconfiguration of society'. The issues that were discussed included current theoretical frameworks, contemporary research projects, issues in and approaches to the design of ICTs, ways of analysing people's experience of these technologies and potential social implications.

This book brings together chapters that we developed from some of the original papers of that conference[4] covering the socio-dynamic character of ICTs, the factors that we should consider when predicting adoption and use, their relevance to people and how they should be evaluated. Two leading questions shaping the choice of material in this book were:

1. *In which ways may ICTs serve as tools in the reshaping of everyday life?*
2. *What social dynamics are involved in the adoption and rejection of ICTs on the personal and organisational levels?*

A sub-question is then: *What is the 'additionality' of ICTs in people's everyday lives and its contribution to their quality of life?* 'Additionality' refers here to the added value or the change potential that ICTs offer in particular socio-economic settings. At the same time, the opposite question is also crucial: *How do the social dynamics of people's lives influence the ways in which they experience these ICTs?*

The aim of this book is to discuss the adoption and use of ICTs in real life settings. In the classical technological and marketing oriented literature, the ICT user is all too often generalised, without considering the specifics of his or her everyday life and work situation. Or else he or she is segmented according to classical socio-

---

1 See http://www.cost269.org/ where various reports from both these early actions can be found.

2 The work of this action can be found on http://wwwcost298.org.

3 COST 298 organised a follow up conference to the one discussed here: *The Good, the Bad and the Unexpected: The User and the Future of Information and Communication Technologies*, Institute of the Information Society, Moscow, Russian Federation, 23–25 May 2007.

4 Other chapters from that conference specifically focusing on the role of users in design can be found in Haddon et al. (2005).

demographic criteria that only provide a partial explanation of adoption and use. This book synthesises and builds upon a selection of the contributions from the above-mentioned conference in order to explore the social dynamic character of the adoption and use of ICTs by individuals, social groups and organisations. The empirical research presented in the book is unique in terms of its breadth, because it provides grounded insights into how and why different kinds of ICTs are, are not, or are only partially, accepted, used and integrated into everyday life.

Part I – Disciplinary Insights into the Social Dynamics of Innovation and Domestication

Much of the research on the patterns of adoption of ICTs and the process by which they are integrated into people's lives (or not) has been conducted within the realm of sociology, using both quantitative and qualitative methodologies or combining both traditions. To a lesser extent, anthropologists have also contributed, especially through ethnographic analysis (e.g. Miller and Slater, 2000 on the Internet; Taylor and Harper, 2005 on the mobile phone). Hence the first part of the book has a focus upon the variety of ways in which other disciplines provide insights. It shows the diverse frameworks and approaches used, within disciplines as well as between them, the methodologies, and the research traditions they draw upon that shapes the very questions asked – questions that in their different ways form considerations that play a role in the decision to adopt or reject new technologies.

Psychologists have often been involved in studies of user interfaces and the usability of ICTs but they have also examined wider issues beyond the design of very particular products. For example, there have been recent psychological studies of behaviour related to the mobile phone (Love and Kewley, 2003; Cumiskey, 2005, 2007). In this first part we start with the chapter by Beckers et al. on computer anxiety in daily life, which is important given its implications for the extent to which any information society will be embraced. One popular notion is that within a short time computer anxiety will be a thing of the past because the younger generation has grown up with the computer and uses it as a self-evident tool. However, Beckers et al. show in a comprehensive empirical study that computers are actually still ambiguous technologies in human society. Although they have become widespread, even younger users still perceive them as frustrating and liable to fail. The chapter addresses questions such as: *Will computer anxiety be a great limitation on the promise of the information society? Is it possible to remedy? Or does it reflect some existential fear about the impact of modern technology on one's daily life and personal identity?*

The second example of the contribution of frameworks developed in psychology is a chapter based on the social representation theory associated with Moscovici. Contarello et al. show that when applied to ICTs, this looks beyond standard questions regarding ICT usage to examine people's images of and evaluations related to these technologies. This is potentially useful in helping us to understand the acceptance of ICTs on a broader and psychological level (as opposed to in terms of practices and a focus on processes within the home that characterised much of early domestication research – Haddon, 2006). The study asks how far ICTs, in terms of perceptions, are completely trusted as a natural part of everybody's life or whether they are still seen as being alien, in many ways contrary to how we feel about the human mind and body – and even something to be feared? Is it true that young people, who have been using ICTs for the majority of their life, have already developed this attitude of trust towards them, taking them for granted? How far do societies differ in this respect? Contarello et al. discuss the results of a comparative study of students in several European countries that looked at these issues.

Economists working within and on behalf of ICT developing firms have been involved in such activities as modelling the take-up of particular technologies and services. In this spirit, the study by Turk et al. shows how microsimulations can reveal different possible adoption patterns regarded Digital TV over a 10 year period. This particular topic is strategic for policy makers because the promotion of DVB-T (Digital Video Broadcasting-Terrestrial) by the EU is part of the European Union Action Plan to further an information society for all. The aim of this study is to evaluate the effects of policy decisions not through making an absolute prediction but rather by developing 'what if?' scenarios showing different possible patterns of adoption under different conditions. Apart from demonstrating a methodological approach, it shows how economists' insights can stretch beyond particular firms.

The research and design efforts of designers, or increasingly of those working in multidisciplinary design teams, are often represented at ICT conferences. But far less of this material is published outside that context. This largely reflects the nature of design work, where it is important to establish the visibility of the work amongst peers quickly, and the conference is a useful vehicle for doing so. Other time pressures and priorities often mean that less of this material is developed into journal articles (for an exception, see Batterbee and Kurvinen, 2005). The chapter by Jensen et al. illustrates this type of contribution, combining research with ideas about how to build upon this to develop future ICT products. It focuses on broken or distributed families, where the physical absence of one parent for periods of time makes it difficult to keep intact and enhance the bonds between parent and child. This qualitative study, based on an interdisciplinary research project in Norway, researched the way in which communication media may act as a parental cord in distributed families. Based on this, they developed product scenarios showing ways in which media like the mobile phone could be enhanced to facilitate bedside chats, enable distant parents to read stories to the children and to be more available when a child needs help and advice.

Part II – The Internet as a Tool to Enable Users to Organise Everyday Life

The chapters in this second part of the book move us, in various senses, towards a more fine-grained analysis of very detailed and specific topics and experiences, which is needed if we want to reflect upon broader claims made about ICTs. They all deal with the use of the Internet as a tool to enhance the quality of life, but they do so in diverse settings: as a facility to support communication via family websites, as a source of legal information to strengthen the position of women and as a way to provide services to the elderly.

Although the Internet literature is now substantial, some strands have clearly received more attention than others. The 'digital divide' is an obvious example of a high profile topic, and much of the early, primarily sociological, interest was in how online communities operate. There have been moves to relate the everyday experience offline to interactions online (Miller and Slater, 2000; Bakardjieva, 2005), also developed in the Carmagnat et al. chapter in this book. Personal websites, as a form of communication, have been one emerging topic: for example, in terms of studies of home-pages (Katz and Rice, 2002), blogs and moblogs (Döring, 2004) and the home pages on social networking sites (Haddon and Kim, 2007). Carmagnat et al. deal with one version of such sites, the family website. They show how they are structured by those offering the service to present ideal, harmonious families, lacking intimate and individual communications and conveying only that which is amusing and inoffensive. In addition, they show the factors shaping families' decisions about what appears online e.g. the politics of who is represented as family, the lack of involvement of some family members, the focus on good news, since bad news is reserved for other channels or forms of communication, etc. Hence the chapter shows why this medium within our communications repertoire is used in the way that it is.

Secondly in this part of the book, Gies examines the specific processes at work on sites offering advice about divorce. This is an example of yet another disciplinary contribution, given that the author is based in a law department and notes implications for how the law, in this case a particular type of civil law, is experienced. This study of websites also makes us aware of connections with, but differences from, older means of legal self-help found in the problem pages of women's magazines, as well as enabling us to explore wider questions of empowerment and the feminisation of the Internet. Specifically, Gies discusses the possibility of assisting women in a way that is new in one professional field: the field of divorce suits where women are often the less informed and more financially disadvantaged partners. She examines legal self-help sites on the Internet that offer these women tools to become legal experts in their own right, examining how it takes on a particular 'feminised' form. But while it offers the potential to empower, she explores how it also has risks, including the risk of creating new digital divides between those who can access this information and those who cannot.

The final chapter in this part of the book deals with a particular group: the elderly. Although there have been studies of the elderly (usually the young elderly) and ICT use (Haddon and Silverstone, 1996; Eve and Smoreda, 2001), there is less on their use of the Internet (one exception being Kanayama, 2003). Sourbarti's chapter reminds us that the elderly are not a homogeneous group by looking at a very specific, albeit minority group of elderly people living in sheltered accommodation. The significance of this is that in such settings staff are present who could potentially support the Internet use of these elderly people. Hence the research considers their views as well as those of the residents themselves. The study shows that although older UK residents are becoming increasingly informed about communal Internet access and are encouraged by family, social networks and care staff to try it out, they considered it mostly to be a new leisure option. They were ambivalent towards the idea of on-line information and the option to request services on-line since they feared it would be alienating and substitute for physical activity and personal social contact.

Part III – ICTs in Organisational Settings: A Tool or a Curse?

The third part of the book examines the organisational and institutional perspective, whereby technology is used as a means for enhancing production and efficiency. At one level ICTs are well established in organisational life across diverse sectors of society – they have become more and more pivotal in various work processes. However, the acceptance and use of ICTs is rather less self-evident than is often assumed: in reality they are sometimes poorly integrated into the practices of many users.

In contrast to private life, in the work situation the choice of adopting or non-adopting is not an individual or family one. Here the social dynamics of ICT use acquire an extra dimension, being subjected to both micro level and meso level influences. On the meso level, interaction within the organisational environment (e.g. clients, managers, shareholders) drives innovation. The more complex the environment, the more complex the work processes. The more demanding the clients, the more impetus there is for innovation. ICTs are supposed to enhance considerably the effectiveness and efficiency of current work and communication processes. Knowledge management and virtual cooperation are becoming increasingly issues that management has to cope with. In the larger organisations especially, computers, the Internet and Intranets form a large part of the technological infrastructure.

However, in these organisations we also have the micro level of influences in operation. When it comes to making use of a technology as a tool to complete your own work, the computer, for example, has been reasonably well integrated into this process. But this does not mean that all innovations are greeted enthusiastically by employees. In the following chapters we shall see, in a variety of organisations, how the social dynamics at the personal and organisational levels play an important role in shaping the acceptance and use of ICTs.

The first of these examines worker participation in the design and implementation phase of a new technological system. This is often said to be a preliminary condition for acceptance of new ICTs by the members of an organisation. However, it does not guarantee that the transition occurs smoothly. The interesting aspect of the study by Halonen is that the workers had an enormous degree of involvement in the process of planning technological change. Yet, ultimately this did not result in the acceptance of new work methods. The main reasons for this were unfamiliarity of the workers with the computer as a tool and the absence of any perceived need among the workers to change their traditional ways of working.

Shifting focus, in many organisations the main task of workers is to provide services to the clients of the organisation. The introduction of ICTs often means a depersonalisation of social contact and a change in the autonomy of the worker as regards making decisions. The chapter by Loos gives an account of the mixed attitudes towards the introduction of an Intranet into a human services institution. On the one hand, the introduction was applauded as it was seen as means to facilitate the sharing of professional knowledge. On the other hand, there was a fear that it would disrupt person-to-person relationships and hamper the professional autonomy of the social workers concerned.

Finally, the introduction of new technology often results in a profound change in job descriptions, breaking up old work groups and teams. Rintala's chapter shows how new technology reduced person-to-person contacts between workers and how the loss of direct social contact resulted in relations becoming more stressed, led to the emergence of feelings of helplessness and helped create new social conflicts. However in this new situation where there was decreased cooperation and increased loneliness some compensation was found in terms of new forms of collaboration, changing interaction at an interpersonal level into group interaction.

Part IV – The Future: The Boundaries between Work and Non-work Life

The fourth part of the book deals with ways in which ICTs affect the boundaries of work and non-work life. One of the assumptions in some of the more utopian claims is that in the future ICT will dissolve the boundaries between working life and private life, enabling individuals to work from the home, anytime. What may be expected in this respect? One literature that clearly deals with this is that on telework, given the (probably disproportionate) visibility of this topic in various national policy documents over many years as well as over 30 years of research. Many of these studies are primarily framed by thinking about the work dimension. There is much less research where the main focus is on consequences for home life (one exception being Haddon and Silverstone, 1994) and few studies give weight simultaneously to the influence of and implications for both home and work. The two chapters in this part of the book do just that.

There is far less research on SMEs (Small and Medium Sized Enterprises), even less on micro-enterprises, compared to telework, despite the fact that it is, as Pierson's chapter suggests, a larger phenomenon. In contrast to the telework studies, this literature is very much framed in terms of thinking of this work experience as businesses. Furthermore, but also true of telework, there is a limited amount of research looking at ICTs and micro-enterprises, although we are now starting to see studies of mobile phones and SMEs in third world countries (e.g. Donner, 2004). Making the link with telework, while some telework studies do in practice include self-employed people working at home (reviewed in Haddon and Brynin, 2005), they do not usually conceptualise them as SMEs nor emphasise the extent to which the process of decision-making is like that of businesses.

Using qualitative and quantitative research, Pierson explores how 'business' decisions within micro-enterprises about acquiring ICTs are sometimes more like decisions made by private individuals than large organisations. On the one hand, they are influenced by a range of business considerations, including the particular business climate but also the business culture, and here we start to move into the realm of social networks more familiar in studies of everyday (private) life. But those decisions are also influenced by various personal characteristics of the entrepreneur (rather than resulting from a collective process of negotiation in a larger enterprise) and by the domestic setting. Through survey results, Pierson shows the complex layers of influences at work on adoption decisions, which vary for different ICTs.

The De Jong and Mante-Meijer chapter is at one level more straightforwardly a telework study, locating itself within that literature and providing empirical research looking at a very particular group of teleworkers working for organisations, rather than teleworkers more widely defined. However, the study follows up a dimension not usually considered in teleworker research – the meaning of the experience – as well as the different ways in which teleworkers manage the boundaries between work and home life. As regards the influence of work on both meanings and practices, these are affected by the attitudes and policy of different types of work organisations. At the same time, it is important to consider what these employees bring to the experience themselves. If we can diverge to make a link with other arenas of study, this would be the equivalent in media studies of how the background of audiences affects the way that they interpret texts. Out of the various possible relevant elements of people's lives, the study demonstrates specifically the influence of life stage on the experience of telework, its meaning for them and hence their orientation to these working arrangements.

Part V – Future Developments

In the fifth and final part of the book we come to some potential future developments of ICTs, or at least some examples of guidelines about how they might develop, reflecting on current issues and problems that have been identified in the two chapters that follow. Both, in their different ways, reflect on ethical questions and hence how ICTs should be designed.

Bărbat et al. ask the ethical question about the use of software 'agents' that could be used to influence behaviour, persuading people to change their habits. The benefit of 'agents' is that they provide role models for the individual to behave in a certain way and this use has been developed especially in the medical world. Examining the example of e-therapy, Bărbat et al. argue how ethical norms have to be taken into account in the development of that type of agent to insure that any misuse is avoided and goes on to suggest practical ways in which this could be implemented in design.

Drawing on the results of several European IST projects, Gladstone acknowledges the benefits of ICTs for the visually impaired but goes on to note the disparity between the promise of technology and the actual limited improvements in quality of life that occur. Through research examples, Gladstone demonstrates that one problem is that the design often fails to take a holistic approach, concentrating on particular well-defined problems without looking at the wider picture of people's activities, the wider context of their lives. Other problems include the conflicts of interest between different users, and financial costs. Looking beyond disabled people, the author notes how many of the issues apply to the population more generally and how design should therefore take certain principles into account.

References

Bakardjieva, M. (2005), *Internet Society: The Internet in Everyday Life* (London: Sage).

Batterbee, K. and Kurvinen, E. (2005), 'Supporting Creativity – Co-experience in Mobile Multimedia Messaging', in Haddon, L., Mante, E.A., Sapio, B., Kommonen, K-H., Fortunati, L. and Kant, A. (eds), *Everyday Innovators: Researching the Role of Users in Shaping ICTs* (Dordrecht: Springer).

Cumiskey, K. (2005), '"Can you hear me now?" Paradoxes of Techno-Intimacy Resulting from the Public Use of Mobile Communication Technology', in Nyíri, K. (ed.), *A Sense of Place: The Global and the Local in Mobile Communication* (Vienna: Passagen Verlag).

Cumiskey, K. (2007), 'Hidden Meanings: Understanding the Social-Psychological Impact of Mobile Phones through Storytelling', in Goggin, G. and Hjorth, L. (eds), *Proceedings of the Conference Mobile Media 2007*, Sydney, 2–4 July.

Donner, J. (2004), 'How Mobiles Change Microentrepreneurs' Social Networks: Enabling and Amplifying Network Contacts in Kigali', *Proceedings of the Conference 'Mobile Communication and Social Change'*, October 18–19, Seoul, Korea.

Döring, N. (2004), 'Mobile Weblogs – Moblogs', paper presented at the workshop 'Mobile Communications and a Culture of Funds: Trends and Concerns', Science Museum, London, 19–20 July.

Eve, M. and Smoreda, Z. (2001), 'Jeunes Retraités, Réseaux Sociaux et Adoption des Technologies de Communication', *Retraité and Société, 33*, 22–51.

Haddon, L. (2006), 'The Contribution of Domestication Research to In-Home Computing and Media Consumption', *The Information Society, 22*, 195–203.

Haddon, L. and Brynin, M. (2005), 'The Character of Telework and the Characteristics of Teleworkers', *New Technology, Work and Employment, 20* (1), 34–46.

Haddon, L. and Kim, S-D. (2007), 'Mobile Phones and Web-based Social Networking – Emerging Practices in Korea with Cyworld', *The Journal of the Communications Network* 6 (1), January–March 2007, 5–12.

Haddon, L., Mante, E.A., Sapio, B., Kommonen, K.-H., Fortunati, L. and Kant, A. (eds) (2005), *Everyday Innovators: Researching the Role of Users in Shaping ICTs* (Dordrecht: Springer).

Haddon, L. and Silverstone, R. (1994), 'Telework and the Changing Relationship of Home and Work', in Mansell, R. (ed.), *Management of Information and Communication Technologies: Emerging Patterns of Control* (London: Aslib). Also in Heap, N. et al. (1995) (eds), *Information Technology and Society: A Reader* (London: Sage).

Haddon, L. and Silverstone, R. (1996), *Information and Communication Technologies and the Young Elderly*, SPRU/CICT Report Series No.13, University of Sussex, Falmer.

Kanayama, T. (2003), 'Ethnographic Research on the Experience of Japanese Elderly People Online', *New Media and Society* 5 (3), 267–88.

Katz, J. and Rice, R. (2002), *Social Consequences of Internet Use* (Boston: MIT Press).

Love, S. and Kewley, J. (2003), 'Does Personality Affect Peoples' Attitude Towards Mobile Phone Use in Public Places?', in Ling, R. and Pedersen, P. (eds), *Front Stage/Back Stage: Mobile Communication and the Renegotiation of the Social Sphere*, Conference Proceedings, 22–24 June 2003, Grimstad, Norway.

Miller, D. and Slater, D. (2000), *The Internet. An Ethnographic Approach* (Oxford: Berg).

Taylor, A. and Harper, R. (2005), 'The Gift of the Gab? A Design Oriented Sociology of Young People's use of "MobilZe!"', *Journal of Computer Supported Cooperative Work* 12 (3), 267–96. Also available at <http: //www.surrey.ac.uk/ dwrc/Publications/index. html>.

PART I
Disciplinary Insights into the Social Dynamics of Innovation and Domestication

Chapter 1

Computer Anxiety in Daily Life: Old History?

John Beckers, Henk Schmidt and Jelte Wicherts

Introduction

The vast proliferation of ICTs has given rise to the idea that most users feel comfortable with these new technologies. Many designers of ICTs seem to assume that their (prospective) users have achieved a certain degree of computer literacy, the competence to use ICTs to extend their own capabilities and spheres of action. At the least there is an underlying assumption that users have an interest in and a willingness to work with these new technologies. And should this not be the case, designers often assume that those users who are averse to technology must belong to an older generation or that they have little education. However, from the onset of using computer technology it has been shown that computers evoke a vast range of emotions, sometimes elation but also anxiety. It is the latter phenomenon, computer anxiety, that is the subject of the study reported in this chapter. The study will address the following questions:

1. *Is computer anxiety prevalent among young and educated computer users?*
2. *Can computer anxiety be readily changed or is this anxiety of an enduring kind?*

Computer anxiety

Computer anxiety can be defined as a feeling of fear and apprehension felt by individuals when they use or consider using computers (Simonson et al., 1987). Computer anxiety has been studied intensively over the past three decades. Most scales used to measure computer anxiety cover various factors, such as lack of confidence in learning to use a computer, dislike of computers, avoidance of computers (Loyd and Gressard, 1984), anxiety aroused by, for example, looking at computer printers and printouts (Marcoulides and Wang, 1990), or anticipatory anxiety caused by knowing that one has to use the computer (Brosnan, 1998b). Summing up previous research, Beckers and Schmidt (2001) suggested that at least six dimensions are involved in the construct of computer anxiety: computer illiteracy, lack of self-efficacy, heightened physical arousal, feelings of dislike and a positive and negative set of beliefs about the role of computers in everyday life. The occurrence of computer anxiety is often related to age, where older people are supposedly more anxious then younger people and the level of education: the less educated, the more anxious. Compared to the young, older people are supposedly used to other ways of working, suffer from interference between old and new learning, are less adaptable, have a smaller short time memory capacity, less visual scanning ability, less developed motor (read typing) skills, etc. All these factors are supposed to have a negative impact on the way a computer is used. Indeed, a number of studies have found an inverse relationship between both age and computer anxiety and computer anxiety and level of education (Beckers et al., 2003; Hollis 2007, Laguna and Babcock, 1997).

Validity studies demonstrate that although computer anxiety is a robust phenomenon, its exact nature is not clearly defined (LaLomia and Sidowski, 1993). An important issue that remains ambiguous is whether computer anxiety is to be considered predominantly a temporary state that emerges when one is confronted by such a machine, or whether it can be seen as a trait of an individual. Traits are personal characteristics that express themselves in enduring, predictable behaviour, for example curiosity or outgoingness. (Harrington et al., 1990). This distinction has an important bearing upon the question of how one may deal with redressing or eliminating computer anxiety. By definition, a temporary state anxiety will pass away, usually when the source that has evoked the anxiety has been removed. For example, when you are driving a car in a desolated area and you see that you are running on empty, it may cause an acute feeling of anxiety. The moment you arrive at a petrol station, the anxiety will be gone. Within the realm of using computers there are indications that by giving special training, social support and user-friendly software this type of state anxiety can be remedied. In some cases the computer anxiety will go away simply by putting in more hours in working with a computer (Simonson et al., 1987; Rosen and Maguire, 1990; Rosen et al., 1993; Bohlin and Hunt, 1995; Laguna and Babcock, 1997).

A trait-like anxiety may be far more difficult to redress since the source of the anxiety may be of an instinctive or existential nature. To return to the example of driving, some people feel anxious the very moment they think about having to sit in a car. They feel vulnerable, out of control, risking their lives.

Deane et al. (1995) argue that computer anxiety is part of a trait anxiety that manifests itself as a heightened state anxiety only in the presence of relevant stressors. Gaudron and Vignoli (2002: 320) found that:

> students who have high levels of computer trait anxiety show a greater increase in state anxiety than those who have low levels, only when trait anxiety and type of situational stress (for instance interacting with a computer) are congruent.

Objectives

The present study was carried out to establish whether computer anxiety is prevalent among young and educated computer users as it is a common belief that among this group computer anxiety has been extinguished as a result of having been exposed to the computer from an early age.

The second objective was to investigate whether computer anxiety is more of a permanent attribute of a person, a manifestation of a more general anxiety affecting other aspects of the life sphere as well, or a temporary anxiety that arises only in response to a particular situational stressor.

To those ends, a study was conducted in which levels of computer anxiety among groups of participants were compared with their responses to a measure of trait anxiety and to a measure of state anxiety. One group of the participants had to fill in the state anxiety questionnaire while using a computer, whereas the other group had its state anxiety measured through a pen and paper procedure. It was expected that if computer anxiety was trait-related, a significant relationships should be found between computer anxiety and trait anxiety under both conditions. In other words there should be little effect of having to fill out the form on a computer. Furthermore, for those students who used a computer to fill out the state test, there should be a higher correlation between computer anxiety and state anxiety than in the situation where state anxiety is measured by pen and paper.

Method

Participants

To assure that the participants in the study were young and educated computer users a sample was drawn from first year psychology students at the University of Amsterdam. As was borne out by the composition of the sample, the average student in the Netherlands becomes acquainted with a computer at an early age and uses a computer regularly in his or her studies. The total sample consisted of 525 students, 172 male, 353 female. The average age was 21.16 years old. The average age at which students used a computer for the first time was 10.95 years old. Thirty-nine per cent rated themselves as fairly to highly skilled in using a computer, 20 per cent as neither skilled nor unskilled.

Measurements

To test our theoretical ideas, several instruments were used. (Inherent) trait anxiety was measured by a shortened version of the Dutch Profile of Mood States (Wald and Mellenbergh, 1990; Ark et al., 2003). This questionnaire measures the general frame of mind of people, distinguishing the following mood states: depression, tension, power, fatigue and anger. The various moods states are described by means of a list of 32 mood descriptions, such as 'feeling attractive', 'feeling active', 'feeling scared', 'feeling tired', 'feeling patient'. The sum of the scores from the answers to these questions is taken to be what McNair et al. (1992) refer to as the 'Total Mood Disturbance Score'. The test was administered in two versions. In version 1, respondents indicated to what extent the description applied to the mood state they experienced during recent days including the day of the test, by using a five point scale (0 = absolutely not, 4 = very well). This rating is indicative of the amount of trait anxiety experienced in general. In the state version of the test, the respondents were asked to give their ratings based on the way they felt just at that moment. The latter answers are indicative of the person's state anxiety.

Computer anxiety was measured by the Beckers and Schmidt Computer Anxiety Scale (BSCAS). This scale measures six latent factors underlying computer anxiety (Beckers and Schmidt, 2001). These six factors are: (1) computer literacy (in terms of acquired computer skills), (2) self-efficacy (confidence in one's capacity to learn to use computers), (3) physical arousal in the presence of computers (such as sweaty hand palms, shortness of breath), (4) affective feelings towards computers (like or dislike of computers), (5) positive beliefs about the benefits for society of using computers, and (6) negative beliefs about the dehumanising impact of computers.

The scale contains 32 Likert-type items,[1] consisting of statements on computers that could be scored between 1 (entirely disagree) and 5 (entirely agree). Computer literacy was referred to by items such as *I find it easy to make computers do what I want, I have difficulty in understanding the technical aspects of computers*. Self-efficacy was referred to by items such as *Everyone can learn to use a computer, as long as one is patient and motivated*, and *I am confident that I can learn computer skills*. Examples of physical arousal items are *I feel suffocated when I am in front of the computer, My heart beats faster when I think about working with a computer*. Affective feelings toward the computer were measured by items such as *Life will be easier and faster with computers* and *Computers are nice to work with*. Beliefs about the benefits of personal computers especially for the good of society were measured by items such *as Computers are bringing us into a bright new era* and *Computers create economic stability*. Beliefs on the dehumanising power of computers were measured using items such as *Soon our lives will be controlled by computers* and *People are becoming slaves to computers*.

Procedure

The anxiety tests were part of an overall testing programme for first-year students. In week 1 of their arrival at university, students received the computer anxiety questionnaire and the trait version of the Profile of Mood States test measuring how they felt over the past few days, both in a pen and paper format. In week 4 the Profile of Mood States test was again presented, this time in the state version measuring how they felt at that moment. As described earlier, in order to be able to investigate the effect of a computer induced stressor, the state version of the Profile of Mood States was administered under one of two conditions. One group (n=236) took the test in pen and paper format (Condition 'Pen and Paper'), the other group (n=289) took the test in a computerised format (Condition 'Computer Format'). Both tests were highly similar with respect to layout, instruction and answer format.

---

1 Items in a Likert scale usually contain a statement. The respondent is asked to evaluate this statement and to indicate whether he or she agrees with it. Traditionally a five-point scale is used.

Statistical Analysis

The data were analysed using Pearson product-moment correlation. This measure, expressed as a coefficient, indicates the strength and direction of a linear relationship between two variables. The coefficient may range between -1 and +1. The strength of the relationship is expressed by the size of the figure. The figure 0 signifies that the two variables that are being compared have no relationship with each other at all. The figure 1 signifies a perfect relationship; any change in one variable is matched by a corresponding change in the other variable. The direction of the coefficient indicates whether the relationship is negative or positive. A negative coefficient indicates that when one variable increases in magnitude the other variable decreases. A positive coefficient indicates that when one variable increases in magnitude, the other variable also increases.

Results[2]

Distribution of Computer Anxiety Scores

Figure 1.1 shows the distribution of the anxiety scores of the total sample. The mean score is 8.58 (*SD*=1.80[3]), where the maximum value of the anxiety scale is 24. An earlier study conducted by the authors that used a representative sample of the Dutch population, found a mean score of 9.99 (*SD*=1.96) (Beckers et al., 2003). This score was based on a list of 77 items, including the items used for the BSCAS measure. When the mean computer anxiety score of this population was calculated by using the 32 items of the BSCAS measure, a score of 9.66 (*SD*=2.64) was found, almost identical to the mean score based on the more exhaustive list of 77 items. This means that the BSCAS measure – scores of the general Dutch population – can be used as a benchmark, with which the scores of the students can be compared.

The mean average computer scores of the student sample and the sample from the Dutch population differ significantly (t-test for independent means, t > 1.96[4], *p* >.05[5]). This indicates that the student sample is less anxious then the sample drawn from the whole population. However, it also indicates that even among a well educated group of young computer users, computer anxiety exists and, indeed, that it is a phenomenon which approaches a normal distribution (represented by the smoothed curve in Figure 1.1). This indicates that about 68 per cent of the sampled students had a computer anxiety score that ranged between 10.38 and 6.78.

---

2 A subset of the data sampled has also been used in a double study as reported in Beckers et al., 2007.

3 Standard deviation is a measure of the spread of data about the mean and is expressed in the same units as the data.

4 The t-test is used to establish whether the means of two normally distributed populations are equal.

5 The p-value is the probability of obtaining a certain result based on chance alone.

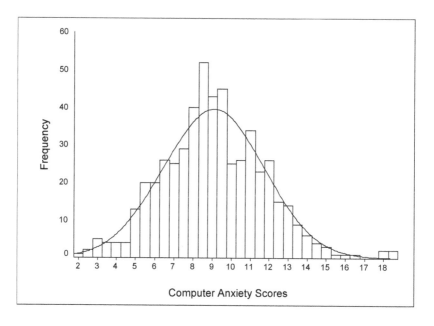

N=525

Figure 1.1   The distribution of computer anxiety scores

The relation between trait anxiety and computer anxiety

Figure 1.2 contains the correlations of the three anxiety factors involved for the computer format and the pen and paper conditions. It can be readily seen that in both conditions computer anxiety has a significant correlation with trait anxiety with a coefficient of .23. It can also be seen that trait anxiety and state anxiety correlate significantly, with a coefficient of .43 in the computer format condition and .44 in the paper and pen condition. Thus we can say that the relationship between trait and state anxiety is stable over the two experimental conditions. In other words, there is no effect from having to use computer. However, there is a remarkable drop in the correlation coefficient between computer anxiety and state anxiety when answering the questions with pen and paper. This falls to a correlation coefficient of .12, when compared to the computer format coefficient of .22. In fact, the correlation between computer anxiety and state anxiety when the students are doing the pen and paper test is no longer statistically significant. On the basis of these results it may be concluded that:

1. Computer anxiety and trait anxiety are indeed related. In other words, the premise of Deane et al. (1995) that computer anxiety is part of a trait anxiety is supported by our findings.
2. In addition, the premise of these authors that computer anxiety manifests

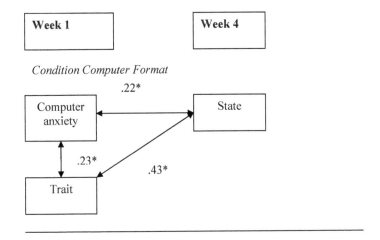

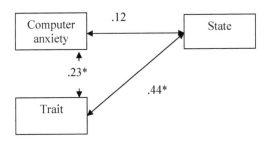

*p < .01

Figure 1.2   Correlations between computer anxiety, trait anxiety and state anxiety

itself as a heightened state anxiety only in the presence of relevant stressor, which in this study was produced by conducting the test on the computer, we find to be supported as there is a significant relationship between computer anxiety and state anxiety.

General Discussion

Firstly, the findings indicate that, contrary to the lay expectations, computer anxiety is present among educated, young and experienced computer users. Secondly, computer anxiety is partly related to trait anxiety and this relationship holds true over the two conditions i.e. whether answering with pen and paper or on a computer. State anxiety

Table 1.1   **Correlations between computer anxiety, trait anxiety and state anxiety**

	Computer anxiety	Trait	State
Condition Computer Format (n=289)			
Computer Anxiety	–	.23*	.22*
Trait	.23*	–	.43*
State	.22*	.43*	–
M	7.51	8.45	5.95
SD	3.87	2.69	3.82
Condition Pen and Paper (n=236)			
Computer Anxiety	–	.23*	.12
Trait	.23*	–	.23*
State	.12	.44*	–
M	8.75	8.12	5.97
SD	2.58	4.16	3.72

* $p < .01$

however is related to computer anxiety only when a computer is actually used, in this case by filling in a (simple) personality test by means of the computer. Moreover, in the pen and paper condition where no computer is present this relationship is not statistically significant anymore.

These findings suggest that for some users computer anxiety really consists of at least two components, one of an enduring nature and one component that only becomes activated by actually using the computer. So one research question would be: *what type of user experiences a combination of the two anxieties?*

Another important question would be: *what are the triggers that elicit these two kinds of anxieties?*

Endler et al. (1991) suggested that trait anxiety has at least three dimensions: individuals are prone to become anxious in situations of ambiguity, social evaluation and physical danger. So the question arises as to whether computer anxiety is derived from a fear of any of these situations or from a combination of them. Ambiguity is often present in working with computers, as well as the fact that one's work with a computer is evaluated by colleagues and superiors (Weil et al., 1990). The threat that a computer poses in terms of a physical danger is debatable, but the rising numbers of people suffering from RSI and eyesight fatigue indicate that working with computers is not risk free. Therefore a case could be made arguing that computer anxiety is in fact composed of a combination of these three elements of a trait anxiety: ambiguity, social evaluation and physical danger. However, Worthington and Zhao (1999) proposed another line of thought, in particular that the existence of computer anxiety was based on an existential fear, a fear about the impact of modern technology on one's daily life and personal identity. Both perspectives underline the basic premise of this chapter that computer anxiety is an elusive phenomenon that cannot readily be dismissed as a condition that afflicts only a few or the dull and ignorant.

There is a case to be made for professional designers, product developers and marketers to take into account the fact that their products and services may invoke feelings of anxiety among their users. The variables that cause or heighten computer anxiety have been studied extensively. An important precursor of computer anxiety has been found to be the perceived lack of control that users have while working with their computer (Beckers and Schmidt, 2003). This feeling of a lack of control can arise as a result of being confronted as a user with jargon that obscures the true nature of the action to be taken or by having to use buttons and menus that will take long and extensive training to understand. With the Internet revolution it was hoped that Internet users would enter a realm of sites designed exclusively to provide them with the right content, which could be easily found by well-designed search engines and accessible by transparent websites that are easy to navigate. However, these laudable goals have not been met.

Will computer anxiety ever go away? On an individual level anxious users can be supported in various ways. Of course there are many training courses that can help one to know how use software in a proper way. There are also courses that go beyond instruction and may help you to do your own troubleshooting. Many people benefit from having a buddy around who is knowledgeable about computer technology. And in the area where computer anxiety is an expression of a deeply rooted fear of technology or life in general therapeutic counselling may offer relief. However it is our premise that as long as the ICT industry does not meet the intrinsic need of many users to be 'in the driver's seat' computer anxiety will stay. At present, we see a giant confrontation within the industry of companies such as Microsoft, which has its roots in developing computer software and Google, whose future is aligned with the revolution caused by the Internet. In spite of the fact that both companies claim to work for the benefit of their customers, various major issues that deal directly or indirectly with the phenomenon of computer anxiety are not adequately addressed. One of the foremost issues is the privacy of the user. Both Microsoft and Google possess very detailed information about their users, what there preferences are, what their actual behaviour is, who they relate too, etc. There is no transparency about what they do with all this information, nor do they seem hindered by any legislation.

The privacy of a user is also threatened by security issues such as hacking and damages done by a multitude of viruses. The cost of spam is crippling to many companies.

Lastly, skills acquired as a computer user become obsolete in a short time and need to be continually refreshed. Though standardisation is the fashionable word, it is fair to say that an average user of software has to learn over and over again the functionalities of new releases or devices.

By now our Western society has become so digitised that nearly every action in daily life somehow involves the use of a device that is intrinsically a computer. Whether you pay your bills through the Internet, watch TV, listen to music, drive a car or make a call to a friend, it is all supported by ICTs. Technology push is a reality, and in line with the view of Mark Brosnan, computer anxiety can be seen as a legitimate reaction of human beings to threatening changes in their daily life as a result of increasingly pervasive technology (Brosnan, 1998a), a technology, we may add, that is now intrinsically global.

References

Ark, L.A. v.d., Marburger, D., Mellenbergh, G.J., Vorst, H.C.M. and Wald, F.D.M. (2003), *Verkorte Profile of Mood States (Verkorte POMS)* (Lisse: Swets Testing Services, the Netherlands).

Beckers, J.J., Mante, E.A. and Schmidt, H.G. (eds) (2003), *Computer Anxiety among 'Smart' Dutch Computer Users* (New Brunswick: Transaction).

Beckers, J.J. and Schmidt, H.G. (2001), 'The structure of computer anxiety: a six-factor model', *Computers in Human Behavior* 17, 35–49.

—— (2003), 'Computer experience and computer anxiety', *Computers in Human Behavior* 19, 785–97.

Beckers, J.J., Wicherts, J.M. and Schmidt, H.G. (2007), 'Computer Anxiety: "Trait" or "State"', *Computers in Human Behavior* 23, 2851–62.

Bohlin, R.M. and Hunt, N.P. (1995), 'Course structure effects on students' computer anxiety, confidence and attitudes', *Journal of Educational Computing Research* 13 (3), 263–70.

Brosnan, M.J. (1998a), *Technophobia: The Psychological Impact of Information Technology* (London: Routledge).

—— (1998b), 'The impact of psychological gender, gender-related perceptions, significant others, and the introducer of technology upon computer anxiety in students', *Journal of Educational Computing Research* 18 (1), 63–78.

Deane, F.P., Heinssen, R.K., Barrelle, K., Saliba, A. and Mahar, D. (eds) (1995), *Construct Validity of Computer Anxiety Measured by the Computer Attitudes Scale* (Amsterdam: Elsevier Science).

Endler, N.S., Parker, J.D., Bagby, R.M. and Cox, B.J. (1991), 'Multidimensionality of state and trait anxiety: factor structure of the Endler multidimensional anxiety scales', *Journal of Personality and Social Psychology* 60, 912–26.

Gaudron, J.-P. and Vignoli, E. (2002), 'Assessing computer anxiety with the interaction model of anxiety: development and validation of the computer anxiety trait subscale', *Computers in Human Behavior* 18, 315–25.

Harrington, K.V., McElroy, J.C. and Morrow, P.C. (1990), 'Computer anxiety and computer-based training: A laboratory experiment', *Journal of Educational Computing Research* 6 (3), 343–58.

Hollis, L.A. (1997), 'Training older adults on computers: Implications from goal setting and aging research', *Dissertation Abstracts International: Section B: The Sciences and Engineering* 57 (8-B), 53–62.

Laguna, K. and Babcock, R.L. (1997), 'Computer anxiety in young and older adults: Implications for human-computer interactions in older populations', *Computers in Human Behavior* 13, 317–26.

LaLomia, M.J. and Sidowski, J.B. (1993), 'Measurements of computer anxiety: A review', *International Journal of Human Computer Interaction* 5 (3), 239–66.

Loyd, B.H. and Gressard, C. (1984), 'Reliability and factorial validity of Computer Attitude scales', *Educational and Psychological Measurement* 44 (2), 501–05.

Marcoulides, G.A. and Wang, X.B. (1990), 'A cross-cultural comparison of computer anxiety in college students', *Journal of Educational Computing Research* 6 (3), 251–63.

McNair, D.M., Lorr, M. and Droppleman, L.F. (1992), *Manual for the Profile of Mood States* (San Diego: Educational and Industrial Testing Service).

Rosen, L.D. and Maguire, P. (1990), 'Myths and realities of computerphobia: A meta-analysis', *Anxiety Research* 3, 175–91.

Rosen, L.D., Sears, D.C. and Weil, M.M. (1993), 'Treating technophobia: A longitudinal evaluation of the computerphobia reduction program', *Computers in Human Behavior* 9, 27–50.

Simonson, M.R., Maurer, M., Montag Torardi, M. and Whitaker, M. (1987), 'Development of a standardized test of computer literacy and a computer anxiety index', *Journal of Educational Computing Research* 3 (2), 231–47.

Wald, F.D.M. and Mellenbergh, G.J. (1990), 'De verkorte versie van de Nederlandse vertaling van de Profile of Mood States (POMS)', *Nederlands Tijdschrift voor de Psychologie* 45, 86–90.

Weil, M.M., Rosen, L.D. and Wugalter, S.E. (1990), 'The Etiology of Computerphobia', *Computers in Human Behavior* 6, 361–79.

Worthington, V.L. and Zhao, Y. (1999), 'Existential computer anxiety and changes in computer technology: What past research on computer anxiety has missed', *Journal of Educational Computer Research* 20 (4), 299–315.

Chapter 2

ICTs and the Human Body: An Empirical Study in Five Countries[1]

Alberta Contarello, Leopoldina Fortunati, Pedro Gomez Fernandez,
Enid Mante-Meijer, Olga Vershinskaya and Daniel Volovici

Introduction

There is already a vast literature on the spread, adoption and integration of ICTs in everyday life by different groups (De Gournay and Smoreda, 2003; Katz, 2003; Ling, 2003; Mante-Meijer and Heres, 2003; Vershinskaya, 2003; Haddon 2003, 2004; Turk et al., Chapter 3 in this book), on their relationship with people's well-being (Contarello, 2003; Hamburger, 2004; Contarello and Sarrica, 2007) and on their role in the texture of family and parental relationships (Jensen et al., Chapter 4 in this book). Meanwhile, negative consequences of their diffusion, such as computer anxiety (Beckers et al., Chapter 1 in this book) or lack of trust (Huang et al., 2003) have also been investigated. However, the topic of interest in this chapter is the discussion, renewed over the last few years, of the 'artificialisation' of the human body (Fortunati et al., 2003) and of the body as itself being both a 'natural' and 'artificial' technology (Fortunati, 2003 et al.; Oksman and Rautianinen, 2003). In this context, we are increasingly confronted with new technologies getting closer to the human body, and even penetrating it by means, for instance, of microchips under the skin (Haraway, 1991; Maldonado, 1997, 2003; Longo, 2003).

Parallel with these theoretical discussions exploring the co-construction and mutual incorporation of technical projects, cultural meanings, bodies and objects (Callon, 1991; Latour, 1992a, 1992b; Mantovani, 2001), empirical research has been carried out from the perspective of social representation theory. The first step in this direction was an Italian study in which the relationship between new technologies (for example the Internet, mobile phone and computer) and the human body were explored (conducted by Contarello and Fortunati in 2002 and published in 2006). As

---

1 Partial results of this research were presented at the conference *The Good, the Bad and the Irrelevant: The User and the Future of Information and Communication Technologies* organised by COST Action 269 and the University of Art and Design in Helsinki, 3–5 September 2003 (Contarello et al., 2003) and at the conference *UNESCO between Two Phases of the World Summit on the Information Society*, St. Petersburg, 17–19 May (Contarello et al., 2005). See also Contorello and Fortunati, 2006.

a second step, a methodological discussion[2] was held in 2002 involving colleagues from different countries as well as from different disciplinary backgrounds (social psychology, sociology, industrial design, artificial intelligence, engineering, computer science, economics, linguistics and so on). This led to an extended study, discussed in this chapter, which broadened the field of research to other nations.

We adopted a socio-dynamic approach (Doise et al., 1993) as we considered it to be the most suitable in order to understand the modalities of how we, at a socio-psychological level, integrate new technologies into our lives. This also takes into account the dynamics of the social structure. People's representations of both these technologies and the human body were explored via a free-association exercise. This allowed us to detect the information component and the semantic field of representation for both ICTs and for the human body. Individuals' particular positioning in regard to these representations of ICTs was then studied further, looking at the importance given to bodily presence within communication. People's familiarity with new technologies and their sociological/cultural positioning in terms of gender and nationality were also analysed. The present chapter presents a comprehensive analysis of our results regarding the five participating countries: Italy, Romania, Russia, Spain and the Netherlands. The opportunity to conduct a joint project involving scholars from these locations allowed us to grasp a preliminary picture on the wider European area, touching its four cardinal points and incorporating the particular contribution of Russia.

We can thus move towards integrating theoretical discussions regarding the domestication of the new technologies (Silverstone and Hirsch, 1992; Haddon, 2003; Oudshoorn and Pinch, 2003) with data we have on the increasingly close relationship between ICTs and the human body that is present in everyday feeling and thinking. Exploring how the layperson constructs meanings with regard to the artificialisation of the human body became for us a priority, especially considering that there is a lack of empirical research on the theme. For these reasons we analysed the social representations of the human body and its transformations in everyday life (as well as in different contexts via 'intelligent' machines) in order to examine shared positions on these themes. Within the range of communicative technologies we focused our attention on the Internet, as emblematic of the ever growing weight of mediated communication, and on the mobile phone, because of its extraordinary and rapid spread in everyday life. Thus our aim was to investigate how individuals perceive the co-construction of new technologies, in particular the Internet and the mobile phone, and the human body; as well to examine the role of national experiences and identities in this process.

To sum up, the research outlined here explored the social representations of ICTs in five countries. It monitored how new technologies – mainly the Internet and the mobile phone – were perceived and considered in relation to the human body, adopting the theoretical framework offered by social representation theory, as developed by Moscovici (1961/1976). A social representation is defined as a form 'of knowledge which is socially elaborated and shared, and which has the practical aim of constructing a common, social reality' (Jodelet, 1989: 36). To become an object

---

2 At the COST Action 269 meeting held in Montegrotto (Padova, Italy), 7–9 November.

of social representations, an *issue* has to exist, framed in a specific *context*, socially *shared* (Farr and Moscovici, 1984) and in the presence of *polymorphism*, where different features, values and voices are provided by different groups (Moliner, 1996). In our case, we charted the views of young women and men of different nationalities living and studying in Italy, Romania, Russia, Spain and the Netherlands. In these different environments, we explored how different access to and use of the Internet and the mobile phone, as well as the different importance given to body-to-body (face-to-face) presence, interact with emerging views of the human body and of the two technologies under study. In particular, we focused on the different components of the representation – information, attitudes and representational field – adopting a combined qualitative and quantitative methodology.

Method

Nearly seven hundred respondents (N=654) took part in the research: 280 from Italy, 120 from Romania, 100 from Russia, 123 from Spain and 31 from The Netherlands. Of the respondents, 56.9 per cent were female and 43.1 per cent male. The participants were university students most equally divided between humanities and social sciences on the one hand and engineering and natural sciences on the other. The data were collected in 2002–2003.

The first component 'information/content' and the third component 'representation field' (i.e. the symbolic and emotional 'texture' or connotations relative to the topic; Bellelli, 1990) were investigated via free associations (Di Giacomo, 1980; Le Bouedec, 1984). The second component 'attitudes towards technologies' was measured via an *ad hoc* Semantic Differential Scale in the case of ICTs (Osgood et al., 1957) while Orbach and Mikulincer's (1998) Body Investment Scale measured 'investment in the human body', i.e. our respondents' experience of their bodies. An extended presentation of the procedure can be found in Contarello (2003).

The authors of the present research, whose work was checked by bilingual speakers, provided questionnaire translations and back-translations. The Italian version was first translated into English. The English version was adopted in The Netherlands and in Romania, allowing respondents to give free associations either in English or in their own native language. A Russian translation was prepared from the English version and a Spanish translation from the Italian one. Translations and back-translations were checked and synonyms and antonyms were identified by the authors in a joint meeting in 2003 and in subsequent exchanges. The presence of scholars from the various countries under study allowed the researchers, as required in comparative research, to control cultural bias and naiveties. The specific software we used (SPAD.T) helped us by offering an equivalence procedure through which it was possible to gather lexical forms from different languages. Finally, data entry and processing were carried out by the same coder, in an identical way for all the countries.

The Content of the Representations

If we consider only the distinct and valid words associated with the first technology, the Internet, we see that those words mentioned more frequently refer to a framework of information/communication. The Internet is first of all described by its parts and functions with email in an outstanding position (see Table 2.1). Secondly, it evokes the world of searching, but also of relationships. Moreover, it is linked to the sphere that some sociologists call 'actualisation' (Keyes, 1998), that is, its important role in the dissemination of news and information on current affairs, its increasing speed and its globalisation. Interestingly enough no negative features seem to appear in the content of the Internet representation, in these most frequent responses, while references to fun and to entertainment indicate aspects of play and the games connected to it.

As regards the mobile phone, after references to its major functions and structure, this technology is represented in terms of its communication aura and the constellation of its more frequently recognised qualities. It is useful, comfortable, necessary and quick, linked with messages, connections and dialogue. The association with friendship further evokes the relational world that the mobile phone is able to manage. Brands are also frequently mentioned, which may serve to help the new adolescents' 'tribes' acquire group identities, as researched by Lobet-Maris (2003). Nor should we forget one of the most important features of the mobile phone – costs – which points clearly to an element of concern by the respondents.

The human body is perceived as a beautiful and unique machine, in which every part is intertwined with others within a highly complex but delicate system. It is our link with life and personal identity. It is perceived as beautiful and perfect: a wonderful 'natural machine', which it is necessary to take care of, but which at some point degenerates.

Table 2.1   The most frequent associations related to the Internet, mobile phone and the human body (the most frequent 21 words in each case)

Internet	Information, communication, computer, email, Internet-parts, speed, global, site, useful, search, fun, new, knowledge, chat, contact, journey, progress, people, wide, magnitude, technology
Mobile Phone	Function, communication, cost, useful, friend, comfort, necessary, mobile-structure, annoying, sound, speed, brand, fashion, values, message, connection, contact, reachability, dialogue, calls, freedom
The Human Body	Beauty, mind, body-parts, machine, complex, unique, perfect, physics, identity, mortal, sensitivity, wonderful, great, research, delicate, to-care, efficient, soul, instrument, curious, well-being

Attitudes

As mentioned above, the measure of the attitudes towards ICTs was operationalised through a Semantic Differential Scale. For each technology, the correlation matrix between the seventeen items scale thus constructed was submitted separately for a factor analysis. A principal components procedure, followed by Varimax rotation, showed that in both cases, with a good degree of reliability (alpha=.75 for the Internet: =.71 for the mobile phone), a single first factor emerged expressing a shared general evaluation followed by other less stable factors (alpha<.50). For this reason in the following analyses we will consider only the first general evaluation factor.

A first clear result was that all our participants held a positive evaluation of the technologies being considered. As regards the Internet, that evaluation (expressed in terms of the Internet being agreeable, amusing, desirable, useful and worthwhile) was quite positive (M=5.42, on a seven-point scale). Meanwhile, mobile phone (described as agreeable, amusing, desirable, worthwhile, pleasant, harmless and easy, M=4.95) was also well accepted, although with slightly less enthusiasm. However, there were differences between countries as regard this factor. The post-hoc Scheffé test highlights the fact that the positive evaluation appeared to be more intense for Romanians, while Italians and Russians were relatively less enthusiastic about both technologies.

Considering the overall profiles of the two technologies we noticed similar patterns in the five countries. As illustrated in Figure 2.1 (Pearson-r correlations between countries as regards both the Internet and the mobile phone result were significant with p<.01), a single pattern with very minor variations emerges regarding the mobile phone: overall it is perceived as being fast, useful, worthwhile, easy, important for fostering communication – but also expensive.

Turning now to the respondents' experience of their own body, an exploratory factor analysis performed on the correlation matrix between the five-points items showed the predicted pattern, with minor changes. As foreseen, four thematic kernels appear, showing good reliability values for the first three of them. These three are Body Love (alpha=.83), Feeling Comfortable with Physical Proximity and with Touch in Interaction (Comfort in Touch) (alpha=.70) and Body Care (alpha=.67). On the whole, our participants seem to have quite a good relationship with their body. They are moderately satisfied with their own appearance (Mean=3.85; median= 4.00), they take care of their body (M=3.90; m=4.00), they enjoy physical contact and they do not keep their distance when talking and interacting in interpersonal relationships (M=3.24 m=3.20). We entered these variables into the study of the representation fields as illustrative variables. Participants were subdivided, either side of the median value, into those with a high and low love of their body, those who were comfortable with touching and those who cared for their bodies.

Uses and Practices

As was expected, the new technologies in question were very common among young adult university students. The vast majority owned a mobile phone, but there were

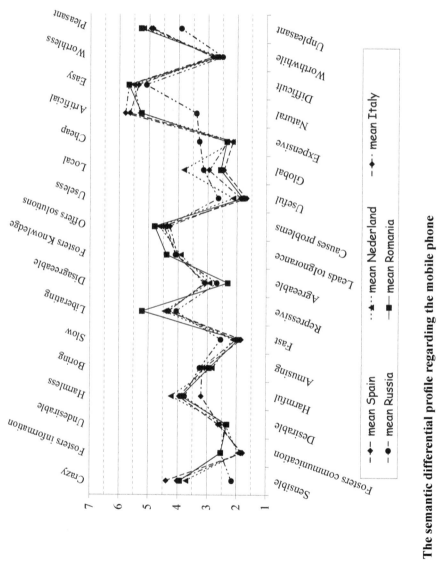

Figure 2.1   The semantic differential profile regarding the mobile phone

some differences between the five countries. According to our data, these ranged from 71 per cent in Russia to 100 per cent in the Netherlands (80 per cent in Romania, and 98 per cent in both Spain and Italy). Most of the respondents had an email address (the Dutch 100 per cent, the Romanians 98per cent, the Spaniards 93 per cent, the Italians 81 per cent, the Russians 62 per cent) and an Internet subscription (the Dutch 81 per cent, the Romanians 55 per cent, the Spaniards 89 per cent, the Italians 82 per cent, the Russians 58 per cent). There was some variation between the five countries in terms of frequency of use both for the mobile phone (voice calls and SMSs) and for the Internet (emails and subscriptions). This has to be taken into account in the analysis of uses and practices as illustrative variables. The data are also of interest because they might help to draw a picture of the phenomenon during a phase when the Internet and the mobile phone were experiencing a high market penetration.

The Representation Field of the Internet, the Mobile Phone and the Human Body

From correspondence analysis, we illustrate here the results of the three key stimuli: the Internet, the mobile phone and the human body. The matrices 'categories x participants' were submitted to a correspondence analysis, following the Asparm procedure of the SPAD.T package (Lebart et al, 1989). Both in the case of the Internet and the mobile, the matrix is 67 x 654 (we retained only lexical forms with absolute contribution =1.49, i.e.100/67); in the case of the human body the matrix is 66 x 654 (threshold =1.51). In the following discussion each factor derived from the analyses is described, and the two ends of each continuum are given a name.

The Internet

As regards the Internet, on the basis of the Scree test we can consider the first three dimensions. The first factor opposes, at one pole, 'The web between journey, communication and study', and at the other 'A useful and wonderful innovation'. The second factor contrasts a view of the device as being 'Playful and hot' with it being 'Cold and absorbing' (see Figure 2.2).

The third factor draws a distinction between 'Eros and fun', on the one side, and a 'New global chance' on the other. Different positions are endorsed by the various participants in this study. These vary in terms of their nationality, their evaluation of ICTs and their investment in the human body. The main results regarding active and illustrative variables are shown in Figure 2.2. Interestingly enough, the first factor opposes a descriptive to an evaluative stance. Individuals with a low evaluation of the Internet and an average degree of comfort with touch make more evaluative statements, whereas we find those with a high evaluation of the Internet and a low degree of comfort with touch make more descriptive statements. Moreover, respondents from the participating countries do not make the same choices: they choose different polarities of the above mentioned factor. The Italian respondents evoke a view of the Internet as being the net that is found at the intersection between journey, communication and study, while Romanian, Spanish and Dutch respondents

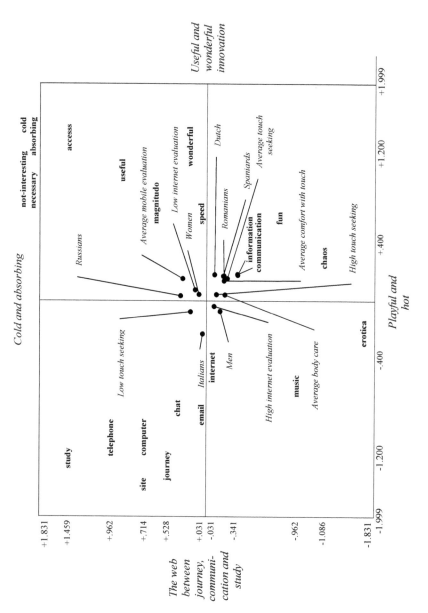

Figure 2.2   The Internet in five countries – a correspondence analysis of first and second factors

celebrate with enthusiasm this new medium as a useful and wonderful innovation. In relation to the second factor, Spaniards and Romanians refer to its playful and lively anarchy, adding to this picture elements of fun and excitement. Individuals with a high or medium degree of comfort with touch also position themselves at this polarity. In contrast, the Russians see the Internet as being the absorbing and useful presence of a necessary device, as do respondents with a low degree of comfort with touch. Minor differences are found as regards gender, which only features in relation to this second dimension of a cold-hot dichotomy. Women tend to stress elements such as absorbing study and interest while men mention lively play and fun. The third factor opposes a vision of the Internet perceived as an advanced and global medium able to foster knowledge and create community to another vision of it, based on eroticism and fun. The first vision is supported by Romanians and individuals with an average score for body care, while the second is supported by Italians and those respondents with low score for body love. This finding suggests that pornography and the Internet are mostly linked together by people with a lack of acceptance of their own body.

The mobile phone

Once again, there appeared to be three factors that were most important for the mobile phone. As in the case of the Internet, the first contrasts a descriptive representation of the technology (yet again stressed by Italians) to an evaluative perspective (once again expressed by Russians, Spaniards and Dutch). The former approach links the device to its constituent parts and functions, highlighting its role in information gathering and knowledge production. The latter nearly equates it to 'life', but also views it as a global artefact with a pragmatic value, even if it is not always useful. The first perspective is expressed by individuals with a high evaluation of the Internet and the mobile phone, while the latter is stressed by respondents with a low evaluation of the Internet and the mobile phone. We named this factor 'A material device for information and knowledge' *vs.* 'A global helper for life'. The second factor from this analysis indicated the strengths and weaknesses of the mobile phone, contrasting 'Vital contacts in work and mobility', a conception shared by Russians and respondents with low score for body love, with 'Critical views of a handy device', a conception shared by Italians and those with a high score for body love. The third factor contrasted 'New problems' with 'New potentials'. We found praise for a technology that opens possibilities both for work and leisure (a vision shared by Italians and Russians, respondents with a low score for being comfortable with touch and an average score for body care, and those with a low evaluation of the Internet and mobile phone). But we also found some concerns in terms of the inconvenience and potential harm the Internet might lead to, expressed especially by Romanians and Spaniards, those with high score for being comfortable with touch and those with a high evaluation of the Internet and mobile phone. Again respondents assume different stances depending on their nationality, familiarity with the device and attitudes towards embodied forms of communication.

The human body

As regards the human body, we present here the first four dimensions from the correspondence analysis, which we named 'Description *vs.* Evaluation', 'Relational features *vs.* Constituent parts', 'Mortal remains *vs.* Perfect means for knowledge', and 'House of the soul *vs.* Great and unique system'. Views of the human body tend to be anchored in sociological variables (nationality) and psychosocial ones (evaluations of ICTs, investments in the body). As illustrated in Figure 2.3, the body is mainly perceived as being a wonderful machine, but one that is delicate and perishable.

Here the answers of the respondents reflected different philosophies and approaches. There is a split between those (Russians and Dutch) who merely describe it (while having a higher evaluation of technologies) and those respondents (particularly the Italians) who sing the praises of a wonderful and perfect device, and who have a low evaluation of both the ICTs in question. Furthermore, those who merely describe the body are characterised by an average score for body love and care, while those who evaluate the body are marked by high score for body love and an average score for being comfortable with touch. Interestingly, Italians, who, as we saw above, express a descriptive vision of the Internet and mobile phone, tend by contrast to evaluate the human body. In relation to the second factor, there is an opposition between those who stress its relational features (mainly women) and those who provide a description of its parts (men, Russians). As regards the third dimension, references to beauty and the perfection of the body are found mainly in the Italians' answers. Meanwhile, Russian, Spanish and Dutch participants see the body as being something that is beautiful and ugly at the same time, which contains and wraps ourselves and which is destined to die. It might be interesting to note that our respondents mention the role of research, not technology, in connection with the human body, and particularly its beauty and perfection. Last, in relation to the fourth factor, we found an opposition between a more materialistic view of the body as a great and complex system and the perspective whereby it is inhabited by the mind and the soul.

Conclusions

Although the debate on the artificialisation of the body has been quite lively at an international level, this perception of the human body as artificialised does not seem to emerge among our particular respondents. Meanwhile, technologies, particularly the mobile phone and the Internet, which might be considered the emblem of artificiality, are actually seen in a positive way. The content of the representation reveals, on the one hand, a largely positive image of these technologies and, on the other hand, a very enthusiastic view of the human body. Respondents note both the higher aspects of the latter, but also its fragility. Some points should be stressed:

a) by 2002–2003 when the data was collected the Internet had already acquired a communicative soul in addition to the informative one.

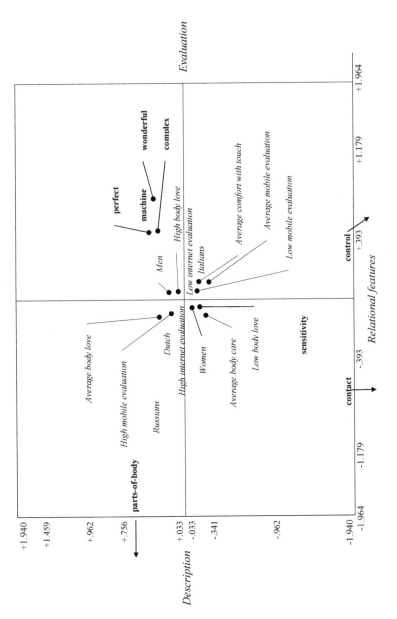

Figure 2.3   The human body in five countries – a correspondence analysis of first and second factors

b) the human body is a 'machine', a device, an instrument. But it is also a very 'special' one, far removed from technology. It is the model that has inspired all machines and technologies, yet it is unique and cannot be imitated by technology. Only the contrary can be true.

Thus, when we speak of an 'extended human' the concept should not be taken to mean an artificialisation of human beings. On the contrary, from the shared knowledge of everyday life captured in this research, the fact that technologies are getting closer and penetrating the human body should be interpreted as a naturalisation of the technologies and thus a naturalisation of that which is artificial, rather than the other way around.

The relationship between bodily experience – at least as presented in our research – and the organising principles that appear to govern people's 'social thinking' related to the Internet and the mobile phone do not show any clear pattern and appear difficult to interpret. It might be that the scale adopted, originally devised to measure self-destructive behaviour but later used successfully to measure normal conduct, is not suitable in our particular case. This research does not allow us to clearly say how bodily experience relates to the new technologies, at least at the representational level. This is a crucial point that has to be left for further research.

Considering the role of the various countries as shown in the correspondence analysis, different positions emerged regarding the two technologies under scrutiny. However, on the whole, and particularly as regards attitudes towards the Internet and the content evoked by it, the general trends are more significant than the variations. With the help of our data we would like to stress the importance of demystifying the outspoken rhetoric regarding these new technologies that makes them appear a 'deus-ex-machina' in most situations. In contrast, the role of these devices – and of ICTs more generally – as tools to be mastered should be made explicit. It is mainly through familiarity with these devices that we recognise the new opportunities they offer, but that familiarity also allows us to reshuffle priorities as regards the agendas we set in everyday life.

References

Bellelli, G. (1990), 'La tecnica delle associazioni libere nello studio delle rappresentazioni sociali: Aspetti cognitivi e linguistici', *Rassegna di Psicologia* 8, 17–27.

Callon, M. (1991), 'Techno-Economic Networks and Irreversibility', in Law, J. (ed.), *A Sociology of Monsters: Essays on Power, Technology and Domination* (London: Routledge).

Contarello, A. (2003), 'Body to Body: Co-presence in Communication', in Fortunati, L., Katz, J. and Riccini, R. (eds), *Mediating the Body: Technologies, Communication and Fashion* (Mahwah: Erlbaum).

Contarello A., Fortunati L., Gomez P., Mante E., Vershinskaya O. and Volovici D. (2003), 'Social representations of ICTs and the human body. A comparative study in five countries,' *The Good, the Bad, the Irrelevant: The User and the Future of*

Information and Communication Technologies. Conference proceedings, COST Action 269, Helsinki, September, 3–5, 2003. Available at: <http//goodbad.uiah.fi>.

Contarello A., Fortunati L., Gomez P., Mante E., Vershinskaya, O. and Volovici, D. (2005), 'General Trends in Digital Culture', *UNESCO between Two Phases of the World Summit on the Information Society*, St. Petersburg, 17–19 May 2005.

Contarello, A. and Fortunati, L. (2006), 'ICTs and The Human Body: A Social Representation Approach', in Law, P., Fortunati, L. and Yang, S. (eds), *New Technologies in Global Societies* (Singapore: World Scientific Publisher).

Contarello, A. and Sarrica, M. (2007), 'ICTs, Social Thinking and Subjective Well-Being. The Internet and its Representations in Everyday Life', *Computers and Human Behaviour*, 23, 1016–32.

De Gournay, C. and Smoreda, Z. (2003), 'Communication, technology and sociability: between local ties and "global ghetto"?', in Katz, J. (ed.), *Machines That Become Us* (New Brunswick: Transaction).

Di Giacomo, J.P. (1980), 'Intergroup alliances and rejections within a protest movement: Analysis of the social representations', *European Journal of Social Psychology* 10, 329–44.

Doise, W., Clémence, A. and Lorenzi-Cioldi, F. (1993), *The Quantitative Analysis of Social Representations* (Hemel Hempstead: Harvester Wheatsheaf).

Farr, R. and Moscovici, S. (eds) (1984), *Social Representations* (Cambridge: Cambridge University Press).

Fortunati, L., Katz, J. and Riccini, R. (eds) (2003), *Mediating the Human Body: Technology, Communication and Fashion* (Mahwah: Erlbaum).

Haddon, L. (2003), 'Domestication and Mobile Telephony', in Katz, J. (ed.), *Machines That Become Us* (New Brunswick: Transaction).

—— (2004), *Information and Communication Technologies in Everyday Life: A Concise Introduction and Research Guide* (Oxford: Berg).

Hamburger, A.Y. (2004), *Internet and Personality* (Oxford: Oxford University Press).

Haraway, D. (1991), *Simians, Cyborgs and Women: The Reinvention of Nature* (London: Routledge).

Huang, H., Keser, C., Leland, J. and Schachat, J. (2003), 'Trust: The Internet and the Digital Divide', *IBM Systems Journal* 42 (3), 507–18.

Jodelet, D. (ed.) (1989), *Les Représentations Sociales* (Paris: PUF).

Katz, J. (ed.) (2003), *Machines That Become Us* (New Brunswick: Transaction).

Keyes, C.L. (1998), 'Social Well-Being', *Social Psychology Quarterly* 61 (2), 121–40.

Latour, B. (1992a), 'Where are the Missing Masses? Sociology of a Few Mundane Artefacts', in Bijker, W.E. and Law, J. (eds), *Shaping Technology/Building Society: Studies in Sociotechnical Change* (Cambridge: MIT Press).

—— (1992b), *Aramis ou l'amour des techniques* (Paris: La Découverte).

Lebart, L., Morineau, A., Becue, M. and Haeusler, L. (1989), *Système portable pour l'analyse des données textuelles (SPAD.T)* (Paris: Cisia).

Le Bouedec, G. (1984), 'Contribution à la méthodologie d'étude des représentations sociales,' *Cahiers de Psychologie Cognitive* 4, 245–72.

Ling, R. (2003), 'Fashion and vulgarity in the adoption of the mobile telephone among teens in Norway', in Fortunati, L., Katz, J. and Riccini, R. (eds), *Mediating the Human Body: Technology, Communication and Fashion* (Mahwah: Erlbaum).

Longo, G.O. (2003), 'Body and Technology: Continuity and Discontinuity', in Fortunati, L. Katz, J. and Riccini, R. (eds), *Mediating the Human Body: Technology, Communication and Fashion* (Mahwah: Erlbaum).

Lobet-Maris, C. (2003) 'Mobile phone tribes: Youth and social identity', in Fortunati, L., Katz, J. and Riccini, R. (eds), *Mediating the Human Body: Technology, Communication and Fashion* (Mahwah: Erlbaum).

Maldonado, T. (1997), *Critica della Ragione Informatica* (Milano: Feltrinelli).

—— (2003), 'The Body: Artificialization and Transparency', in Fortunati, L., Katz, J. and Riccini, R. (eds), *Mediating the Human Body: Technology, Communication and Fashion* (Mahwah: Erlbaum).

Mante-Meijer, E. and Heres J. (2003), 'Face and place: The mobile phone and internet in the Netherlands', in Fortunati, L., Katz, J. and Riccini, R. (eds), *Mediating the Human Body: Technology, Communication and Fashion* (Mahwah: Erlbaum).

Mantovani, G. (2001), 'The psychological construction of the Internet from information foraging to social gathering to cultural mediation', *CyberPsychology and Behavior* 4 (1), 47–56.

Moliner, P. (1996), *Images et Représentations Sociales* (Grenoble: PUG).

Moscovici, S. (1961/1976), *La psychanalyse. Son image et son public* (Paris: PUF).

Oksman, V. and Rautianinen, P. (2003), 'Extension of the hand: Children's and teenager's relationship with the mobile phone in Finland', in Fortunati, L., Katz, J., Riccini, R. (eds), *Mediating the Human Body: Technology, Communication and Fashion* (Mahwah: Erlbaum).

Orbach, I. and Mikulincer M. (1998), 'The body investment scale: Construction and validation of a body experience scale', *Psychological Assessment* 10 (4), 415–25.

Osgood, C.E., Suci, G.J., Tannenbaum, P.H. (1957) *The Measurement of Meaning* (Urbana: University of Illinois Press).

Oudshoorn, N.E.J. and Pinch, T.J. (eds) (2003), *How Users Matter: The Co-Construction of Technologies and Users* (Cambridge: MIT Press).

Silverstone, R. and Hirsch, E. (1992), *Consuming Technologies: Media and Information in Domestic Spaces* (London: Routledge).

Vershinskaya, O. (2003), 'Information and communication technologies in Russian families', in Katz, J. (ed.), *Machines That Become Us* (New Brunswick: Transaction).

Chapter 3

The Adoption of Terrestrial Digital TV: Technology Push, Political Will or Users' Choice?

Tomaž Turk, Bartolomeo Sapio and Isabella Maria Palombini[1]

Introduction

In the European area the introduction of digital technologies in terrestrial television services is named DVB-T (Digital Video Broadcasting Terrestrial), and it is one of the objectives of the European Union Action Plan 'eEurope 2005: an information society for all' (European Commission, 2002). The following terms are also used:

— DTT (Digital Terrestrial Television). Over-the-air broadcasting of digital television signals, using locally available radio spectrum.
— DTV (Digital TV). The transmission of television signals using digital rather than conventional analogue methods.
— DVB (Digital Video Broadcasting). A set of standards that define digital broadcasting using existing satellite, cable, and terrestrial infrastructures.

DVB-T was designed to carry video, audio and programme data for television. But it can carry much more than just TV, including: electronic programme guides; teletext; parts of the Internet; broadband multimedia data, news, weather; interactive services; software updates and games. DVB-T allows for a better use of transmission media and involves an increase in the number of channels (4 to 6 times the number of existing analogue channels) and a better audio/video quality. Services can also be dynamically reconfigured.

In most European countries digital terrestrial television is being launched between 2006 and 2010. But while DTV may bring many benefits both to consumers and to industries, its development may not depend only on the market. Hence, governments must consider the situation carefully in order to evaluate if and how they have a role in promoting this innovative technology.

The difficult economic environment, the fact that the channels that are currently transmitted on analogue terrestrial networks do not have any interest in promoting

---

1 The content and the opinions expressed in this chapter are those of the authors and do not necessarily reflect the view and the position of the Italian Ministry of Communication, nor do they imply its agreement with them.

digital terrestrial television and the difficulties as regards finding adequate financing to build digital terrestrial networks may cause a delay in the expected analogue switch-off. Without the widespread penetration of DTV, analogue switch-off will not be considered by local governments (European Commission – Andersen, 2002). And there are further complications. Pay-TV plays an important role in the digitisation process since pay-TV operators currently account for a large portion of digital households. Yet the introduction of digital terrestrial services brings free-to-air and public service broadcasters into the digital TV market.

Meanwhile, the development of the Internet could represent a real threat for traditional media. The impact of the Internet on traditional media is clearly correlated with the ability of the Internet to propose a real-time worldwide database covering both traditional media services and new services. It is very difficult to predict the exact amount of 'viewing' time that will shift from one media to another, but it is reasonable to believe that the Internet will have a strong substitution effect on TV viewing time. Certainly heavy users are more likely to shift leisure time from television to the Internet. Meanwhile, the impact of the Internet on media consumption will continue to increase due to the fact that Internet websites will develop increasingly equivalent or better services compared to traditional media services with an equivalent, or even better, quality of service. This trend will continue, fuelled by the overall penetration of broadband Internet made possible through the development of devices such as 3G mobiles, PCs, etc.

On the other hand, although the Internet is clearly competing with TV for leisure time, both media are in some sense also very different and therefore not quite true substitutes (European Commission – Andersen, 2002). TV is passive while Internet surfing is active. TV is often a social medium while Internet is personal. TV is mostly used for entertainment while the Internet is often used for information gathering. The majority of online users watch TV while online. Lastly, TV will itself become more and more interactive.

In theory Interactive Digital TV (iDTV) represents an intermediary medium between traditional TV and the Internet. The developments of digital TV and bi-directional networks have driven the development of iDTV[2] in some countries (such as the UK). iDTV's most popular elements are gambling, interactive advertising and the expanded choice of programming. Internet access, email via television, e-banking, etc., however, have proved less popular among users, partly because they relate to a business context.

It seems particularly interesting to study the process of DVB-T adoption at this time and to identify the factors and the mechanisms that influence the users' decision to switch to the new technology. Moreover, it is very important to understand the role that public interventions might have in facilitating the transition and influencing the

---

2 Terrestrial digital television can be accessed either by purchasing a set top box, which is basically an adapter that simply connects to the existing TV and aerial socket, or by purchasing a digital TV set. The latter is definitely more expensive, but more advanced too. Users should be able to use their existing rooftop aerial, depending on its age and precise location but they may need to get it checked. In some areas a 'wideband' aerial is needed.

processes of imitation mechanism among social networks of users. In this study we used microsimulations to research the dynamics of the DVB-T adoption process.

Microsimulations

Microsimulation modelling was first introduced by Orcutt (1957) and has since received much attention from researchers studying sociological phenomena. Wolf (2001: 2) suggests the following definition of microsimulation in the field of social science applications:

> Microsimulation consists of drawing a sample of realisations of a prespecified stochastic process.

Since the microsimulation models can be deterministic, we may use another description of the purpose of microsimulations (where stochastic influences are usually omitted):

> (...) to study complex systems by representing each of the microscopic elements individually on a Computer and simulating the behaviour of the entire system, keeping track of all of the elements and their interactions in each time period. (Levy et al., 2000: XIII).

The basic idea in microsimulations is that we choose microscopic elements (agents) of the same or different type or class (for example, people, households, firms in social studies) and develop the relationships between them, or the rules as regards their behaviour, usually over time. The rules can be developed in a form of one or more statistical models, with their parameters derived from real data. The rules relating to agents' behaviour can be also described in other ways (for example, decision trees). For simulation purposes, the set of agents with their attributes is then created, usually based on real cases.

Microsimulations enable social scientists to carry out experiments, which would otherwise be missing from their analytical toolset. The observed population and the set of rules can be created virtually. The real power of microsimulation is twofold. First, we can gain knowledge from the systematic study of rules and the comparison between simulated populations and real society. Second, we can estimate the direct and indirect effects of different policies since the dynamics of socio-structures in time can be well described and animated.

Although other analytical models can be used for predicting future developments in DVB-T adoption, we found that the microsimulation approach has some appealing characteristics. There are at least two obstacles facing classical analytical models. The first is that models, especially macromodels, are built upon assumptions which may or may not hold in reality. The second is that in attempting to manage without such assumptions, the models can become complex and difficult to analyse (Levy et al., 2000).

Our analysis of DVB-T adoption has the following main steps:

a) Preliminary analysis and data collection. Since the microsimulation model uses a population of agents and the set of rules, data describing the real society should be collected and assembled either directly or indirectly. On one hand, we can get feedback from people directly using questionnaires or other methods, in order to assemble the necessary datasets and to develop the set of rules. On the other hand, one can establish a 'virtual society' of agents with data collected indirectly from other sources (for example, surveys, census data). Data can also be provided in aggregate form, from which the population of agents with their attributes can be derived according to a chosen method (see, for instance, Ballas et al., 1999).

b) Relationships among agents and system dynamics. In longitudinal data analysis there is a choice of several models from which one can obtain the decision rules for microsimulation model development, for example models of duration and of event sequences, linear models for continuous outcomes and models for discrete-outcome panel data (Wolf, 2001). These are so-called data-driven microsimulation, which differs from the context-driven microsimulation that was used in this study. In context-driven simulation the set of behavioural rules is deduced in a different way using a distributed 'artificial' intelligence approach. Rules are not necessarily derived from statistical modelling that relies on empirical data. Instead, each agent's behaviour is described in other ways, for instance using decision trees. This approach is sometimes called 'theoretical modelling' (Burch, 1999). We have chosen the latter option, since in practice the quality of any dataset we collected would not be good enough to provide the estimated parameters, if we are considering discrete-outcome panel data.

c) Programming and running the microsimulation model. The microsimulation model can be programmed after data has been collected and the decisions about the set of rules to be used have been taken. Different programming environments can be used for this purpose. When choosing the right toolset, we found that it must have the following: sufficient data import and export capabilities; tools for microdatabase development and analysis; a broad set of methods for defining rules; the option of allowing a quick pre-analysis of results for test purposes; an object oriented programming language. The microsimulation environment should also contain the necessary tools for debugging and searching for errors, whether in terms of syntax or of pertaining to semantics. We found that all of the requirements are met by the Universal Micro DataBase System microsimulation environment (Sauerbier, 2001).

This step also includes the verification and the validation of the model. During verification the computer program is tested to see if it is coded in a proper way according to the microsimulation model. Validation of the model is a more complex task, since it involves checking whether the simulation model actually reflects reality (Banks et al., 2000). During the validation phase the model is calibrated for parameters that, empirically, are relatively hard to establish in an exact manner.

If the set of rules is not established in a way that leads to a complete model, then the model must be calibrated iteratively. One should be careful when taking this step, since calibration is itself strongly connected to the established set of rules within a model. The parameters operating within the model should also be observed to operate in reality. Finally, the calibration process is strongly connected to the validation of the model. If the model is finally validated, it can be used in predicting the behaviour of agents in the real world.

d) Examination of the results. After calibration the model can be used to test different scenarios and different populations of agents. In the latter case, those parameters within a model that are population specific should be either measured exactly or estimated empirically. When this is not feasible, one can still re-calibrate the model. The results should always be seen in the light of the sensitivity of the model to its parameters. If the parameters are not point estimates, the resulting values should be given as probabilistic distributions.

e) Further research on household behaviour. We expect that some decision rules that we have incorporated into our model will be clear enough given the knowledge that we currently have about the observed population. The simulation model should always be compared to real data and through this comparison we can refine the basic questions in order to discover the missing pieces and hence to redesign the microsimulation model.

Field Research and Model Implementation

The main purpose of our simulation model was to research the dynamics of DVB-T adoption processes. In principle the model should also be useful for making predictions about the effects of different policy options. Since the adoption of ICT products is a complex process, we focused primarily on the act of buying a suitable device that is DVB-T capable.

Since adoption can follow different patterns in respect to different technological possibilities we have described the phenomenon using two variables. The first variable shows the number of digital TV sets in a particular household, while the second shows the number of set top boxes in a household. The timeframe of the microsimulation model should be at least 10 years, in this case from 2003 to 2012, to allow it to reach some predictions. Although many developments took place in the field since this research was carried out in 2003, the following content should be regarded as an exercise to demonstrate how microsimulations could inform policy at particularly strategic moments in time.

Data was collected by means of a questionnaire exploring the wishes and attitudes of potential users of DTV in Italy, as well as their willingness to pay for the service. After a basic statistical analysis of the sample, we estimated the set of variables that might influence the final decision of the household as to whether to adopt a certain DVB-T device or not. Although the questionnaire included the decision variables about the willingness to adopt DVB-T, further analysis revealed that the quality of values obtained would be questionable if the rules were to be derived on the basis of discrete-outcome panel data.

Since the household behaviour needs to be described by a set of rules, we firstly developed two different decision trees to test our understanding of the decision process within a household. The first tree is an 'ideas tree', built with the intention of organising variables that were later to be included in the simulation process. The second tree is an 'evaluation tree', derived as a simplification of the first tree and used to test the 'ideas tree' by using empirical data from the real households.

The first step was to extract from the questionnaire the variables to be considered in the adoption process and to organise them into homogenous groups. Table 3.1 presents a list of selected variables and their classification.

Table 3.1   Selected variables and their classification

1	BASIC
1.1	DTV
	This is the top variable, and it represents the user's decision to buy a set top box or a digital TV set.
1.2	Switch over date
	National governments will decide the date after which all television programmes will be broadcast in digital form. As the switchover date gets near, users will accelerate the transition to digital devices.
2.	FINANCIAL
2.1	Income class
	This variable refers to the income of the household.
2.2	Set top box price
	Manufacturers suggest that there will be three classe of set top boxes: basic (50 to 150€), intermediate (120 to 200€) and advanced (200 to 400€). The higher the cost, the more the functionality of the set top box, including its interactivity.
2.3	DTV set price
	The price of a digital TV set will range from 1000 to 2.500€.
2.4	Monthly expense
	This variable measures the users' willingness to pay for digital TV services, including pay-per-view and interactive applications.
2.5	Government subsidy
	National government are very likely to subsidise the purchase of a basic set top box in order to support the transition to DTV.
3.	QUALITY OF SERVICE
3.1	Interactive services
	Interactivity will increase the appeal of digital TV channels, but it requires a return channel (telephone line, ISDN, xDSL or optical) and an advanced set top box or TV set.
3.2	Customisation
	Services and advertisements can be personalised based on users' tastes, but this could also be perceived as an intrusion in one's own privacy.
3.3	User friendliness

	The user friendliness of set top boxes, TV sets and remote controls will be an important factor in users' acceptance of DTV.
4.	MEDIA
4.1	Use of traditional media
4.1.1	The Internet
	This variable measures the number of daily hours spent on the Internet. It raises an interesting question: are people who spend a long time on the Internet more incline to switch to DTV or are they not so interested?
4.1.2	Traditional TV
	This variable measures the daily consumption of TV programmes in the family.
4.1.3	Pay TV
	The ownership and use of pay TV will certainly influence the decision to buy terrestrial DTV.
4.2	Entertainment appliances
	These variables refer to the possession of appliances for entertainment purposes within the household. They are a proxy for measuring the technological orientation of users.
4.2.1	Traditional TV sets
4.2.2	Videorecorder
4.2.3	DVD player
4.2.4	Home theatre
4.2.5	Game console
4.2.6	Digital camera or camcorder
4.2.7	Hi-Fi
5.	DEMOGRAPHICS
	These variables describe the composition and the activities of the households, suggesting potential interest in new TV services.
5.1	Social network
5.1.1	No. of friendly households
	This variable helps define the social network of a household. It is used to build the population in the microsimulations.
5.1.2	No. of friendly households with DTV
	Imitating friends and relatives can be an important factor in the adoption process.
5.2	Household composition
5.2.1	No. of household members
5.2.2	No. of members less than 18 yr
5.2.3	No. of members more than 65 yr
5.2.4	No. of male members
5.3	Household activity
5.3.1	No. of students
5.3.2	No. of employed people
5.3.3	No. of domestic workers
5.3.4	No. of people with no activity

A simplified tree was used to test hypotheses about the decision process. Three different household types were tested, using very different characteristics in order to explore opposite scenarios (see Table 3.2).

Table 3.2   The evaluation of the decision tree with three different households

	Low end family	Average family	High end family
DTV (decision to buy)	Nothing	Set top box	TV set
Switch over date	More than 1 yr	More than 1 yr	1 yr to go
Financial			
Income class	≤ 10,000 €	10,000 - 40,000 €	≥ 40,000 €
Government subsidy	No	Yes	Yes
Quality of service			
Interactive services	High availability	Low availability	High availability
Customisation	High	Low	High
User friendliness	Medium	High	High
DTV	Nothing	Nothing	Nothing
Media			
Use of traditional media			
Traditional TV	> 4 hours per day	> 4 hours per day	2-4 hours per day
Pay TV	Non owner	Non owner	Owner
Entertainment appliances	1 – 5	6 - 10	6 – 10
Demographics			
Social network			
Fr. families with DTV	< 10	< 10	< 10
Importance of fr. adop.	4	5	5
Household composition	6 – 11	6 – 11	6 – 11
Household activity	0 – 10	11 - 19	11 – 19

The first household is a low income family in a year when the switch-over to digital television is still a long time away. Their decision is not to adopt. The second household is an average income family, whose members watch a good deal of television and possess a range of electronic devices. Their decision is to buy a set top box if it has the government subsidy. The third household is a high income family in a scenario where the household has access to good quality services and interactive devices. Their decision is to buy a digital TV set.

Starting from the raw data in the questionnaires, a few indices were calculated that were to be used when programming the microsimulations. The indices were calculated during the simulation for each household since they are based mostly on household attributes.

The household composition index was calculated by adding up household members, including members younger than 18, members older than 65, students, domestic workers, members with no activity. Employed members were subtracted. The range was from 0 to 25. This household composition index gives us an idea of the total number of family members present in the home, which should be reflected in a willingness to watch television.

The entertainment appliances index was calculated by adding up the number of devices owned, covering video recorders, DVD players, home theatres, games consoles, digital cameras/camcorders and hi-fis. The range was from 0 to 6. This entertainment appliances index measures the household's orientation towards buying entertainment technology.

The quality of service index was calculated by adding up interactivity (0=low, 1=high) multiplied by the importance of interactivity to users, customisation (0=low, 1=high) multiplied by the importance of customised services to users, and user friendliness (0=low, 1=medium, 2=high) multiplied by the importance of user friendliness to users. The range was from 0 to 20. This quality of service index measures the appeal of digital TV to the potential user, weighted according to his/her interest levels.

The TV usage index was calculated by adding the levels of TV usage (1=less than 1 hour, 2=1 to 2 hours, 3=2 to 4 hours, 4=more than 4 hours) of all the household members. The range was from 1 to 20. The TV usage index is a measure of the hours spent watching television by the entire family.

The imitation index was calculated my multiplying the number of households already possessing digital TV (ranging from 0 to the population size) by the importance of imitation as a factor influencing the adoption of digital TV (ranging from 1 to 5), and dividing the figure by the size of the entire population. The range was from 0 to 5. This imitation index is a measure of the households that already have digital TV weighted by the importance of imitation as a factor in adopting digital TV and normalised over the entire population.

The decision tree developed above was used later on only as a framework for showing the reasoning within a household in certain circumstances. Only some branches were explored. These were selected according to the importance of the variables on that branch in relation to a particular decision in a particular situation.

The next step was to construct a range or 'space' of states that each household can achieve. The state of a household is described with a vector (a, b), where 'a' represents the number of digital set top boxes and 'b' represents the number of digital TV sets within a household. A household can move from one state to another (for instance, from state (0, 1) to state (1, 1)). This range or space of states, together with transitions, can be represented as a graph where the nodes are the state of a household at a certain moment in time and arches represent transitions from one state to another, i.e. adoption or non-adoption.

We assumed that, according to the temporal horizon of the simulation, the maximum number of set top boxes in a household is 3 and the maximum number of digital TV sets is 2.

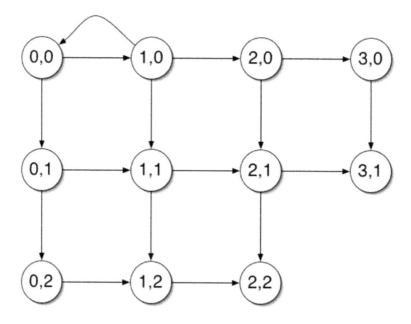

Figure 3.1　Transition diagram

Transitions are governed by rules that were programmed according to the following criteria:

State (0,0)

The transition to (1,0) can arise through many different factors within user profiles. The factors to be taken into account are the presence of a public subsidy to buy a set top box, the entertainment index, the approach of the switchover date, subscription to pay TV, the TV usage index, the household composition index and finally the imitation index.

The transition to (0,1) depends on the price of a digital TV set in relation to income and on the entertainment index, which should be high in order to induce the purchase.

State (1,0)

The transition to (2,0) depends on the number of traditional TV sets in the household that still have no set top box and on one or more of the following: the switchover date is very near, there is a high household index or a high TV usage index.

The transition to (1,1) depends on the price of a digital TV set in relation to income and on the entertainment index, which should be high in order to induce the purchase.

The transition to (0,0) depends on a low quality of service and random factors that lead users to abandon the digital technology.

State (0,1)

The transition to (1,1) depends on the number of traditional TV sets in the household that still have no set top box and one or more of the following: the switchover date is very near, there is a high household index or a high TV usage index.

The transition to (0,2) depends on the price of a digital TV set in relation to income and on the TV usage index and the household composition index, which should be high to motivate the household to purchase digital TV.

State (0,2)

The transition to (1,2) depends on the number of traditional TV sets in the household that still have no set top box and on the household index. If this has a high value it indicates a pressure to have another digital TV.

State (2,0)

The transition to (3,0) depends on the number of traditional TV sets in the household that still have no set top box, on the TV usage index and on the income, which should not be at the lowest level if we want the household to purchase digital TV.

The transition to (2,1) depends on the price of a digital TV set in relation to income, on the TV usage index and on the household composition index, which should be high in order to induce the purchase.

State (1,1)

The transition to (2,1) depends on the number of traditional TV sets in the household that still have no set top box and on income, which should not be at the lowest level if we want the household to purchase the digital TV

The transition to (1,2) depends on the price of a digital TV set in relation to income, on the TV usage index and on the household composition index, which should be high in order to induce the household to purchase the new technology.

State (1,2)

The transition to (2,2) depends on the number of traditional TV sets in the household that still have no set top box and on the household index. If this has a high value it indicates a pressure to have another digital TV.

State (3,0)

The transition to (3,1) depends on the price of a digital TV set in relation to income and on the quality of service, which should be high if we want to make digital TV attractive and motivate its purchase.

State (2,1)

The transition to (3,1) depends on the number of traditional TV sets in the household that still have no set top box and on the income, which should not be at the lowest level if we want to motivate households to acquire digital TV.

The transition to (2,2) depends on the price of a digital TV set in relation to income, on the TV usage index and on the household composition index, which should be high in order to produce a motivation for purchase.

A few exogenous variables were also modelled. The price of digital TV sets was assumed to decrease over the time horizon being considered, from a maximum of €2,500 to a minimum of €.1,000 The interactivity, customisation and user friendliness levels were assumed to be increasing during this same time period. The switchover date was assumed to be 2010. Since the switchover date and the possibility of getting a government subsidy are dependent upon the policy chosen, we have used different years for their implementation.

After testing the decision tree with these sample households, we started to implement the microsimulations in order to study the adoption process within an entire population. A database containing 99 households was developed, including all data collected through questionnaires. The database with agents thus contained real data. The number of households was near to 100, so the absolute numbers obtained in the results were near to the percentage value if comparisons are made with the whole population.

We developed a computer program in the chosen environment UMDBS (Sauerbier, 2001). The program was tested, then all parameters were calibrated. The rules for transitions contained certain threshold index values, according to Table 3.3. Some of the threshold values were set arbitrarily, and we ran three different microsimulations with different values for each of them. The scenarios varied from optimistic (Min) to pessimistic (Max). The results of those scenarios are given in next section, together with results from other scenarios describing different policy issues.

Results and Discussion

One of the most important parts of the examination of the results from a microsimulation is the analysis of the model's sensitivity. After checking the parameters of the model we found that the model was sensitive to some threshold values, which are given in Table 3.4. This sensitivity shows that our future research should be focused on determining the importance of the entertainment appliances in a household and the importance of the household members' social networks, since

Table 3.3   Scenarios showing the basic setup of exogenous variables and their differences

Scenario	Description	Household indices threshold values*)	Subsidy starting year	Switch over year
Min	Different options for household indices	Min	2004	2010
Med		Med	2004	2010
Max		Max	2004	2010
Subs - without	Without subsidy	Med	-	2010
Subs - 2005	Subsidy starting from 2005	Med	2005	2010
Policy - without	No policy (neither subsidy nor switch over date)	Med	-	-
Switch - 2006	Switch over date 2006	Med	2004	2006

*) See Table 3.4 for explanation.

Table 3.4   Threshold values for indices, used in rules within a microsimulation program

	min	med	max
household composition index	4	5	6
entertainment appliances index	2	2	3
imitation index	2	2	3
TV usage index	8	9	10
price - income ratio	0,3	0,3	0,3
quality of service index	5	5	5
troubles (probability of abandoning of the digital technology)	0,05	0,05	0,05
switchover time (time in years to switchover date)	1	1	1

Table 3.5   Digital TV set prices for entry model, included in all microsimulations

Years	2003	2004	2005	2006	2007	2008	2009	2010	2011	2012
DTV Set price	2500	2500	2400	2200	1900	1600	1300	1000	1000	1000

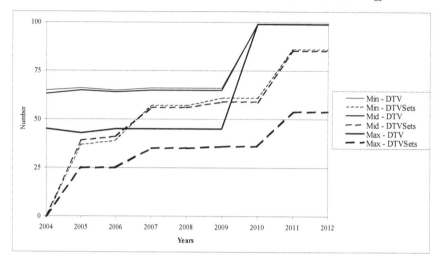

Figure 3.2   Results from the simulation runs for sensibility testing

these provide the household with information about and impulses towards acquiring new technological possibilities on the market. The results show that the predictions of the Max scenario are not close to the predictions of the other two scenarios (Min and Med). Scenario Max is different from Min and Mod in terms of the threshold values for the entertainment appliances index and for the imitation index. Other parameters in the scenario are obviously not so crucial, but we should keep in mind all the complexity of relationships among variables and rules. The results from running the three simulations, which were created to calibrate the model and to test the model's sensitivity, are given in Figure 3.2. Because it is the most representative scenario, the Med scenario was finally chosen for comparison with the other simulation runs, which represent different policy options.

The results were further examined in relation to four different policy scenarios and compared to the Mid scenario. All scenarios include the same parameters and threshold values as the Mid scenario (see Table 3.3, Table 3.4 and Table 3.5); they only differed in terms of the following:

— 'Subs – without' was developed from the premise that there is no government subsidy;
— 'Subs – 2005' established the government subsidy in the year 2005 (other scenarios presume that the subsidy started in 2004);
—'Policy – without' indicated the prediction of adoption when there was no policy (neither in relation to subsidy nor to switchover date);
— 'Switch – 2006' is created for illustrative purposes only – the switchover date was deliberately set to soon, but under circumstances when a subsidy started in 2004).[3]

---

3 As we explained earlier in our chapter, the study was conducted in 2003.

Table 3.6 shows the number of households in a given state in the year 2012 under different scenarios. The importance of a state in all the scenarios is measured by the sum of the households in a given state across all scenarios. We can see that by the end of the simulated timeframe the most preferred states involved having one DTV set and one, two or three set top boxes. In the non-extreme scenarios (Subs – 2005 and Mid) the important states were also (2, 0) and (1, 0), obviously for the households that were just trying to prolong the life of their traditional TV appliances.

Table 3.6   The number of households in a given state in the year 2012 under different scenarios

	Subs - without	Subs - 2005	Policy - without	Switch - 2006	Mid	Sum
(3, 1)	27	29	14	36	29	135
(2, 1)	31	29	1	20	28	109
(1, 1)	27	27	1	27	27	109
(0, 0)	1	0	43	0	0	44
(0, 1)	0	0	35	0	0	35
(2, 0)	6	6	5	8	7	32
(1, 0)	6	7	0	7	7	27
(2, 2)	0	1	0	1	1	3
(3, 0)	1	0	0	0	0	1
(0, 2)	0	0	0	0	0	0
(1, 2)	0	0	0	0	0	0

Conclusions

In order to decide if a policy of subsidies helps to support the diffusion of a new technology (from a government point of view) our model permits us to simulate users' behaviour once some basic user attitudes have been tested through empirical data. The results obtained enable us to compare the different adoption trends in relation to various public policies. Without subsidies, adoption was not so fast, although more than 50 per cent of households decided adopt the technology. The no policy scenario ('policy – without') showed that without a switchover deadline, the new technology was unlikely to succeed, unless better quality is provided in comparison with traditional services and competing price options.

The three scenarios without subsidies showed the level of interest in buying DTV sets in the year 2004, but in the following years it does not look as if DTV will become a mass service, because the number of households does not increase significantly, and only wealthy users will benefit from it. The scenario with subsidies starting from 2004 and a switchover takes place in 2006 showed the most rapid rate of adoption, of course. And with respect to the policy with subsidies starting from 2005, at the beginning the number of households with at least one DTV appliance remained almost the same, whereas the difference from subsidies was represented by the number of buyers of set top boxes or DTV sets. In the case of subsidies starting in 2004, all users may have become acquainted with the new technology from the first years when DVT was available, and not only the wealthy ones.

Such standalone results are still not sufficient to show that one policy is better than another, because to evaluate them we need to consider both their economic and their social impacts. If a government's aim is to favour a rapid mass transition to DTV, then the cost of subsidies may be less relevant. On the other hand, through a modest incentive one can stimulate a rapid diffusion scenario which allows the government to recover any costs sustained through tax revenues from the appliances sold or from other economic effects.

The above simulation experiments represent an important aspect of this complex evaluation because they provide outcomes in terms of different adoption trends, which can be used to estimate the various economic impacts. Besides such analysis, other factors should be considered, deriving, for instance, from the substitution effects in relation to other technologies. The influence of Internet surfing on the adoption of digital TV should be investigated further, where this kind of analysis could also be conducted using microsimulation tests.

References

Ballas, D., Clarke, G. and Turton, I. (1999), 'Exploring Microsimulation Methodologies for The Estimation of Household Attributes'. Paper presented at *The 4th International conference on GeoComputation*, Mary Washington College, Virginia, USA.

Banks, J., Carson II, J.S., Nelson, B.L. and Nicol, D.M. (2000), *Discrete-Event System Simulation* (Englewood Cliffs: Prentice-Hall).

Burch, T.K. (1999), *Computer Modelling of Theory: Explanation for the 21st Century* (London, Ontario: Population Studies Centre – University of Western Ontario).

European Commission (2002), *eEurope 2005: An information society for all*, COM 2002-263.

European Commission - Andersen (2002), *Outlook of the development of technologies and markets for the European Audio-visual sector up to 2010*, June 2002.

Levy, M., Levy, H. and Solomon, S. (2000), *Microscopic Simulation of Financial Markets* (San Diego: Academic Press).

Orcutt, G. (1957), 'A new type of socio-economic system', *Review of Economics and Statistics* 39 (2), 116–23.

Sauerbier, T. (2001), *UMDBS: Universal Micro DataBase System, Benutzerhandbuch* (Darmstadt: Technische Universität Darmstadt, Fachgebiet Statistik und Ökonometrie).

Wolf, D.A. (2001), *The Role of Microsimulation in Longitudinal Data Analysis*, Center for Policy Research, Maxwell School of Citizenship and Public Affairs (New York, Syracuse: Syracuse University).

Chapter 4

The Flexible Room: Technology for Communication and Personalisation

Marianne Jensen, Heidi Rognskog Mella and Kristin Thrane

Introduction

Family patterns are changing and so is the role of ICTs in our daily lives. This chapter describes the research results from the analysis of communication needs in distributed families, and then goes on to examine how we transformed our new knowledge to applications designed to meet these identified needs. Through the creation of the the Flexible Room we wanted to develop demonstrators that would serve as examples of new services that can fulfil the needs of distributed families for communication and flexible dwellings. The demonstrators that were presented in the laboratory 'Home of the Future' were: 1) distributed fairytale reading, 2) electronic wallpaper, 3) a scent interface and 4) an intelligent lamp used to communicate.

This chapter can be seen as a case study showing some of the processes involved in actively taking user inputs into account in the innovation process. It also shows how those participating in the design process collaborated, both at the level of interdisciplinary teams and in terms of collaboration between firms (whose products could be seen as being complementary). Furthermore, although the chapter will show that many of the product ideas that have been generated have not been carried out, some elements from the ideas have reached the market in one form or another.

Distributed Families

Distributed families are those in which family members live in different households or where some family members spend time outside the home. Distributed families can be distributed in both time and space. Time distributed families can, for example, be families where one of the parents works shifts or works at a remote location such as an oil platform. In this chapter, we will focus on families that are distributed in space such as those where parents are divorced and the children move between the respective homes of their parents (Jakobsen et al., 2003; Hjorthol et al., 2006). In Norway, 25 per cent of all children under the age of 15 have two homes, i.e. the re-established home of their mother and of their father. An increasing number of parents choose to share the responsibility and care for their children equally after a marital disruption.[1] Thus, the children spend alternate weeks in each home (Jensen, 2003). It is clear that this type of family setting creates new communication needs, both for the parents and for the children. ICTs may provide extended possibilities for communicating across distances and enhancing the presence of family members in each other's lives (Hjorthol et al., 2006; Ling, 2006).

As with the broader issues considered in this book, there are still many issues with regard to the adoption and use of ICTs. We are still working out how technologies fit into our everyday lives and they are still finding their place within the context of pre-existing structures and institutions such as the home and the family. Like the other authors in this book, we are trying to examine the factors affecting the adoption and use of these technologies in mundane situations. As with other technologies, in order for adoption to be successful technologies must meet user needs and capabilities and it is important that the interfaces are intuitive and self explanatory (see also Beckers et al., Chapter 1 in this book). These are the issues that will be examined in this chapter.

Methodology

For our empirical data we have carried out 12 in-depth interviews and three focus groups[2] with divorced or separated parents. The in-depth interviews were carried out at the informants' homes. We interviewed parents with visiting rights, with main custody and with joint care. An example of visiting rights would be when the child is with the parent one day a week and every second weekend. This is the most common situation for the children of divorced parents, but it is changing more and more towards joint care between the parents. We interviewed both men and women. We carried out one focus group with fathers who had visiting rights, one with women who had main custody, and one focus group with both men and women who had joint care. The focus groups were carried out in the Home of the Future. In 2001 we also had a workshop with children. We invited ten children between the age of six and nine years old to come to Telenor to play and talk about their life and ideas for the telephone in the future. The idea about bedtime storytelling that we present in this chapter came up during this session.

This project started out using a range of qualitative research methods to explore and identify the needs of spatially distributed families as regards communication and coordination. The use of qualitative methods answers more 'what?', 'why?' and 'how?' questions as opposed to questions of 'how many?' (Glazer and Strauss, 1967; Fog, 1997; Kvale, 1997). The in-depth interviews gave informants the opportunity to describe their daily lives. Many of the interviews were conducted in the informants' own homes where the researchers were able to observe the physical surroundings, the homes and how the informants organised their everyday lives. In contrast, focus groups are especially suitable when the purpose is to study people's attitudes to

---

1 Obviously we are simplifying the situation here since there are many parents who were never married, there are children born into the new relationships, etc. However, for the sake of clarity we choose to use these categories.

2 See also Loos, Chapter 9 in this book.

services (Nøtnæs, 2001). In fact, they are commonly used in market research but they are also becoming more accepted and used in social science studies. One disadvantage is the tendency for moral evaluations to develop in the group, which can lead to the establishment of 'group thinking'.

In this study the focus groups provided valuable insight into different attitudes to family organisation and to ICT services, and helped us see how distributed families communicate. After analysing the material where needs and user behaviour were revealed, we started to work on generating ideas for products and concepts that could fulfil the needs of distributed families. This process was carried out in a series of multidisciplinary workshops. The use of representatives from different professions covering a variety of perspectives is a well used method in the development of new services (Hagadon, 2003). In this project we invited external partners from outside Telenor, such as IKEA[3] and Husbanken[4] to collaborate in finding solutions to meet the user needs that had been identified. The results were documented as scenario descriptions. In all the workshops and through developing the scenarios, we used the analyses from the empirical data as inspiration and as a backdrop.

During the scenario mapping, we created the child personas[5] Thea and Thomas. As young members in a distributed family they become representative characters in the distributed families. A wider group of researchers who have been working with projects related to the Home of the Future became engaged in the final realisation of the concepts presented in this chapter as 'The Flexible Room'. These researchers were designers, artists, HCI specialists and technologists bringing together their skills to implement the scenarios as installations and demonstrators. Again we would like to stress the importance of multidisciplinary teams the process of service development.

The demonstrators are not complete and finished applications or services, but serve rather as visualisation tools showing examples of possibilities. When presenting the demonstrators for external audiences the Thea and Thomas background story made it easier to communicate the idea behind, and the purpose of, the demonstrators. The Home of the Future laboratory, in conjunction with the dissemination of the research results as demonstrators, also served to attract potential external partners.

Results from the Empirical Study

Our results show that the use of communication media serves as a parental cord in distributed families. Distance creates a challenge for parenting by limiting the possibilities for being present in children's everyday activities. Communication

---

3 Two IKEA designers came to Telenor for a joint workshop.

4 The Norwegian State Housing Bank, which has responsibility for national housing policy.

5 Personas are fictitious characters created to represent different types of user within the targeted demographic group that might use a site or product. Personas are given characteristics and are assumed to be in particular environments based on known users' requirements so that these elements can be taken into consideration when creating scenarios for conceptualizing a site (Cooper, 1999).

media such as the telephone, the mobile phone with messaging services and the Internet are widely used to compensate for the limitations represented by distance.

The age of the children is significant with regards to mediated communication. Younger children may be uncomfortable with the disturbance that a calling parent may constitute and withdraw from communication because their mind is occupied with other activities (for example, watching TV or playing with friends). Hence, parents with younger children expressed the need for more non-intrusive and 'richer' communication technologies than did parents of older children. For the parent actually living with the child in a space distributed family, communication between the child and the remote parent is not always looked upon positively. It may threaten their own individual privacy and even upset the child. In addition, depending on the nature of the relationship between the ex-partners, the intrusion into his/her life in order to chat with their child may tap into other unresolved issues between the parents.

By the same token, children who are reaching their adolescent years challenge the patterns of communication. They are spending more time away from the home, and they may need more expressive support as a result of maturing emotionally and going through various ups and downs. Thus, 'parents with visiting rights' experience a greater need for communication media during their children's adolescent phase. Often the visitation agreements have ceased to work and the children decide for themselves where to stay.

We asked a father with visitation rights the following question:

'Are you in contact with your child every day?'

He replied:

'Yes, I send her "I love you", "Miss you", and that sort of thing. She is going through a turbulent period at the moment, so she needs to have a father present.'

The quotation above illustrates the types of issue and the way that the father tries to maintain at least a 'virtual presence' in the life of his child, regardless of distance.

In addition, the interviews revealed the need to have a variety of channels available through which to keep in contact with the non-resident parent, as well with the child. The level of conflict in the family, the age and the nature of the communication task in question can all influence the choice of communication media.

In the families that had broken up, the need to re-establish two homes means that there may be a strain on household budgets and a subsequent reduction in the size of the homes. For instance, in our analysis, we found a slight tendency whereby families that had split up had more limited space in their households. There were, for example, several children sharing a bedroom either with the parent or a sibling, something that is less common in intact families. In addition, the use of space in the household varied depending on where the children were living at the moment. Both these situations create a need for flexibility, which was our point of departure in the workshop involving IKEA and The Norwegian State Housing Bank.

Workshops on Definition of The Flexible Room

The aim of the iterative workshops was to provide input into the development of a future-oriented installation in the Home of the Future laboratory. We were interested in demonstrating the flexible use of space and the role of technology for personalisation. In the work sphere, the 'clean desk' policy becomes more and more common in office environments – you tidy your desk everyday, and tomorrow you might sit at another desk. The idea behind the 'clean desk' policy is to rationalise the use of space since not all employees are present all the time. But how would this work in the private sphere, and for distributed families?

The 'clean bed' policy was introduced in the workshop as a conceptual tool for expanding thinking with regard to the use of technology and the use of space in the private sphere. We posed the questions: *Is it possible to use technologies to personalise a domestic environment that is high in flexibility, where family members come and go? Can technology replace a personal space?*

We defined the child personas Thomas and Thea in a distributed family in order to create a context for the use of space and technology in the Home of the Future. In order to highlight the issues of coordination and the need for flexibility, the scenario included two children with the same father but two different mothers. These children lived every other week at their mothers' homes. The workshop concentrated on the following three themes: ways to divide the rooms, flexible furniture and personalisation.

Figure 4.1   The 'clean bed' policy, showing cupboard with bedding and personal items to complement the 'clean bed'

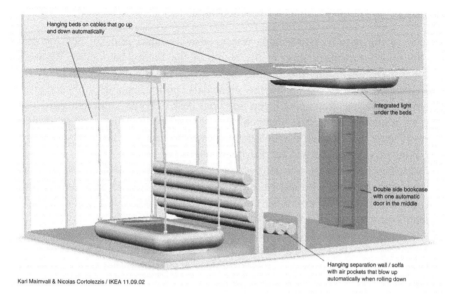

Figure 4.2   **Solution for a flexible room (IKEA 2002)**

The illustration embraces and builds upon several of the ideas from the workshop with IKEA and the Norwegian State Housing Bank at Telenor. The beds could, for instance, be put in different positions depending on the number of children in the house. However, the ideas for furniture were never built or implemented directly. When refining the results from the workshop, Telenor R&D prioritised three areas as guiding the development of the demonstrators for the Home of the Future: technology for social communication, technology for personalisation and technology for privacy.

The Flexible Room: Four Demonstrators

From the focus group findings and scenario building, including the personas Thea and Thomas, we started with the descriptions of some challenging situations they could experience that could be resolved using new technology. The request for new communication channels and the wish to personalise their environments were the two most important factors that we wanted to reflect in the technology based demonstrators installed in the Home of the Future in December 2002.

Being an ICT research organisation there was an emphasis on using new challenging interfaces based on telecom technology rather than focusing on the use of space that was more connected to physical furniture and interior design. However, we want to point out that it will be important to look at how to design new immersed interfaces in the intersection between the structure or architecture of the home, its interior design and new communication technology. Therefore we found ambient technology to be a useful area for exploration.

As an example, the families had described the mobile phone as being a parental cord, therefore we wanted to expand the communication experience through incorporating pictures and video in that communication channel. Another example from our findings is the situation when several children share a bedroom with parents or siblings, but not necessarily at the same time. By using new technology and multimedia, we wanted the family members (Thea and Thomas) to be able to change or customise the room's atmosphere according to their interests, taste and character.

Ambient displays

Changes in scent and lighting in the surroundings can be a source of information and a means of personalisation (Aarts and Stefano, 2003). Ambient displays provide alternatives to existing interfaces like PC connected screens. Ambient displays cover interfaces that are not currently thought of as constituting interfaces, but that may serve other functions such as being wallpaper, furniture, lamps, vases, etc. We believe that this type of display can be especially suitable for the home environment.

We wanted to provide examples of new interfaces that use senses other than those we normally think of when considering ICTs today. Not all information and communication needs to be in the form of text, images or sound. Changes in smells/scents, lighting or tactile changes in surroundings can give us information without demanding too much of our attention (Nyseth et al., 2004).

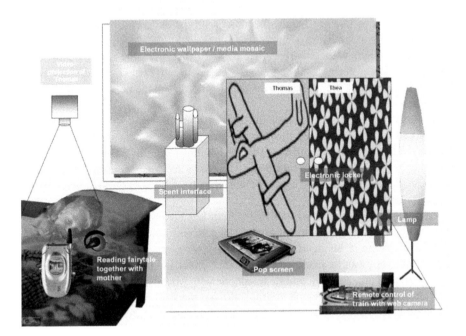

Figure 4.3   Ideas about the demonstrator room (IKEA 2002)

The ambient interface can also cover different types of needs compared to traditional user interfaces. It is possible to create an atmosphere and a sense of closeness through communication in a relatively intrusive way. A phone call from the remote mother can interrupt an ongoing activity and is less flexible compared to a message '*I love you – thinking of you*' on the lamp before going to sleep.

Changes in smell/scent and light constitute a type of information in the surroundings that is not suitable for all types of applications. This is because they operate in the background, at the edge of people's awareness and attention.

The sketch (Figure 4.3) shows some of the demonstrator ideas that we came up with during the workshops on scenario mapping. All the ideas could in some sense address the challenges to which distributed families are exposed. We chose the following ideas to be developed as demonstrators in the Flexible Room: 1) distributed fairytale reading, 2) the electronic wallpaper, 3) the scent interface and 4) the intelligent lamp.

1) Distributed fairytale reading

To show how technology can support social communication in distributed families, we wanted to examine the use of audiovisual solutions such as video communication in real time between the homes. When this proposition was posed to the 'Distributed Families' focus group the response was clear: opening the home to an ex-partner with real-time video access in a shared family space was not desirable. However, when asked if video contact with the children via a personal mobile terminal was a good thing, the attitudes were more positive. It was very clearly stated that mobile telephones are necessary for being in contact with the children during the periods when they are not at the home of the parent.

In the workshop with children aged 6–9, a 7-year-old girl told us how her father read bedtime stories to her on her mobile telephone in the evening. She was, however, disappointed that she could not see the pictures in the book from which he was reading.

This story provided the foundation for showing how close contact between parents and children can be reinforced through the use of richer media than mere voice telephony. This led us to examine extended functions such as MMS (multimedia messaging services) on mobile terminals. The MMS service was introduced in the Norwegian market in 2002 and commercialised in 2003, so at the time it was a new service concept in the market.

We came up with a demonstrator that is built around a bedside situation. On the bed a video sequence of Thomas falling asleep is projected onto the bed. He has a mobile telephone in his hand and a hands-free set connected to his ear. A voice reading a fairytale can be heard from a speaker under the bed. Thomas' mother is reading. On the bed, there is a mobile telephone with MMS function. On the display on the mobile, we see images photographed from the storybook.[6] Thomas' mother takes photographs of the illustrations from the children's storybook and sends them to Thomas while she is reading.

---

6 The story is called *Kafe haletippen* by the artist Bjørn Rørvik.

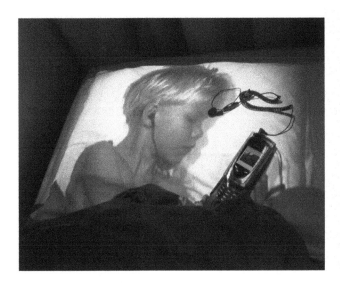

Figure 4.4   Distributed fairytale reading

This type of application via MMS examines how we might think of intimate and close-up experiences in various home-based user situations. Through the previous experiences of customer visits to the Home of the Future, we know that this type of installation creates a framework for discussion. Critics will raise questions such as *'How early should children be allowed to use a mobile telephone?'*, *'Is it right to sell mobile telephones as a substitute for contact between parents?'*, etc. It is important to bring these attitudes to the fore, in order to identify factors which may influence the adoption of new services. Nevertheless, we saw that sending images by mobile telephones was a potentially useful application in a distributed family.

2) The electronic wallpaper – media mosaic

In the scenario we set up the situation whereby Thomas and Thea live in the flexible room on alternate weeks. Because of this, it would be desirable to change the surroundings according to their individual wishes and tastes. The electronic wallpaper consisted of video images, and was a solution that allowed for the various tastes, interests and the different characters of Thomas and Thea. Video sequences representing the child's interests are shown on the wallpaper. For example, Thomas likes exotic animals while Thea likes flowery wallpaper. Thomas has also made his own wallpaper, consisting of video images of his favourite toys and the environment at his mother's home. One can imagine that the children will also compose their own images (rock stars, football players, film clips, etc.).

The wallpaper showed images that have another tempo and degree of brightness than that which we would normally experience when looking at media such as film or television. The wallpaper worked as a visual mosaic. There are other requirements that this electronic wallpaper needs to meet. It should create a calm atmosphere and

Figure 4.5   Electronic wallpaper with exotic animals (Africa wallpaper)

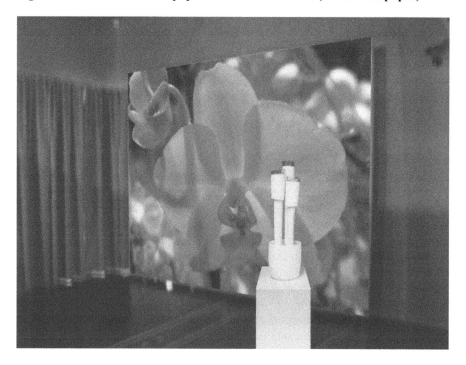

Figure 4.6   Electronic wallpaper with orchids

should be in the background, integrated into the home's interior, unlike the medium of TV that is supposed to capture our attention. The different motifs in the wallpaper gave the room diverse atmospheres, styles and characteristics.

In the demo, we also showed how a web camera could send images from other rooms in the apartment or, indeed, from Thea's or Thomas' other homes. The wallpaper then functioned as a channel of communication between the homes. In the demo, we showed how Thomas was in touch with his mother via the web camera video projections integrated into the wallpaper. The wallpaper could change mode and also functioned as a projection area for other media sources in the home (for example, it could be a screen for DVD films or for a games console).

3) The scent interface

Scent is a very strong elicitor of personal memories and associations and may be an important factor when dealing with the issue of personalisation. In the Telenor installation, we developed a scent interface that allowed us to vary the aroma in the room according to whether Thomas or Thea was the current occupant.[7] Examples of the scents we used in the installation in the Home of the Future were a floral fragrance, mint and lavender. These could also be coordinated with the video images presented on the wallpaper.

To illustrate how this interface might be used, in the scenario the scent of lavender filled the room when Thomas' mother tried to contact him through the web camera. When Thomas smelt the scent of lavender, he knew that his mother was at home and trying to contact him. When Thea entered the room, we smelt the floral fragrance. When Thomas entered the room, we smelt the mint fragrance.

The scent interface was designed to be an abstract plant shape and was a sculptural object with three 'flowers'; one for each of the scents.[8] Scent was also a reinforcing element in the demonstrator adding to the experience of peace and calm that is generated by the background images.

4) The intelligent lamp

The scented flowers constituted an independent object, but we can exemplify how information can be integrated into existing interiors and objects in these surroundings through the intelligent lamp. The intelligent lamp became an interface that facilitated interaction between people and also between people and IT systems using PC like e-mail or messaging services.

The lamp was divided into three sections: one red, one green and one yellow. The brightness could be adjusted. Changes in light with different colour combinations provided information that remained in the background and did not demand too much of one's attention.

---

7 Scent containers and a Tini-server, lighting and a fan were built into a sculptural vase. The diffusion of scent was controlled over a WEB- or WAP-interface (Nyseth et al., 2004).

8 The sculptural vase was designed by N. Khalayl, J. Romm and L. Haaland for the Design Exhibition Form 2002 in Oslo, Norway.

Figure 4.7   Communicating lamp

The communicating lamp functioned as an extended interface connected to the Internet. Instead of getting messages or reminders on the PC interface, Thea or Thomas got reminders or messages through the lamp from their remote parents. Different light combinations meant different things, like '*I miss you*', '*Call me*' or a notification that there was an e-mail waiting from the remote parent.

Concluding Remarks

The principle that new media sources in the home can allow us to create personalised rooms and facilitate interpersonal communication has been the guideline for the work done in the project and was manifested through the project demonstrators. The choice of demos that we ultimately developed was based on needs expressed by potential users, in addition to the points raised during interdisciplinary workshops. Those users expressed a desire for personalisation, solutions for security and privacy, as well as social communication. Each installation encompassed two or more of these elements.

We particularly wanted to explore new interface technologies. Along with the electronic wallpaper, we wanted to show how scent and light sources could be a part of the stream of information in the home. When we set out to design the intelligent lamp and the scent interface, it was important not to place too much emphasis on the information to be represented. It was important to have an open and experimental attitude to give both visitors and ourselves a broader horizon to speculate about what was possible with regard to the representation of personal information in the Home of the Future (Nyseth et al., 2004). This said, the arrangement of the interior of the room that can reinforce a sense of it being a private and intimate sphere and give a feeling of having come into a real home were lacking in The Flexible Room.

One can discuss the extent to which the solutions we selected adequately engaged with the findings that have come out of interviews and focus groups in the 'Distributed Families' project. We believe, however, that we captured certain elements which reflected the reality of these people but which were, at the same time, forward-looking. On the other hand the concepts were never formally tested with real users after finalisation. The project ended before we were able to get any closer to a final solution.

Today, we see a continuation of the general trend as regards the increase in divorce rates and children's increased access to mobile phones at younger ages. In 2005, seventy-five per cent of 10-year-olds and fifty-two per cent of nine-year-olds had access to a mobile phone (Telenor R&D/ Statistics Norway). Subsequent research showed that children with divorced parents tended to have access to mobile phones at younger ages than children with intact families, and that the divorced parents use the mobile phone as an important tool for keeping in contact with their children to a larger extent (Hjorthol et al., 2006).

The realisation of the small rabbit-like robot Nabaztag in recent years (http://www. nabaztag.com/en/index.html) shows that objects and services are being developed and introduced into the market that coincide well with our line of thinking in the Flexible Room project. Nabaztag is a 23 cm tall rabbit with movable ears, coloured light and voice that is constantly connected to the Internet. It provides access to other Internet users, other rabbits, or mobile phones. The Nabaztag provides information about weather, incoming e-mails, or you could simply program the rabbit to provide access to your personal information. It can be used for social communication as well as to display information between individuals in the home environment. The Nabaztag represent a new interface technology, acts as a supplement to PC and mobile terminals and opens up opportunities for personalised technology.

Another example of interactive furniture that has since been developed elsewhere is the Japanese research project Teleshadow that is used as a non-intrusive way for friends to stay in touch. The system projects a video of what people are doing at home via the net into their friends' houses. Instead of showing images in full motion and colour, Teleshadow turns them into shadow outlines projected on the inside of a small decorative lamp. The invention was inspired by Japanese history where the rooms of Japanese homes were originally divided by paper walls. The thin walls preserve some privacy but the shadows cast on the paper as people moved about also acted as a reminder of that person's presence. This research project was shown at the Siggraph computer graphics convention held in San Diego in August 2007 (http://www.siggraph.org).

Nabaztag and Teleshadow are experiments using alternative display solutions that, like ours, are ambient and non-intrusive. They present a different way to exchange communication and information within social networks such as friends or families. Both projects stand as examples of developments along the same lines as the ideas that we wanted to emphasise in the Flexible Room.

The results from The Flexible Room could have been taken further in the innovation process. Some interesting and promising concepts were identified, but the ability to take the concepts into a commercialisation process was not present at the time. However, many of the research issues and services that were developed in the Home of the Future and The Flexible Room can be seen as precursors for later research activities within Telenor Research & Innovation. As an example, we can mention the Telenor R&I project Connected Objects which builds on M2M (machine to machine) and wireless communication technology.

In the market today we see that the price of projectors aimed at consumers has dropped and a considerable number of projectors have been sold in the Norwegian domestic market.[9] We also see that video images used to create atmosphere and ambience are now available to a larger extent in the market (for example, live bonfire, fish swimming in fishbowl). Coming back to the broader issues in this book, our work indicates that there are many questions and issues associated with the eventual adoption of new technologies. Even though we have what seem to be unlimited possibilities, these still need to be worked into the daily lives of individuals so that they make sense and are seen as being useful in that context. The Home of the Future allowed us the opportunity to examine some of these possibilities in a somewhat freer context. This, in turn, gave us the chance to gather the thoughts and reflections of individuals when confronted with these ideas. By conducting this mapping exercise we were able to better understand the constraints and possibilities of the technology vis-à-vis users' everyday lives and sensibilities.

Acknowledgements

The demonstrators presented in this chapter are central deliverables from the work with Home of the Future in Telenor, and the result of a group effort. In particular we would like to thank the project manager Arnfinn Nyseth for his efforts as a driving force behind The Future Home, and the members of the Future Media Research Group at Telenor for contributing to the realisation of the demonstrators described in this chapter. This chapter has presented results from the interdisciplinary research project 'Distributed Families' at Telenor R&D 2002, where the demonstrators are conceptualised around the notion of 'The Flexible Room', an installation in the Home of the Future, Telenor R&D's laboratory for development of new ICT solutions in an everyday setting in the period 2000–2004. Today the Home of the Future can be seen as the 'The Futuristic House' at the Open Air Museum at Maihaugen in Lillehammer: http://www.maihaugen.no/.

---

9 The Consumer Electronics Trade Foundation in Norway estimates the sale of projectors for the home market to be about 7400 in 2006.

References

Aarts, E. and Stefano, M. (2003), *The New Everyday View of Ambient Intelligence* (Rotterdam: OIO Publishers).

Cooper, A. (1999), *The Inmates are Running the Asylum* (SAMS).

Fog, J. (1997), *Med Samtalen som Utgangspunkt. Det Kvalitative Forskningsinterview* (København: Akademisk forlag).

Glazer, B. and Strauss, A. (1967), *The Discovery of Grounded Theory* (New York: Aldine).

Hagadon, A. (2003), *How Breakthroughs Happen: Technology Brokering and the Pursuit of Innovation* (Harvard Business School Publishing Corporation).

Hjorthol, R.J. et al. (2006), *On the Move – in the Car – with the Mobile Phone: a Study of Communication and Mobility in the Daily Life of Families with Children* (Oslo: TØI/Telenor).

Jakobsen, M., Jensen, M. and Thrane, K. (2003), 'Communication and Coordination', *Distributed families*, R43, 2003 (Telenor R&D).

Jensen, A.M. (2003), 'More children live with dad – towards a turning point', *Samfunnsspeilet*. 03/2003 (Statistics Norway).

Kvale, S. (1997), *The Qualitative Research Interview* (Gjøvik: Ad Notam Gyldendal).

Ling, R. (2006), 'Flexible coordination in the Nomos: Stress, emotional maintenance and coordination via the mobile telephone in intact families', in Kavoori, A. and Arceneaux, N. (eds), *Cultural Dialectics and the Cell Phone: Essays in Social Transformation* (New York: Peter Lang).

Nyseth A. et al. (2004*), The Future Home*, Telenor R&D Report No 24, 2004.

Nøtnæs, T. (2001), *Introduction to the Use of Focus Groups*, SSB note paper 2001/24.

PART II
The Internet as a Tool to Enable Users to Organise Everyday Life

Uses of the Family Internet Sites: A Virtual Community between Intimate Space and Public Space

Fanny Carmagnat, Julie Deville and Aurélia Mardon

Introduction

Family websites or 'family Intranets' in France have expanded remarkably since 2000. Within a period of two years they grew from a few hundred to several hundred thousand sites, encouraged by the free and easy creation of a site with only a few clicks. The growth of digital camera penetration in France is another sign of the importance of photography in family communication. Family Internet sites can be defined as sets of personal web pages that are common to a family group and that are accessible only to this group. The services offered differ little from one supplier to another. They allow families to create thematic photographic albums, launch discussions by posting messages, chat and send e-mails to everybody who wants to know notifying them of the birthdays of family members.

Our hypotheses concern the sociology of the family but they also question the status of virtual spaces on the Internet. Are family relationships affected by this new means of communication? Do family websites encourage relationships with remote members of the family? Do they help renew relationships with relatives with whom contact has been lost? Can this new means of communication be a substitute for other, more traditional, means of maintaining contact, such as family meetings, sending e-mails or phone calls? Our final question relates to these family websites' identity. They are spaces reserved for a restricted number of members. But do these private family spaces not have some characteristics of a public space?

Methodology

A qualitative study was conducted in 2001 into the uses of family websites that were offered on subscription by two main providers *notrefamille.com* and *familoo. com* (Carmagnat, 2000; Deville and Mardon, 2002). This study included an online questionnaire and thirty in-depth interviews with websites initiators and their families. The ethnographical part of the survey consisted of observations of the life of some family websites, as the investigators were 'invited' to view some sites for a couple of months.

The Composition of Family Websites

The answers to the online questionnaire showed that about half of the family website creators (administrators) were women. As they are more involved in family relationships, they may be particularly attracted by this use of the Internet (Bott, 1957; Picrou, 1992; Smoreda and Licoppe, 1999). One of the providers, *Familoo*, seems to attract young people, mainly aged between 25 and 34 years old (40 per cent), while most of the site creators on the other one, *Notrefamille*, are aged over 40 (56 per cent). They may have chosen this particular site because it is more tuned to genealogy. Half of the creators of family websites have children at home, mostly babies or young children under 2 years old, teenagers and young adults over 15.

A few of the family sites were first created at the time of the birth of a child, but most of the administrators said that they initiated their sites without a connection to any specific event. During the interviews they usually said that they had decided to make their own family website when they first discovered the provider's offer. Many of them had felt a need for such a form of communication. Some of them had tried to create a family site by themselves or else already had a personal website. Almost all users mentioned the fact that some of their relatives lived far away from them and thought that the site facilitated better communication with these relatives. Young parents also wanted to share news and the photos of their children with their wider family. The questionnaire about *Notrefamille* asked about the reasons for the creation of the website. Most of the people chose all the possible answers, which were 'interest in genealogy', 'to strengthen family links', 'to spread family documents easily', and even 'as a game'. These specific reasons seem to signify a general attachment to the family.

Who is Part of the Family?

All the members of the family website were 'invited' to visit it by its creator. These administrators were the only ones allowed to choose who counted as being family members and it was quite a responsibility. The administrator was the centre of the group of parents and friends who were invited to visit the site, who tied them together, but who had to be careful to offend no-one. Administrators may have had to include people they did not like very much. They also had to consider the situation of distant relatives and any family feuds. Each family website was accessible to a specific combination of relatives. Most of the sites included the creator's brothers and sisters (55 per cent), 45 per cent included the administrator's spouse or companion, or his cousins, about a quarter or a third included the father and mother, the children, other relatives or friends. Less than 15 per cent included the father- and mother-in-law and the grandparents.

In most of the families, some choices were obvious: the closest relatives, brothers and sisters, parents, and quite often cousins, uncles and aunts were invited to visit as soon as they had access to the Internet. They may have even been registered on the family website before they used the Internet, in anticipation of a future connection, or for symbolic reasons, to indicate that no one had been left out. Up to a point, which is not the same in all families, the decision to send out an invitation required some serious reflection. Some people were too remote, from a genealogical or an affective point of view, to be automatically included. And most of the creators did not want their family website to grow too large. The creator's own companion may not have been part of the site, particularly when the couple had formed too recently or when the site was made for the creator's family. Some couples also shared the same electronic address, giving the impression that both of them participated when in fact only one of them used the site. The choice of the members was based on two motivations: many of them belonged to the same generation as the creator or else they had a close family link to him. Brothers and sisters and cousins, who are invited to be part of many sites, had both characteristics. In fact, many sites were based on a strong relationship between brothers and sisters. The most frequent members, except the husband or wife, also shared a common ancestor. Some users of the family website even referred to this ancestor, talked about his life and his place in the family, and sometime showed his portrait, which was occasionally placed on the first page of their site.

The backbone of family websites often seemed to be a particular lineage within the family. If men rarely hesitated to give their own name to the site, married women had a choice to make. Some of them chose their maiden name, because their site was oriented towards their own family, or even the name of an ancestor. When the site had been created at the birth of a baby, it was often linked to the two family lines of the parents and bore both their names.

The Reasons for Choices

The combination of relatives invited onto the site depended on the administrator's age, which determined his or her position in the life cycle. Creators aged under 25 years old invited mainly their brothers and sisters, then their mother and father. Brothers and sisters were still the main guests for creators aged between 25 and 59, but husbands or wives took the secondary position. Children came first or second in the sites initiated by people aged over 50. Their rank was a logical consequence of the creator's age; they were more likely to be found on the website when the creator was older, because the children were themselves older, used the Internet and may have left home. Old parents or grandparents were often left out of the website. They were supposed to be too old to adapt themselves to the new technologies. '*They are 87 and it's really the kind of stuff…*', said one user. Another one started with a statement that soon proved to be a supposition: '*They don't understand! Especially on my father's side, they wouldn't understand*', and her mother's family was also evoked with the same ambiguity: '*They don't understand the principle of the Internet. They wouldn't understand these pictures can be seen from any computer in the world, or the principle of the mail, too. It's not obvious to them*'. Seniors may be a minority on the net, but our questionnaire showed that people over 60 and even 70 have created sites. Some of them may have done this at the end of their working life, but certainly not the older ones. In France, studies have shown that old people are ready to use new technologies as soon as they think it can be useful for them (Caradec, 2001).

But it seems that family websites are used more to communicate within a generation than between generations, even if intergenerational links have tended to be renewed and have grown these last years (Attias-Donfut and Segalen, 1998; Attias-Donfut et al., 2002).

In everyday life as experienced on the web the relationship with the family 'in-law' was ambiguous. It could be strong or weak, easy or difficult. In each particular case you had to find 'the right distance' (Lemarchant, 1999). The administrator's father- and mother-in-law were included in only 12 per cent of the sites, but they were often present when the site was mainly about a baby. In this case, the site creators mentioned *the family*, including both family lines, and referring to *my family* when they talked about their own line. We have no statistics about the brothers- or sisters-in-law, and more generally about those members of the spouse's family who belonged to the same generation. It would have been interesting to know if they were less likely to be included than the spouse's parents because the site's creators had fewer obligations towards them, or if they were more often members because they belonged to the creator's generation. The choice depended on the kind of relationship between the two families. When it was good, this fact could often be seen on the site. We noticed that the more the site creator's spouse used the site, the more his or her family was included on it.

We saw all kind of situations. In some cases the father, mother, brother- or sister-in-law were full and active members on the family website, some others had been politely invited but did not use it, and on many sites they were not included. In these cases, the creators often felt obliged to justify their choice and evoked various, and sometimes vague, reasons. Some argued that their spouse's family did not use Internet, or were not Internet-oriented, or that they did not foster the family relationship ('*they are not keen on family*'). Others said that their website was made for one specific part of the family, or that it could not include everyone. In some cases, the users wanted their site to be very intimate and thought that this was not possible if there were too many members. They sometimes felt close to some members of their family-in-law, but not enough to invite them.

Each creator decided where to draw the boundary. One of them, for example, included most of his wife's family, but decided that his children's parents-in-law would stay out. He said that they are certainly allowed to see the website when visiting the children, and seemed to appreciate this, but they were not close enough to him to be included. About a third of the websites included people who were not part of the family. On the other hand many users thought that friends could not be part of a family website. Some of them said that the site was specifically made for the family. Others thought that it would have been too difficult to communicate if their site had included friends and relatives who did not know each other. Some parents would have felt lost, and, as noted by one user who had refused to put a photo of a friend on her site, '*people won't necessarily understand, and they are not necessarily interested in knowing who my friends are, either*'. Family and friends generally belonged to different spheres, and many of the users who had invited friends to have access explained their choice by the fact that these friends belonged to the familial sphere: they may have been only friends, without kinship link, but '*they are just like family*'. Some website creators had tried to include friends who had not had this kind of strong relationship with the family, but in these cases there was not much participation on the sites. The deciding factor to include someone was his or her belonging to or assimilation within the family, although the degrees of assimilation varied. We could not deduce a general rule from these cases, but this was a consequence of the diversity of families in France nowadays.

The relationships inside a family can be difficult. Sometimes, the family website can help this, sometimes not. A woman who we met, for example, was in conflict with her brother but she could communicate with him through her site because it allowed her to keep her distance. But the family website did not solve all feuds: she also had divorced parents who would not talk to each other, even on the Internet. Hence, she had decided to create two sites, one including her mother, the other including her father. Some users created several sites because they were included in various circles that had no particular reason to communicate with each other, even if there were no conflicts. Some of them had made one or two sites for their family, because of a divorce or because the two parts of the family did not share the same interests. But some had also made one for their friends, or for their classmates. The friend websites did not usually work very well, because the members did not all know each other. The classmate sites tended to become a way to share news about work.

The Uses of Family Sites

The members of a family site had the option to upload material to and take part in the site by bringing photos and news. Most of the administrators would have liked all members to participate, but in fact only a few members became active. The administrator remained, generally with his or her brothers, sisters and cousins, the more active member. Friends, uncles, aunts, and children rarely participated. However, a few conflicts had occurred when an administrator tried to encourage family participation. Several reasons can explain the low interest of members and the power that the administrator kept over the site. Technical difficulties or lack of equipment played a role. But the ambivalent nature of the site was the main reason. The site may have been collective, but it was particularly the expression of the family network in which the administrator was at the centre. That said, on some sites we could observe the equal participation of all members. However, this was because those sites had relatively few members and they felt close to each other.

Women and men administrators managed their family site in the same way but thought about their use of their Internet in very different ways. Women never referred to a technical activity managed through their computer and described its use in a modest way. Some men talked about having a passion for computing, and described their technical interest in the computer. The administrators managed their sites from home and often did this alone in front of their computer in order to create some quiet time. The second place from which the website was managed was the office. This was a way of introducing a familial and private dimension into their working lives, bringing some pleasure in work, as shown by Monjaret (1996). In reality, communication was from one person to a group or to another person, but the fiction of a group communicating with another group could be assumed when the administrator signed the message both for himself and his spouse. Using the chat facility was more often the occasion to communicate collectively. Husband, wife and children could participate easily in this convivial communication, which was a kind of a virtual family gathering.

The administrators managed their sites at work too, because of the ease, the money it saved and the pleasure it brought to work. The husband or wife of the administrator rarely participated. Sometimes they uploaded photos to and wrote messages on the site, or wrote something with the administrator, but their activity was always less important than the activity of the administrator. This weak participation was linked to the fact that the administrator took charge of all the communication with the rest of the family.

The creation of a family site was not a substitute for other ways of communicating within the family, but instead extended them. In fact, communication via the site was always positive. Bad news or intimate talk appeared in channels of communication that were less shared, like telephone, email or sometimes letters. For some families with members living far away from each other, chat makes communication easier. For example, Véronique Morin had decided to set up an appointment to chat with her sister and mother who lived very far away from each other. Thus, the site allowed people to maintain a link in spite of the geographical distance and often multiplied communication options because of its low cost features.

Our study points out that the site was a tool to restore the family network. It made building or re-building communication possible with those members of the family amongst whom communication had ceased, mostly cousin or uncles and aunts. It acted as a mediator in several ways. Members were free to accept or refuse contact. Communication via the site was 'asynchronous', and thus less disturbing than the telephone. The site created a symbolic and virtual space where each member knew he had a place but also knew that he was not forced to participate. Also, the site allowed members to create a certain distance when communicating. A contact was activated and maintained, but it did not necessarily lead to direct links. Thus the site may have enabled the invigoration of a family network but it did not have huge implications for its members. It seemed like an ideal way to maintain ties with family members who lived far away or who did not get on well with each other. For the family that seemed harmonious, the site was considered to be a tool that could reinforce family contacts and ties.

An Ideal Family Show

The family sites that people subscribed to on *familoo.com* or *notrefamille.com* seemed to be electronic versions of ideal family meetings. On these websites, any reference to negative or troubling elements, any topic that could reveal dissent, any mention of unhappy events was all banished. The very format offered by the site providers, as seen in the contents of the headings, was inclined to dissolve differences and avoid any conflict. Thus, the amount of scope given to members for presentation on *Notrefamille* was limited. They could choose, from a pre-given list, their subjects of interest such as hobbies, cooking, or pets. Their portrait was only allowed to be impersonal. They could announce what their preferred colour was or decide if they were 'sentimental', 'curious', 'optimistic' or 'independent'. But the website avoided asking about the political or religious orientations of members.

Since communication on the site was collective in nature, the news topics were often of a very general and consensual nature. The sites did not allow any room for unspecified intimate and individual communications. If the offers of the two site suppliers had implicit rules regarding usage that furthered harmony, this appears to be in perfect coherence with what the families were able to practise on their site. For example, the header 'Discussion' did not allow them to discuss topics that concerned them deeply. And in practice the users did choose light subjects, generally in the form of jokes or derision. The implicit rule that was never transgressed in the cases studied was that one should use the site for amusing and inoffensive subjects. But even if contributors to the family sites recognised that the messages that they posted in the discussion area were by choice general and harmless that did not mean that they judged the whole content of their site to be insignificant or without any interest. On the contrary, they expressed a strong attachment to this virtual space where one can see the photographs of children and ancestors and communicate with distant relatives linked by communal ancestors. These sites, as in the case of any family meeting, had their excluded people, their private discussions, their favourite relationships and their family secrets. In fact, a recurrent difficulty was the situation that could arise if two people were on the same site who were on bad terms with each other. In this case, the manager of the site had to decide if he (or she) should invite them all, or only one of them (and if so, which), or none of them.

The most outstanding fact about the contribution of the sites to family sociability was that their creation renewed contacts with relatives with whom contact had been lost, and revealed unknown relatives. The other noticeable fact was that the people renewing contact through the website could have communicated by other means – by mail, by telephone calls, by visiting – but in practice they had not. Less intrusive than telephone – as noted above – and with fewer implications than personal letters, the family site sent out invitations without forcing people to accept them. Just as on a family tree each has his or her rightful place, the members of the same family group have their place in their site without having to assert it.

The Role of Photography

Photographs play a central role in the constitution of family memory (Bourdieu, 1965; Barthes, 1980). Even more than the presence of the members on discussion forums, sending photographs was the sign of their real participation in the life of the site. Photographs were organised by topic in virtual albums. These topics included pictures of ancestors or places of the origins of the family, holidays or travels, family events such as marriages, births or family celebrations, and children. Traditionally, old family photographs have held a central place in a family's devotion (Muxel, 1997; Cohen Hunther, 1999). They were formerly gathered in paper albums or displayed on mantelpieces. In these family websites they were now offered for family contemplation, virtually always present on the Internet.

The ego-centred origin of the sites, comparable with that of family trees, carried within it a contradiction, which resulted in the low participation of many of the invited members. The site was posted like a virtual space pertaining to the entire family group, but only one person, the initiator of the site, designed the range and the limits of this group. Each site had a different tone. Some were devoted to the conservation of the family memory and emphasised the genealogy aspects, while some others were, in contrast, dedicated to family communication. Some sites could also merge these two functions.

Conclusion

Family sites are to be understood as lying between public spaces and private places. They are not places for intimate circles since they are strongly constrained by implicit rules and they address the wider family group and not only the members of the nuclear family. Neither are they public spaces for the expression or construction of opinion. Instead, they are defined as community spaces. Modelled after family meetings, the family websites combine a cautiousness in the use of language, in order to maintain family togetherness, with a strong emotional content attached to the material on the sites, links to childhood, family origins and beginnings and the place which one occupies within a family lineage and within a wider family group.

References

Attias-Donfut, C. and Segalen, M. (1998), *Grands-parents: la famille à travers les générations* (Paris: Odile Jacob).

Attias-Donfut, C., Segalen, M. and Lapierre, N. (2002), *Le nouvel esprit de famille* (Paris: Odile Jacob).

Barthes, R. (1980), *La chambre claire, notes sur les photographies* (Paris: Editions de l'Etoile, Gallimard).

Bott, E. (1957), *Family and Social Networks: Roles, Norms and External Relationships in Ordinary Urban Families* (London: Tavistock Publications).

Bourdieu, P. (1965), *Un art moyen. Essai sur les usages sociaux de la photographie* (Paris: Editions de Minuit).

Caradec, V. (2001), '"Personnes âgées" et "objets technologiques": une perspective en terme de logiques d'usage', *Revue Française de Sociologie* 42 (1), p. 117–48.

Carmagnat, F. (2000), *Les usages des Intranets familiaux, les utilisateurs de 'Notrefamille.com'*, rapport FTRD, June 2000.

Cohen Hunther, J. (1999), *La mémoire familiale* (Paris: Collection Logiques sociales, l'Harmattan).

Deville, J. and Mardon, A. (2002), *Internet et relations familiales: enquête auprès d'utilisateurs de sites familiaux*, rapport FTRD, April 2002.

Lemarchant, C. (1999), *Belles-filles. Avec les beaux-parents, trouver la bonne distance* (Rennes: PUR).

Monjaret, A. (1996), 'Les communications téléphoniques privées sur les lieux de travail', *Traverse* No. 3 Force des liens. Parenté, travail et genres 1996, 53–63.

Muxel, A. (1997), *Individu et mémoire familiale*, Collection Essais et recherches (Paris: Nathan).

Picrou, A. (1992), *Les solidarités familiales. Vivre sans famille?* (Toulouse: Privat).

Smoreda, Z. and Licoppe, C. (1999), 'La téléphonie résidentielle des foyers: réseaux de sociabilité et cycles de vie', *Actes du 2nd colloque Icust Arcachon (France),* 7–9 June 1999, 401–09.

Chapter 6

Legal Self-help and the Internet

Lieve Gies

Introduction

Who do people turn to when they are confronted with a serious legal problem? Those who can afford to pay for professional legal services or are eligible for publicly funded legal aid could opt to engage a lawyer, while others may turn to the voluntary sector. However, a major English study (Genn, 1999) has found that 35 per cent of people who are faced with a 'justiciable' problem, that is, a 'problem for which there is a potential legal remedy' (Pleasence et al., 2003: 14), at some point attempt to tackle it without any professional help. Meanwhile a small, yet nevertheless worrying, 5 per cent is believed to do nothing at all. Considering that access to justice is one of the cornerstones of a democratic society, such figures make sobering reading. A possible solution is to expand state-funded legal aid provisions so that everyone, rich and poor alike, would be able to take advantage of professional services. But such a policy is almost certain to impose a considerable burden on the public purse, making it a rather unattractive option.

'Electronic Paths to Justice'?

Could 'electronic paths to justice', as Widdison (2003) asks, be a possible alternative? Could ICT be deployed to reach out to self-helpers, not through tailor-made advice from a lawyer but in the form of 'unbundled' (Giddings and Robertson, 2003: 103) legal services, a pared-down type of legal assistance whereby, with the aid of technology, individuals can gain access to interactive sources of advice and information? This would seem to be a sensible compromise, for while it requires self-helpers to be closely involved in solving their own problems, they are not being abandoned completely by the legal profession. Previously, legal practice had ignored the 'latent legal market' (Susskind, 1996), a segment of the legal services market in which there is a demand for inexpensive and easily accessible legal advice, because it was not profitable. However, it is now thought to represent a major growth market, so much so that in Britain, even supermarkets are keen to jump on the bandwagon. The concept of 'Tesco lawyer' and 'Tesco law', inspired by the British supermarket chain Tesco, has entered the legal jargon as a derogatory term. Yet it is also a symbol of considerable professional disquiet about the deregulation of the legal services market (Clementi, 2004). Consider, for example, the following comments by the UK Centre for Legal Education (UKCLE):

Shoppers can now choose from groceries, finance and insurance, telecoms, wine, electrical goods, DVDs, flowers, books – and legal services. Great news folks, at the moment there are triple ClubCard points on many legal products! Now, when you divorce someone you can gain Air Miles too – what a great way to cure those post divorce blues! At £7.49 it almost seems too cheap not to get a divorce.[1]

Undeterred by the scathing criticism, Tesco is attempting to make a multimedia business out of its 'do-it-yourself' (or 'DIY') legal products. It has its own legal services website[2] which offers DIY legal kits containing books and CD-ROMs guiding self-helpers through the process of drawing up their will, selling their house and arranging their own divorce – to give just a few examples – all without the involvement of a lawyer. While legal self-help books have been around for quite some time, DIY law has undoubtedly received a major boost from ICT.

This chapter considers the implications of ICT for legal self-helpers, focusing mainly on Internet websites that offer assistance with divorce-related matters. Moreover, to avoid technological determinism, that is, an account in which ICT is regarded as the prime mover behind important social changes, I aim to document how DIY law is embedded in a much wider culture of self-help. That culture encourages individuals to 'manage' their own lives and realise their 'full' potential in a range of areas such as their health, personal finance and relationships (Hancock and Tyler, 2004). This will enable me to examine online legal self-help as a communal experience and a potentially gendered practice.

Whilst the potential of new ICT to improve access to justice is evidently very strong, this chapter concludes on a cautionary note. I argue that policy decisions to scale down the availability of state-funded legal aid could mean that tailor-made professional legal advice in the future becomes the exclusive privilege of the most affluent, while other groups in society would be left to defend their legal interests using standardised self-help packages. Moreover, material inequalities may result in excluding the most deprived groups from basic legal information because they lack access to ICT or struggle with elementary skills such as numeracy and literacy.

Legal Advice, Lifestyle and Managerialism

Vuoi contare di piu'? Conta su te stesso![3]

The mass media undeniably play an important role in providing their audiences with factual information about the law. How reliable such information is may be debatable but that does not diminish the fact that self-helpers, not knowing where else to turn for advice, have traditionally found media outlets a useful source of information (Pleasence et al., 2003). Lanctot (1999) describes a fascinating radio experiment in 1930s America which involved lawyers and judges dispensing free advice to listeners

---

1 http://www.ukcle.ac.uk/directions/previous/issue9/tesco.html, accessed 17 January 2007.

2 http://www.tescolegalstore.com, accessed 17 January 2007.

3 Advertising slogan for Italian online bank 'We' which roughly translates as 'Do you want to count on more? Count on yourself!'.

calling in with legal problems. *Good Will Court* was a hugely popular programme which encountered intense resistance from the legal profession, eventually resulting in its cancellation. This pioneering example suggests that lawyers have been traditionally opposed to so-called 'disruptive technologies' (Mountain, 2001). But it also demonstrates the potential of mass media technology to accommodate some of the unmet needs of the latent legal market. Obviously, advice dispensed in such a way requires some compromises: for example, there is no possibility of discussing one's problems in confidence when it is part of a phone-in programme and the advice one gets is almost inevitably of a very general and superficial nature. The arrival of telelawyering helplines that provide one-to-one advice over the phone have been an obvious improvement. For example, it is not unusual for legal advice columns in print media to act as a gateway to helplines that offer readers the possibility of premium-rate telephone access to a lawyer or a call centre employee working under the supervision of a qualified lawyer (Gies, 2004). A decisive step in legal self-help's entry into cyberspace occurred in the mid-1990s with the arrival of 'legal web advisers' offering 'interactive legal advice delivered via Extranet without human intervention using questions to collect facts and then using decision tree analysis to produce answers' (Mountain, 2001, section 1).

The peril and the promise of this brave new world of online legal advice have been summed up by the English Legal Services Commission (2001: 5) in the following way:

> The proliferation of websites offering legal information represents an unrivalled opportunity for members of the public to increase their understanding of the legal process, and of their rights and responsibilities within it (…) One drawback, however, is that users – especially inexperienced users – may be unable to make an informed choice about which sites to access or trust.

This suggests that legal self-help, regardless of whether it is facilitated by 'old-fashioned' media or cutting-edge new ICT, involves an element of risk which, as I explain below, has in no small measure to do with the reliability of information dispensed away from a conventional professional setting. Overcoming the risk barrier requires a cultural climate in which helping oneself is envisaged as an appropriate and responsible course of action. Technological capability alone is insufficient if users lack the self-confidence to carry out parts of a legal transaction unaided. Professional disdain for self-help sources is unlikely to be an incentive whereas an official 'quality mark' for reputable websites carrying legal information and advice is clearly intended to foster confidence in the self-help market. Interestingly, Hancock and Tyler (2004) see self-help as part of a much wider cultural shift involving an extensive managerialisation of everyday life. They comment that:

> [W]estern industrial societies appear to be almost defined by an obsession with the need to seek out experts and sources of life planning in order to make it through the complexity and uncertainty of contemporary existence. What is perhaps most notable about today's examples of such expert advice, however, is the emphasis they place not so much on instructive imperatives, but rather on the facilitation of self-improvement. That is, they

appear to allow us to 'manage' our own lives more efficiently and effectively, than to provide expert solutions per se. (Hancock and Tyler, 2004: 631)

In other words, responsibility for finding a solution to life's problems has been transferred from the expert to the non-expert who is assumed to be able to self-diagnose in a rational way. This indeed appears to be an apt description of the burden that sources of legal self-help impose on users. As Giddings and Robertson (2003) argue, the effective use of a legal self-help service requires users to take a rational and detached view of what may be a deeply emotional or personal issue. For Hancock and Tyler (2004), it is the contemporary lifestyle magazine which most vigorously promotes the managerial self-help ethos in everyday life. However, while men's lifestyle magazines are a relatively recent phenomenon in the publishing market (Jackson et al., 1999), women's magazine dealing with equivalent female lifestyle issues have been around for much longer (Leman, 1980). Providing women with incentives to improve their own lives by becoming thinner, younger-looking and more beautiful wives and mothers who are capable of fulfilling their domestic and professional potential is the bread and butter of women's magazines. In this discourse of self-improvement, the expert obviously plays a central role but it is ultimately down to readers to take control of their destiny and implement the expert's advice.

Contemporary women's magazines do not shy away from tackling a broad range of (controversial) lifestyle issues. A noteworthy example is the British magazine *Vive* which was launched in 2000 (Gies, 2004). What was remarkable about the magazine was that it targeted the divorce market. Its slogan that 'there is life after a break-up' illustrated the magazine's philosophy that with the right level of self-management, marital break-up could lead to embracing a new lifestyle. Strikingly, the family law expert dominated the advice pages in *Vive* and divorce lawyers were the magazine's most important advertisers. The magazine could almost have been mistaken for a specialist legal publication, complete with a glossary of legal terms. Readers were positively encouraged to consider a Tesco-style DIY divorce. In the end, *Vive* evidently failed to find its market: it folded after only four issues. But what made it an interesting experiment is that it tapped into an already thriving self-help culture at a time when the technological capability necessary to put the rhetoric of legal self-help into action was becoming widely available.

The Added Value of Online Self-help Services

Considering that legal self-help already existed in a limited form in popular culture before the Internet, what are the specific benefits that users derive from being able to access online sources of legal advice? A similar question can be asked about the benefits of accessing Internet services more generally: what moves people to go online to carry out specific interactions instead of performing these offline? Convenience seems to be the key to explaining the domestication of the Internet and the services it offers – after all, the Internet is open 24/7 and shopping online potentially saves both time and money. But this has to be weighed up against specific risks. The main risk factor is often associated with the human-machine interface: transacting business online is an anonymous, distant and virtual process which deprives users of the 'vocabularies of bodily idiom' (Goffman, 1963) that accompany face-to-face interaction. This may make it more difficult to verify the trustworthiness and provenance of information, although as Pauwels (2005) rightly argues, it is worth bearing in mind that identity is the object of construction and manipulation in all forms of human interaction.

Harshman et al. (2005) in outlining the challenges of the Internet for professionals, including lawyers and financial advisers, cite the startling case of a 12-year-old American boy who was able to dispense legal advice on a well-known website. Needless to say, the boy was not a lawyer, but that did not prevent him from becoming one of the website's most popular legal experts who received very favourable feedback from users. Greater user awareness and professional accreditation of reputable websites go some way towards addressing problems of identity deception, but it must also be recognised that both in the online and offline 'risk society' (Beck, 1992) the phenomenon of bogus doctors, lawyers, accountants and life-style gurus will probably never be eradicated completely.

Reassuring users about Internet security is only part of the story. For users to be swayed to resort to online services where an offline equivalent is available requires significant benefits which cannot be entirely explained through convenient access and low cost alone. The lowering of the threshold for legal self-helpers is in no small measure down to the capacity of ICT to provide users with a pathway through a topic with which they have little or no previous familiarity. Widdison (2003, section 2) comments that:

> Guidance should integrate as much knowledge and know-how as is necessary in a practical, step-by-step approach to enable self-helpers to solve their legal problems. In order to make all this knowledge digestible to self-helpers, it is suggested that guidance not only be written in lay people's rather than lawyers' language wherever possible, it should also be structured helpfully, making optimum use of the hypertext paradigm.

The interactive and hypertext qualities of various ICT applications would indeed explain why these constitute an altogether more sophisticated and user-friendly resource than are print materials such as books and information leaflets. However, I want to focus on a different aspect of user-friendliness, namely the specific capacity of the Internet to make self-help a communal experience by offering virtual forums where users obtain support from others who are going or have been through similar legal problems. It is arguably the Internet's ability to let users access social support networks that gives it the edge over alternative sources of legal self-help and even makes it more appealing than conventional legal services.

The community-building capacity of the Internet is not limited to legal self-help alone (Bakardjieva, 2003): an interesting parallel can be drawn here with health websites. As well as being able to access a wealth of information at the click of a button, users suffering from an illness or health concern can also fall back on support and advice from fellow sufferers (Orgad, 2004). The ability to offer each other comfort and sympathy is the glue of online self-help communities. Such a sense of belonging and togetherness appears especially important when the problem with which users wrestle is socially isolating, for example, when it is a debilitating illness

(Parr, 2002) or an issue on which there rests a considerable social taboo (Whittle, 1998). While much of the medical information online is provided by healthcare specialists, chat rooms and message boards often act as sites for contesting expert medical knowledge (Parr, 2002). This signals a potentially important shift in the doctor-patient relationship, a shift which Harshman et al. (2005: 232) describe as a 'welcome correction to the asymmetrical relationship that often defines professional-lay interaction'. On the Internet, professionals compete with users who derive their authority not from years of study and training but from having suffered a particular setback or problem in their own lives, which in the eyes of others users may make them the more credible experts.

To what extent are such community-building features also beneficial to legal self-helpers? The psychological burden of tacking a legal problem without professional help should not be underestimated (Genn, 1999) and Internet support groups could be instrumental in making legal self-help a less lonely and daunting experience (Widdison, 2003). For example, the British *ondivorce* website,[4] which is dedicated to divorce-related issues and features one of liveliest message boards of its kind, explains its own success in the following way:

> By allowing you to make contact with others who are, or have been going through the same experiences as yourself, the help and support you will find here are what have made the site unique. Please make use of all its facilities and over time, when you feel comfortable, hopefully you will pass on the benefits of your own experiences to other visitors. Our discussion boards are some of the best used in the UK and, of course, reflect real life situations covering legal, emotional and financial matters (including actual outcomes).

The postings on the message boards of this and other similar websites immediately reveal that there are varying degrees of self-helpers, ranging from users who handle their divorce all by themselves to users who turn to each other for help and advice to supplement professional legal services. For example, one user, having been told by her solicitor that she will need to cite a substantial reason for wanting to divorce her husband after only six months of marriage, asks members of the *ondivorce* community for their advice on what may constitute such a reason.[5] The mixed reactions to her query also demonstrate that message boards do not always involve a meeting of like-minded users who are unconditionally supportive of each other. On the contrary, an ideologically charged topic such as marriage is capable of bitterly dividing users who hold very different views about the circumstances in which divorce is acceptable.

What is the role of the professional in this environment? As Kritzer (1999: 747) argues, it would be wrong to suggest that legal self-help has made the professional expert an endangered species. Lawyers are not being made redundant, but their role is definitely changing. A self-help divorce kit that users can purchase online or elsewhere still requires professional expertise: it has been developed and standardised by lawyers with the aid of technology. However, the cyberlawyer needs

---

4 http://www.ondivorce.co.uk, accessed 17 January 2007.

5 http://www.ondivorce.co.uk/messageboard/mb-index.php?mb_id=2&subject_id=5596, accessed 17 January 2007.

to be aware of the more egalitarian relationship between clients and professionals on the Internet. For example, Harshman et al. (2005) suggest that the reason why the 12-year-old American posing as a lawyer became so popular is because he gave his 'clients' a sense of belonging through his relaxed and informal style. The idea of a partnership between professionals and clients appears key. The *ondivorce* website, for example, was not the brainchild of a lawyer but that of a divorced accountant whose experiences of divorce inspired him to set up a website that would offer advice and support to others in a similar situation: '*At the time, I needed to communicate my thoughts to someone; I was obsessed with it*'. Paul had a real need to get his thoughts down on paper and the person most readily available was his solicitor. '*He was more than happy to be my sounding board, but his support came with the inevitable price tag*', he reflects now. Thinking back, Paul believes his main feeling when he was going through his divorce was loneliness. It was then that the Internet became his focal point. Paul was struck by the impact that the worldwide web is having on the way we communicate. '*I thought that if I could get ordinary people with similar experiences to communicate with each other in some sort of forum, I would have made some progress towards making the process a little less painful for others*', he says. The website does have a clear legal focus, but the fact that it is run by a non-lawyer who is apparently not motivated by financial gain (although the website advertises commercial products and services) enhances its self-help ethos and voluntary atmosphere.

The decentring of the professional expert and the concomitant rise of the user-expert almost inevitably mean that problems are more likely to be approached from a user-centred perspective. Widdison (2003, section 2) observes that: 'it is becoming widely accepted that legal guidance needs to be orientated towards 'life episodes' rather than traditional legal categories'. A layperson's experience of something such as marital break-up is not that it is foremost a *legal* problem; it is likely to be experienced as a personal crisis in which a legal remedy is only part of the solution. What people in such a situation may need, as Paul's testimony above illustrates, is a *holistic* approach, involving many different services such as financial advice, psychological counselling and health advice – in short, the kind of all-encompassing guidance that the managerial life-style magazine aspires to deliver. The Internet puts this into practice by allowing a wide range of services to be bundled and made easily accessible. Many divorce websites act a one-stop virtual advice centre: for example, the divorce website *divorce-online*[6] allows readers to keep a diary of their experiences as they go through divorce and it even offers an online dating service. The Internet, just as the lifestyle magazine, is a place where lawyers appear happy to team up with other experts. For example, the *insidedivorce.com* website, another British divorce site[7] proudly states:

6 http://www.divorce-online.co.uk, accessed 17 January 2007.

7 http://www.insidedivorce.com/divorce-help/Meet-our-team-of-experts, accessed 17 January 2007.

Meet our team of experts, who are here to advise you on all aspects of relationship breakdown and divorce. We've got everything covered, from legal and financial issues to wellbeing and style advice.

The expertise involves drier topics such as finance and the law but also typical life-style themes such as stress relief and 'wardrobe management'. Such a multidisciplinary setup clearly resonates with what observers claim is a reconfiguration of the legal profession (Kritzer, 1999; Boon et al., 2005), a process in which the role of ICT cannot be overlooked.

From a user perspective, online self-help legal websites and, by extension, the latent legal market, present us with an interesting paradox. On the one hand, it involves a trend towards a depersonalisation of legal services. Instead of obtaining advice in a face-to-face setting, clients have to make do with a series of e-mail or telephone exchanges with a lawyer, or possibly just help themselves with a self-help kit, making the relationship with the professional expert both impersonal and distant. On the other hand, what makes the Internet attractive for legal self-helpers is its ability to deliver an all-encompassing service that offers much more that just a legal remedy. It also offers a sense of identity and belonging. In this sense, online legal self-help may actually manage to provide a much more personalised service than does conventional legal practice.

Legal Self-help: Who is being Empowered?

Having addressed the appeal that the Internet holds for legal self-helpers, a final issue worth exploring is the question of who is likely to use online self-help resources. It is appropriate, I believe, to frame this as a gender issue, because legal self-help, most notably through its association with supermarkets, is itself arguably a gendered construct. Indeed, gender may prove relevant in unravelling the legal profession's ambivalence towards DIY law. The fact that Tesco is a *supermarket*, a place to go shopping for groceries and perform a quintessentially female household chore, could go some way towards explaining why it has received such a high level of attention in the British debate on the deregulation of legal services. Could it be that lawyers resist having their profession equated with supermarkets because these are too banal, too everyday, too 'womanly' a space for the sophisticated – and still quintessentially male (Sommerlad, 1994; McGlynn, 1998) – art of lawyering? On a positive note, given that one of the most important advantages of ICT is that it enables the less well-off to access legal advice from the comfort (of discomfort as may be the case) of their own home, it is worth considering that the domestication of ICT in this regard is potentially most empowering for women who cannot easily leave the home because of their care responsibilities and who, compared to men, are more likely to be in less well-paid jobs.

To what extent the use of ICT is gendered and whether it is appropriate to label ICT in gender terms remains somewhat contested (Van Zoonen, 2002). The military-industrial roots of the Internet and its social construction as a predatory space in which pornography thrives with apparent impunity reinforce the image of cyberspace as inherently women-unfriendly (Baron, 2002). Nevertheless, for many women the

Internet has become an integral part of their everyday lives (Sassen, 1999; Franklin, 2001). Despite the risk of cyber-harassment, the Internet offers a physically safe forum where users can confide in complete strangers whilst preserving their anonymity. Women using the Internet find that it is a more suitable way of expressing emotions than are other means of communication (Hardey, 2002). Meanwhile, research on legal self-help has found that victims of domestic violence in particular feel safer communicating by e-mail than in a face-to-face setting (Giddings and Robertson, 2003). This gives considerable weight to the argument that the Internet is a medium which lends itself to distinctly feminine usages and holds great feminist potential (Spender, 1995; Youngs, 1999; Franklin, 2001). Self-help, as we have seen, with its emphasis on mutuality and community spirit but also with its exhortation to manage everyday life, is intimately connected with the lifestyle magazine that is steeped in women's culture. Legal self-help resources thrive on the Internet to a large extent because they offer users the ability to bond with each other and find a holistic solution to their legal problems. In short, they go about problem-solving in a way which is strikingly similar to the approach advocated in women's magazines.

Conclusion

My claim is not that the Internet features legal advice in a format that predominantly attracts women users. I merely say that these online resources resonate strongly with women's make-do culture. The exhortation to help oneself, both in online and off-line cultures, should also not be treated as unequivocally empowering. Just as in women's magazines, it is often a thinly disguised form of commodification of users' experiences. Attractively packaged websites which promise guidance on every imaginable facet of a legal problem are often an advertising front for the services of lawyers and other experts keen to exploit the latent legal market. The holistic approach that self-help websites promote could be interpreted as a very enterprising attempt at redefining legal problems as lifestyle issues requiring the consumption of a wide range of commodities. Getting divorced, instead of just making a couple of visits to a lawyer, now also requires a trip to the shops to acquire a new wardrobe as well as countless (real or virtual) visits to the stress counsellor, hairdresser and dating agencies to get one's life back on track, not to mention the many self-help products that users are encouraged to purchase.

A high-profile legal self-helper who caused furore in the British tabloid press is Heather Mills, the ex-wife of the former Beatle Sir Paul McCartney. Although she retained the services of one of the most prestigious legal firms, she reportedly needed to rein in the cost of her legal bills, which explains why at one point she decided to represent herself in the High Court (Simpson, 2006). Married to one of the wealthiest men in the country, here was a woman reduced to legal self-help because she could not afford to let her lawyers take care of everything. This may be no more than a clever case of media manipulation by Mills, but it is certainly a poignant illustration of a potentially enormous inequality between parties. Can there be an equality of arms between litigants if one party has access to customised professional legal advice while the other has to make do with self-help resources? Should people be led to believe that they are able to settle their own divorce with a self-help kit bought on the Internet? Or, by contrast, do we need to have more confidence in users' skills and should we avoid inflating the importance of professional expertise? Is a law without lawyers a law that users can easily appropriate by using the Internet as a vast repository of legal knowledge? In a time when policymakers become increasingly aware of the potential of technology in easing the burden on courts and state-funded legal aid schemes, it is tempting for them to encourage the proliferation of a culture of legal self-help. However, Giddings and Robertson (2003: 115) observe:

> Rather than being empowered by the availability of such services, they [self-helpers] may end up being abandoned to navigate a complex legal map without the necessary knowledge, skills and confidence.

Dear and Flusty (1999) offer an evocative imagery of the future of information societies that is of immediate relevance to the issues considered in this chapter. They envisage a bifurcated social order that would be based on huge inequalities in access to ICT. The 'cybergeoisie' would have access to state-of-the art top interactive services while 'cyberia' would be populated by a technological underclass of people whose communication facilities would consist of only the most rudimentary technologies. Applying this visionary perspective to the use of ICT in legal practice, it is not difficult to see how an elaborate culture of legal self-help could result in the exclusion of a large number of people who have neither the means to buy the professional tailor-made services of a lawyer nor the literacy to access and successfully deploy self-help legal products. The scenario of a 'digitally divided justice' is not entirely implausible (LAG, 2001). The possible emergence of an elitist cybergeoisie improving its access to legal services that are specifically tailored to its needs (as opposed to standardised self-help legal packages) and instantly delivered through state-of-the-art technology cannot be dismissed lightly. The promise of user empowerment through ICT clearly needs to be balanced carefully against its potentially hugely divisive effects that could actually increase inequalities in access to justice.

References

Bakardjieva, M. (2003), 'Virtual togetherness: an everyday-life perspective', *Media, Culture and Society* 25 (3), 291–313.

Baron, P. (2002), 'The Legal Regulation of Cyberpornography: Law's Quest for Borders in a Borderless World', in Thornton, M. (ed.), *Romancing the Tomes: Popular Culture, Law and Feminism* (London: Cavendish).

Beck, U. (1992), *Risk Society: Towards a New Modernity* (London: Sage).

Boon, A., Flood, J. and Webb, J. (2005), 'Postmodern Professions? The Fragmentation of Legal Education and the Legal Profession', *Journal of Law and Society* 32 (3), 473–92.

Clementi, D. (2004), *Report of the Review of the Regulatory Framework for Legal Services in England and Wales*. Available at: <http://www.legal-services-review. org.uk/content/ report/index.htm>.

Dear, M. and Flusty, S. (1999), 'The Postmodern Urban Condition', in Featherstone, M. and Lash, S. (eds), *Spaces of Culture: City-Nation-World* (London: Sage).

Franklin, M.I. (2001), 'Inside Out: Postcolonial Subjectivities and Everyday Life Online', *Internationalist Feminist Journal of Politics* 3 (3), 387–422.

Genn, H. (1999), *Paths to Justice* (Oxford: Hart Publishing).

Gies, L. (2004), '"Helping Generation Ex": Divorce, Legal Advice in Women's Magazines and DIY Law in Cyberspace', *International Journal of the Sociology of Law* 32, 64–84.

Giddings, J. and Robertson, M. (2003), 'Large-Scale Map of A-Z? The Place of Self-Help Services in Legal Aid', *Journal of Law and Society* 30 (1), 102–19.

Goffman, E. (1963), *Behaviour in Public Places* (New York: Free Press).

Hancock, P. and Tyler, M. (2004), '"MOT your life": Critical management studies and the management of everyday life', *Human Relations* 57 (5), 619–645.

Hardey, M. (2002), 'Life beyond the screen: embodiment and identity through the internet', *Sociological Review* 50 (4), 570–85.

Harshman, E.M., Gilsinan, J. F., Fisher, J.E. and Yeager, F.C. (2005), 'Professional Ethics in a Virtual World: The Impact of the Internet on Traditional Notions of Professionalism', *Journal of Business Ethics* 58, 227–36.

Jackson, P., Brooks, K. and Stevenson, N. (1999), 'Making sense of men's lifestyle magazines', *Environment and Planning D: Society and Space* 17, 353–68.

Kritzer, H.M. (1999), 'The Professions Are Dead, Long Live the Professions: Legal Practice in a Postprofessional World', *Law & Society Review* 33 (3), 713–59.

LAG (2001), 'Digitally Divided Justice?', *Legal Action* (February), 3.

Lanctot, C. (1999), 'Attorney-Client Relationships in Cyberspace: The Peril and the Promise', *Duke Law Journal* 49 (1), 147–259.

Legal Services Commission (2001), *The Quality Mark Standard for Websites* (London: Legal Services Commission).

Leman, J. (1980), '"The Advice of a Real Friend" Codes of Intimacy and Oppression in Women's Magazines 1937–1955', *Women Studies International Quarterly* 3, 63–78.

McGlynn, C. (1998), *The Woman Lawyer: Making the Difference* (London: Butterworths).

Mountain, D. (2001), 'Could New Technologies cause Great Law Firms to Fail?', *Journal of Information, Law and Technology (JILT)*. Available at <http: //elj. warwick.ac.uk/jilt01-1/ mountain.html> (accessed 17 January 2007).

Orgad, S. (2004), 'Help Yourself: The World Wide Web as a Self-Help Agora', in Gauntlett, D. and Horsley, R. (eds), *Web Studies*, 2nd edn. (London: Arnold).

Parr, H. (2002), 'New body-geographies: the embodied spaces of health and medical information on the Internet', *Environment and Planning D: Society and Space* 20, 73–95.

Pauwels, L. (2005), 'Websites as visual and multinodal cultural expressions: opportunities and issues of online hybrid media research', *Media, Culture and Society* 27 (4), 604–13.

Pleasence, P., Genn, H., Balmer, N.J., Buck, A. and O'Grady, A. (2003), 'Causes of Action: First Findings of the LSRC Periodic Review', *Journal of Law and Society* 30 (1), 11–30.

Sassen, S. (1999), 'Digital Networks and Power', in Featherstone, M. and Lash, S. (eds), *Spaces of Culture: City-Nation-World* (London: Sage).

Simpson, R. (2006), 'Heather Mills Represents Herself in Divorce Court to Save Cash', *Daily Mail*, 7 December 2006.

Sommerlad, H. (1994), 'The Myth of Feminisation: Women and Cultural Change in the Legal Profession', *International Journal of the Legal Profession* 1, 31–53.

Spender, D. (1995), Nattering on the Net: Women, Power and Cyberspace (Melbourne: Spinifex Press).

Susskind, R. (1996), *The Future of Law: Facing the Challenges of Information Technology* (Oxford: Clarendon Press).

Whittle, S. (1998), 'The Trans-Cyberian Mail Way', *Social and Legal Studies* 7 (3), 389–408.

Widdison, R. (2003), 'Electronic Paths to Justice', *Journal of Information, Law and Technology (JILT)*. Available at http://www2.warwick.ac.uk/soc/law/elj/jilt/1003_2/ widdison/ (accessed 17 January 2007).

Youngs, G. (1999), 'Virtual Voices: Real Lives', in Harcourt, W. (ed.), *Women@ internet: Creating New Cultures in Cyberspace* (London: Zed Books).

Zoonen, L. van (2002), 'Gendering the Internet: Claims, Controversies and Cultures', *European Journal of Communication* 17 (1), 5–23.

Chapter 7

On Older People, Internet Access and Electronic Service Delivery: A Study of Sheltered Homes

Maria Sourbati

Introduction

The online administration of public sector information and public service delivery has been a priority aim of the European Union (EU) and Member States since the end of the 1990s. Core objectives in the Europe's eSociety policies and national e-government programmes are the electronic delivery of government information, modern online public services, including e-learning and e-health, alongside the fostering of e-commerce (Cabinet Office, 2000; European Commission, 2000). In the context of Europe's visions for the information society Internet access is taken as a manifestation of an inclusive society that addresses both economic and social development and equity issues (Couldry, 2004). In the UK, the public policy objective of universal Internet access was first announced in 2001 as a government commitment to ensuring that 'everyone who wants it has access to the Internet by 2005' (Cabinet Office, 2002). This objective covered access from a range of channels at home and in the community, including personal computers, digital interactive television and public terminals such as street kiosks and community access points in public libraries.

Five years on, despite having set up channels to access public service information online, levels of use of e-government services remained low across the EU, with an average 45 per cent of Internet users visiting public authorities' websites to obtain information in 2005 (Cross, 2005). In the UK, which rates among the most advanced European e-governments, a mere 24 per cent of Internet users (15 per cent of the population) had accessed any e-government service (OxIS, 2005). Policy concern subsequently shifted to the non-use of digital, online media and e-services by vulnerable users of welfare services. In 2005 the EU launched the 'wide deployment' phase of its policies for the information society, prioritising broadband infrastructure to develop a competitive digital economy and an inclusive information society that promotes growth and prioritises better public services (European Commission, 2005: 3–4). In the same year the UK e-government strategy was updated, setting out key actions to 'transform public services using ICT' and 'increase understanding of customer needs and behaviours' by engaging with citizens, business and frontline public servants in order to structure e-provision around 'the needs of key groups – such as older people' (Cabinet Office, 2005: 7–8).

Political interest in Internet access and electronic service delivery is predicated upon a belief in the transformative powers of ICT (Hudson, 2003). Policy discourses emphasise the potential of new ICT applications to modernise welfare provision, transform government and empower citizens. According to the *i2010* initiative of the European Commission the so-called 'ICT-based public services' will promote inclusion and improve public services and quality of life (European Commission 2005, 9). Britain's *Digital Strategy* is for 'public service delivery transformed by modern technology' (Cabinet Office, 2005: 7). This kind of policy vision share implicit assumptions that modern, online media strengthen the position of individuals in society. ICTs are taken here as being inherently progressive and their use as desirable for all (Wyatt et al., 2002). However, these policy goals in e-government seem to be defined without reference to the actual lived circumstances of citizens – how users of ICTs encounter them (Olsson et al., 2003; Olsson, 2006). As with much of the literature about the digital divide, their focus is on 'the generic or ideal user' of digital, online ICTs (Wyatt et al., 2005: 228). Technology-centric policy discourses construct individuals through generalising categories. Two of the most popular, widely used generalisations are the labelling of young people as being 'online experts' (Livingstone et al., 2005) and older people as being 'technophobes' (Riggs, 2004).[1] This chapter discusses practices of media use in sheltered homes for older people in order to question these technology-centric perspectives with their focus on the transformative properties of new ICTs. It questions the claims about such benefits with their emphasis on abstract, generalised individual (non) users of new, online media services.

Underlying these two sets of claims, policy and popular discourses portray the relationship of older people and new ICTs as being problematic: older people are 'have nots'; they stand at the wrong end of the 'digital divide'. On the one hand, within the classical e-government and marketing literature there are assumptions that ICTs are generating tremendous benefits to users. Benefits accruing from Internet access include opportunities for isolated, home-centred older people to contact people and services, increase their sense of security and support independent living in the community (Blake, 1998; Gilligan, 1998; Adler, 2002; Seniornet, 2004). On the other hand, engagement with new ICTs is coded as the domain of younger generations. Older people are customarily positioned as members of a homogenous group, comprising individuals over a certain chronological age, usually from 60 upwards. Older people's engagement with new ICTs is most commonly understood in terms of an analysis of the barriers they face, where ageing, associated with decline, disability and decay, impedes the development of new media literacies (Riggs, 2004; Richardson et al., 2005). In keeping with this framework, the first national, longitudinal study of media literacy undertaken by the UK Office of Communications (Ofcom), which cites as evidence the fact that the ownership of networked computers is lowest among older people (defined as those over 65), standing at 20 per cent of these households as against a national average of 57 per cent, concluded that age features as 'the single

---

1 See also Beckers et al., Chapter 1 in this book.

most significant defining factor' in the ability to learn to use new interactive ICTs (Ofcom, 2006: 11). However, this chapter paints a more complex picture reaching a different set of conclusions. It draws on findings from a small scale qualitative study of older people, looking at the actual practices and perceptions of electronic media use in two sheltered accommodation complexes in London.[2]

Internet Access and E-service Delivery in Sheltered Homes for Older People: Exploring the Realities of (Non)use

The sample of respondents comprised 18 tenants and six care professionals. The residents were older retirees who used a range of welfare services, including health care support. Using observational methods and qualitative interviews, the study examined whether and how Internet access was introduced into the life and everyday practices of residents, and how residents and staff felt about the idea of accessing welfare information and health care support services online.

One of the research sites was an extra-care housing complex with a capacity of 50 self-contained flats. It employed care staff and made networked computers available that tenants could use free of charge. Interested customers could join a weekly Internet Club to take basic computer and web browsing lessons. The club was advertised by the housing trust as an enabling resource for tenants to facilitate independent living, '*to get more in control of their lives so that they didn't rely on other people coming in to help or give care or whatever*'. (Daphne, Community Support Officer)

The other site comprised 250 flats, did not employ community support workers other than wardens and was not wired up at the time of the research.

Experiences and perceptions of the Internet

All except three home-centred and very frail participants from the tenant sample had heard about the Internet from their family and social networks or from announcements made by staff in the sheltered homes and local libraries as well as through national television and the press. Ten of the 18 participants had interacted with a computer at least once. Five of those tenants had accessed the Internet at least once through attendance at introductory courses run on site or in Community Centres, or during visits to relations. In fact, one participant, who owned a networked computer, regularly accessed the Internet from her home. Those tenants who had either given the Internet a try or wanted to do so engaged in social activities outside their home and had family relations and friends who were already online. Their involvement in learning to use the Internet had been encouraged by relatives, friends and community care staff. In other words, the research suggested that there was in practice a range of ways in which older people engaged with the Internet, of experiences of online access, of expectations about the Internet and of perceptions of electronic service delivery.

---

2 The study was supported by a grant from the Joseph Rowntree Foundation. See Sourbati (2004) for a full report and discussion of findings.

Assisted access to communication and entertainment

Four older respondents had logged onto the Internet a few weeks before the research interviews took place, with assistance from community support workers or family members. This first experience of getting online was also their first encounter with a computer. Rosalynn and John had joined the Internet club at their housing complex, Margaret had taken her first computer lesson in the local library and Betty had one experience of Internet access while staying with her son in France. Although not all in this group were fully mobile, all engaged in social activities outside their home, for instance, in Day Centres. Despite encouragement, motivation and assistance, accessing the Internet was far from straightforward. At the time of the research these respondents were learning basic skills such as typing in a password to log on and using the mouse. Although they felt overwhelmed by this new technology they found logging on to the Internet to be an interesting, novel activity, potentially useful – though not necessarily to them – mainly as a leisure option: '*I'm trying to learn it but I don't think I'm doing so well. I am a beginner.*' (Rosalynn); '*I find it very awkward at the moment (...) I'm a new boy. I'd rather use it as, interested in it as a gimmick. It could be useful but not for me at the moment*'. (John); The idea of exchanging emails to stay in touch with family members was also appealing: '*My granddaughter and grandson are in Los Angeles and they say you can send messages. You can communicate cheaper than the telephone*'. (Betty); Some would see the potential of obtaining information online as vaguely useful: '*Information like, Ask Jeeves. Just for the information I think would be of value*'. (Rosalynn)

A desire to access for companionship, entertainment, quality of life

Some participants from the site that did not run a communal Internet facility were very keen to access the Internet. They were younger than most tenants in the sample (their average age being in the early 70s), they had friends who were using the Internet and they had learned basic computer skills during their previous employment or after retirement. Joe had acquired a laptop computer, a freebie from his former employers, in the spring of 2002. In the summer he joined '*a little computer course to learn the basics*' following advice from a friend. Nancy had taken basic computer skills training arranged by the Department of Social Security before she had retired. Tom, who was coordinating a campaign to reinstall an Internet connection in the communal library of his place of residence, had been learning basic computer skills by 'experimenting' with computers in the library for a few weeks back in 2000. Nancy, Tom and Joe spoke with enthusiasm about what they saw as the potential of the Internet to improve their quality of life. To them, Internet access represented an opportunity to engage with new forms of leisure, a form of companionship, more choice in information, an opportunity to communicate with other users and maintain contact with modern society: '*I would love to be able to use the Internet. I'd use it as an entertainment, I could tap into information, companionship. Rather than me sitting at home lonely, it would be something in the corner I could turn on, I can use, I can enjoy, that's the word.*' (Nancy); *It is so ideal because, there's nothing else happening here. There's no social activities taking place, there's nothing at all in the evenings.'* (Tom); *'It's great! For fun, to get in touch with new people, find out about new things.'* (Joe)

Internet access as a dynamic social process

Vera, the only participant in the tenant sample who was routinely accessing the Internet from home, had bought her first computer after retiring in the mid-1990s and installed her dial-up connection in 2001. Getting online was for her a matter of maintaining her lifestyle and involvement in her social environment: *'I think most people I come across are linked up to the net so in that sense one feels quite up to date, you know.'* She described how she had integrated this new ICT into her everyday practices gradually, building on her experience. She used the email facility primarily for social communication and for her voluntary, community work: *'I use email a lot, I usually check it at least once a day. I do a little bit of voluntary work and, I mean it's just so quick isn't it. And it's lovely to keep in touch with people who live a long way away, live abroad.'* Some months before the interview she had started searching the web for content relating to her leisure interests. She noted that she only browsed the web occasionally: *'I am not terribly interested in spending hours surfing the Net. It's very nice if you've got a specific thing you want to search occasionally.'* She spoke enthusiastically of the first time she had visited a website, following the prompt on a BBC Radio 3 programme, to get information about baroque opera: *'I was so thrilled. They had all this sort of information for the four programmes – four programmes on baroque opera – and I thought, God this is just marvellous.'*

Online access to services not fitting daily routines and service cultures

Unlike the generally positive perceptions of the Internet the idea of accessing online health care information and support services alienated most participants. The majority of the older tenants could not conceive of the idea of ordering prescriptions or contacting services such as their local clinic via a networked computer or television. Many pointed out that access to such services was currently being arranged for them by their carers: *'I order from the receptionist what I want. And my carer collects it from the pharmacists.'* (Rosalynn); *'Have you got anything to worry about you can tell the district nurse. And she arranges to see a doctor.'* (Arthur); *'Carers can phone my GP if I want them to come.'* (Maureen)

Many of the younger, more recently retired respondents, including all the Internet enthusiasts, were at best ambivalent towards accessing care related information and services via the Internet. Participants tended to think of online access to care services as a substitute for social contact and physical activity, potentially increasing the threat of isolation: *'It's sort of cutting off something social that you go out.'* (Vera); *'I think it gets terribly insular.'* (Bob). Moreover, Vera questioned the objectives behind electronic service delivery: *'My suspicion is it's to do with a much more limited way of communication and obviously cutting down money.'*

Most frontline community support staff were dubious about it too. Professional care workers, who like their clients were not very familiar with the Internet, could not see any practical returns in the idea of the online administration of various aspects of care provision: '*Saving time for carers, no. Because they are going to need to see the doctor anyway, aren't they. So I don't see how [online transfer of prescriptions] is going to save time, I don't know.*' (Lorna)

However, a few participants from the tenant sample and some of the more senior staff members could envisage a future where online access to health and care-related information and services supported these older Internet users who experienced mobility difficulties: '*I think the booking of appointments and delivery of prescriptions would be an excellent service to be used ... when you're ill and you have that ability to ask for help ... The new elderly if you like, the people that have had some amount of knowledge of the Internet and computer systems are far more ready, able to use it.*' (Bob)

Office-based staff who were using networked computers at work also took a longer term view of the potential of Internet access in care provision: '*It would be a way forward to save time and make service administration simpler*' (Julia, senior officer); '*It's a matter of time. It's a matter of skills, it's a matter of staff understanding [the Internet] and linking it to their work.*' (Sarah, management team member).

At present, as both staff and tenants noted, use of new media services and more general involvement in learning was not part of the inherited culture of care provision: '*We were going to have lessons and teach people how to use the computers in the library. But there's no attempt to encourage greater use of anything.*' (Tom); '*I imagine that there isn't a culture of people going into their office in this work and switching on their PC to use the Internet.*' (Paul, senior staff member)

Discussion and Conclusion

The research reported in this chapter was undertaken in 2002–2003 and had a number of limitations. The sample of older residents was small, yet diverse, in terms of their educational background, levels of income, social status, physical condition and age range. Moreover, the experiences of Internet access of most participants (tenants and staff) were limited. Even so, the study offered some interesting insights into what older residents did or wished to do online, and how they and the care professionals working with them felt about Internet access and electronic service delivery. The findings indicated that the mode and experience of Internet access and perceptions of opportunities and barriers varied significantly across older tenants.

A minority of the very old and frail tenants who had an occasional go on a networked computer assisted by relatives or care staff saw the Internet as potentially useful mainly for personal and social communication and as a recreational activity. However, they found the computer difficult to use without assistance from experienced users and largely irrelevant to their everyday lives.

Some of the younger, more recently retired, residents from the site that was not connected to the Internet were very enthusiastic about the prospect of accessing it, but they had no access facilities at hand. To them, the Internet represented an opportunity to engage in constructive leisure, communicate with other users and maintain contact with modern society. These tenants were keen to join free training schemes and use communal Internet access facilities but they had no clear idea of what Internet access entailed. To Vera, the tenant with a home Internet connection, this new ICT primarily offered a convenient way for managing social communication, and gradually, as she became more experienced, a new means for seeking information.

The attitudes of respondents tended to be more consistent in their discussions about electronic service delivery. Tenants were at best ambivalent towards the idea of online information and service requests. They tended to think of Internet access to health and care information services as a substitute for physical activity, one that threatened to reduce their social and personal contact with other human beings. Far from seeing additionalities here, far from perceiving electronic service delivery as an additional option in service access, many participants were actually worried that the online delivery of aspects of health care support would replace traditional forms of service provision. But a minority of participants could see benefits in services that prolong the ability of users to carry out daily routines independently of care support. At this point it is worth remembering that most frontline care professionals who participated in the research failed to see any utility in online access to e-services. In addition, of the many obstacles faced by the tenants who showed an interest in Internet access, only design related usability issues were related to any actual physiological changes, such as a reduction in vision and a slowing of movement, which are commonly associated with the biological processes of ageing. Perhaps more significant was the lack of new media skills and awareness of the relevance of Internet access to their everyday communication and information seeking practices. This was experienced across non-adopters of all ages. This finding calls into question market and policy research featuring age as 'the single most significant defining factor' in the ability to learn to use new interactive ICTs. As Chapter 1 (Beckers et al.) in this book shows, the popular understanding – that as younger generations have grown up with computers any ambiguous perceptions of new technologies will soon become a thing of the past – can be misleading.

This book in various ways questions the way in which the ICT users are all too often generalised in the classical technological, policy and marketing oriented literature. Older people have been at the receiving end of this trend more than any other (non-) users. This kind of prevalent generalisation about ICT users does not contribute to mapping patterns of user participation and exclusion in Europe's Information Society policy development. To account and provide for the diversity of circumstances faced by vulnerable older users of public services, policy and research attention must shift to the actual lived experiences of age, the situation faced by older individuals, the role played by structural inequities such as levels of income and education as well as by social capital. The fact that it is the older pensioners whose family and social networks are using the Internet who are themselves are more likely to become interested in going online indicates possible inequalities in opportunities to access. But, viewed in a social care context, it underlines the role of care staff in facilitating – or discouraging – frail customers' access to a new service. Professional carers, who can account for the only human relationship that some isolated, homebound older people have, can perform a gate-keeping role in introducing older people to new services (Tetley et al., 2000). The non-engagement of frontline care workers with new ICTs is of course subject to organisational dynamics, the theme of the next part of this book. Internet access has not yet been integrated into the routines of care provision.

To conclude, homogenising categorisations of older people can deny individuals the attention and policy provision that could benefit them. This research indicated that many older residents would like to try the Internet but did not have access to networked equipment and skills training that would enable them to use new online media services. So far in the UK, there has been no national scheme promoting access to Internet technologies and computer skills for older citizens who are not in formal education or employment. In addition to questions regarding investment in facilities and the learning of skills, there are issues of social infrastructure. In order for everyone who wants it to have access to the Internet, human assistance needs to be available to people who wish to access e-services but who need some support. Older people who use care support services can benefit from the option of assisted or 'proxy' use whereby experienced users act as intermediaries, supporting them as they try to navigate through online content options or, if needed, contacting others electronically (Wyatt et al., 2005: 212; Hudson, 2006: 320). Many retired older people do see the benefits of Internet access. The steady growth of Internet use by older adults (see University of Southern California Annenberg School Center for the Digital Future 2004) is yet another indication that the centrality of the Internet to the everyday lives of users does not correlate with age (Loges and Jung, 2001). Older people's perceptions and experiences of benefits do not necessarily correspond to policy claims concerning the advantages of accessing e-government information services (see also Richardson et al., 2005). What participants valued about trying the Internet were advantages that enhanced their quality of life. Most notably, they wanted to sustain connectedness with friends, family and the modern world, find stimulating and constructive leisure and have opportunities to obtain information relating to their interests and hobbies. What they worried about was the possibility that online delivery of healthcare information and support would substitute for human contact and physical activity. The overall message of the study reported here is that policy development must abandon its technology-centric focus and take a broader, interdisciplinary perspective on the diversity of older users, their social material and cultural circumstances, their needs and wishes, and their everyday practices of media (and) service use.

References

Adler, R. (2002), *The Age Wave Meets the Technology Wave. Broadband and Older Americans*, Seniornet. Available at http://www.seniornet.org/downloads/broadband.pdf (accessed December 2006).

Blake, M. (1998), *The Internet and Older People,* British Library Research and Innovation Centre.

Cabinet Office (2000), *e-Government. A Strategic Framework for Public Services in the Information Age* (London: The Stationery Office). Available at http://archive. cabinetoffice. gov.uk/e-envoy/ukonline-estrategy/$file/default.htm> (accessed January 2006).

Cabinet Office (2002), *UK Online Annual Report 2002*, Office of the e-Envoy – The Cabinet Office, November 2002.

Cabinet Office (2005), *Transformational Government Enabled by Technology.* The Cabinet Office, November 2005 Cm6683. Available at <http://www.cio.gov.uk/ documents/ pdf/transgov/transgov-strategy.pdf> (accessed December 2006).

Couldry, N. (2004), 'The Digital Divide', in Gauntlett, D. and Horsey, R. (eds), *Web Studies. Rewiring Media Studies for the Digital Age* (London: Arnold).

Cross, M. (2005), 'Continent at the cross roads', *The Guardian*, 23 November 2005. Available at <http://society.guardian.co.uk/e-public/story/0,13927,1648368,00. html> (accessed December 2006).

European Commission (2000), *eEurope 2002. An Information Society for all. Action Plan prepared by the Council and the European Commission for the Feira European Council, 19–20 June 2000*, June 14, Brussels: European Commission. Available at: <http://europa.eu.int/information_society/eeurope/2002/action_ plan/pdf/actionplan_en.pdf> (accessed January 2007).

European Commission (2005), 'i2010 – A European Information Society for growth and employment', *Communication from the Commission to the Council, the European Parliament, the European Economic and Social Committee and the Committee of the Regions*, COM(2005)229 Final, Brussels, 1/6/2005. Available at <http://europa.eu.int/information_society/eeurope/i2010/docs/communications/ com_229_i2010_310505_fv_en.doc> (accessed December 2006).

Gilligan, R. (1998), *The Current Barriers for Older People in Accessing the Information Society.* Available at: <wwweuromedia.net/editors.asp?EditorID=36> (accessed January 2003).

Hudson, H.(2006), 'Universal access to the new information infrastructure', in Lievrouw, L.A. and Livingstone, S. (eds), *The Handbook of New Media. Social Shaping and Social Consequences of ICTs*. Updated Student Edition (London: Sage).

Hudson, J. (2003), 'E-galitarianism? The information society and the New Labour's repositioning of welfare', *Critical Social Policy* 23(2), 268–90.

Livingstone, S. , Bober, M. and Helsper (2005), 'Inequalities and the Digital Divide in Children and Young People's Internet Use', Findings from the *UK Children Go Online* project. April 2005. Available at <http://personal.lse.ac.uk/bober/ UKCGOdigitaldivide.pdf> (accessed December 2006).

Loges, W. E. and Jung, J. (2001), 'Exploring the digital divide. Internet connectedness and age', *Communication Research* 18(4), 536–62.

Ofcom (2006), 'Media Literacy Audit: Report on media literacy amongst older people', Ofcom, 3 April 2006. Available at <http://www.ofcom.org.uk/advice/ media_literacy/medlitpub/medlitpubrss/older/older.pdf> (accessed December 2006).

Olsson, T. (2006), 'Approaching civic information and communication technology: a critical study of Swedish ICT policy visions', *New Media and Society* 8 (4), 611–27.

Olsson, T., Sandström H. and Dahlgreen, P. (2003), 'An Information Society for Everyone?', *Gazette: The International Journal for Communication Studies* 65 (4–5), 347–63.

Oxford Internet Survey (OxIS) (2005), 'The Internet in Britain', Oxford Internet Institute, May 2005 URL. Available at: <http://www.oii.ox.ac.uk/research/oxis/oxis2005_report.pdf> (accessed December 2006).

'People's Internet Use'. Findings from the *UK Children Go Online project*. April 2005. Available at <http://personal.lse.ac.uk/bober/UKCGOdigitaldivide.pdf> (accessed December 2006).

Richardson, M., Weaver, C.K. and Zorn, T.E. (2005), '"Getting on": older New Zealanders' perceptions of computing', *New Media and Society*, 7 (2), 219–45.

Riggs, K.E. (2004), *Granny@Work: Aging and New Technology on the Job in America* (London: Routledge).

Seniornet (2004), 'Seniornet members' interest survey. Summer 2004'. Available at <http://www.seniornet.org/php/default.php?PageID=7414> (accessed December 2006).

Sourbati, M. (2004), *Internet Use in Sheltered Housing: Older people's access to new media and online service delivery*, YPS for the Joseph Rowntree Foundation.

Tetley, J., Hanson, E. and Clarke, A. (2000), 'Older people, telematics and care', in Warnes, A., Warren, L. and Nolan, M. (eds), *Care Services for Later Life. Transformations and critiques* (London and Philadelphia: Jessica Kingsley Publishers).

University of Southern California (USC) Annenberg School Center for the Digital Future (2004), 'The Digital Future Report. Surveying the Digital Future Year Four', University of Southern California, September 2004. Available at <http://www.digitalcenter. org/downloads/DigitalFutureReport-Year4-2004.pdf> (accessed December 2006).

Wyatt, S., Henwood, F. Hart, A. and Smith, J. (2005), 'The digital divide, health information and everyday life', *New Media and Society* 7(2), 199–218.

Wyatt, S., Thoman, G. and Terranova, T. (2002), 'The came, they surfed, they went back to the beach. Conceptualising use and non-use of the Internet', in Woolgar, S. (ed.), *Virtual Society?* (Oxford: Oxford University Press).

PART III
ICTs in Organisational Settings: A Tool or a Curse?

Chapter 8

Resistance to Innovation: A Case Study

Raija Halonen

Introduction

This chapter provides a case study of an implementation project that was carried out in the mid-1990s. It discusses the power of users, and especially the power of user resistance, to influence the success of implementing a new information system. The material for the case study came from interviews and observations made by the author during the implementation project, which lasted six months. The case study, described in detail to enable readers to get a full conception of the situation, is of the attempt to implement an information system to replace pen and paper recording of a work process in a factory making coatings for cables.

Research Method

The case study (Stake, 2000; Loos and Rintala in this book) as a research method suits this investigation due to the self-contained nature of this innovation within the organisation concerned. The approach used was one of 'reflective practitioner' (Schön, 1983) because the author was fully involved in the information system project, where she had to act both as a member of the project and simultaneously work as an outside expert. The author participated in collecting the material for the study by conducting interviews with the workers and with their foremen in the factory and interviewing the representatives from the managerial level. Four sets of interviews were carried out altogether: before the design phase, during the design phase, during the implementation phase and during the testing phase. During the implementation project the author also made observations concerning the progress of the implementation process. When the first signs of resistance to the new information system became evident, some plans were made to manage the resistance. Actions to reduce this resistance were taken and reflections at the time were noted to be used afterwards during the evaluation of the study.

Innovation, Implementation and User Participation

Before turning to the case study, various relevant considerations will be identified from the existing literature on innovation. First, there is the advice about user participation. Information systems are implemented in organisations to improve the effectiveness and efficiency of those organisations (Hevner et al., 2004). There is a tradition arguing that user involvement in information system development contributes to the success of such implementations (for example, Newman and Noble, 1990). According to some writing in this tradition, users should not only provide data and information input for the expert's creative process, but they should provide expertise in generating the solution (Cairns and Beech, 1999).

User training is a critical task during the implementation process and has a bearing upon any resistance to change (Davis and Olson, 1985). The amount of user training is itself dependent on the degree to which the new information system affects different tasks within the organisation.

There are also other considerations. Before any information or work process can be digitised it should be described clearly enough (Halonen, 2006). Developing and implementing information systems are instances of organisational change (Davis and Olson, 1985) that often lead to changes in personnel structures and work processes (Sahay and Robey, 1996). An example of the latter would be new information that needs to be put into databases and remembering to do this can be perceived as being difficult (Effron, 2004).

Not all writings on innovations have such a focus on users. For example, Nikander and Eloranta (1997) list the 14 most common reasons for project problems and users, as such, are not even mentioned in their list. However, the overwhelming advice is that user participation in strategic change processes is frequently assumed to have a number of consequences for producing positive responses to change and ultimately the success of implementation (Lines, 2004). Our case study reports differently. The design phase was concluded with the help of these users of the system after supervisors had held some discussions with the foremen of the workers. The sad conclusion arising from this implementation project was that the information system was not used despite user training and user involvement from the very design phase because of various forms of resistance from the workers.

Users' Resistance

So what does the existing literature say about user resistance? First, users need reasons to use new applications. Keefe (2003) writes about the importance of focusing on the user, who must not be forgotten in any phase of the system development. One key point he makes is that systems that improve business processes and deliver information faster to workers are not sufficient. Users using the new application must themselves also be motivated to do the tasks that are needed to make the information available. Keefe argues that without motivated users there is no traction to enable the implementation project to succeed.

Second, the implementation process can be supported by recognising in advance the type of potential resistance. Markus (1983) outlines three theories of resistance to change according to the three most important reasons for resistance. It is important to know what kind of resistance is occurring, because the appropriate responses depend on identifying the root cause of the resistance. If the resistance comes from the people actually working with the new innovation, then these users must be trained and persuaded and/or they must be taken into the implementation process as members of the project. If the resistance to change arises mainly from the nature of the system itself, then it is the system that must be developed by improving its usability, adjusting the system within the organisation and maybe increasing the user's role in the process of system design. A third type of resistance to change can arise from the interaction between the organisation and the system. In this case it is the problems in the organisation that should be amended before the implementation phase begins. From a political perspective looking at changes in power-sharing, as well as from a socio-technical point of view, changes in the distribution of work might also offer a solution to any resistance to change that arises from this third possibility.

Markus (1983) then goes on to list some familiar observations regarding user resistance:

1. management support and user involvement in the design process reduce user resistance;
2. systems that are technically good meet less resistance than ones that are not;
3. users resist systems that are not user friendly;
4. if there is nothing wrong with the old system, then users resist change;
5. benefits should exceed costs.

Users working in an organisation adopt the culture that dominates within that organisation (Ayas and Zeniuk, 2001). It is worth asking about the scope for changing that culture, asking if there is space for learning capabilities within an organisation. Newman and Noble (1990) refer to various learning models that can be used where user involvement is seen as an opportunity for designers to educate and inform users about new systems. In fact, in the case reported here, certain types of resistance decreased when that occurred and when the expectations of the system became more realistic. Learning proved to be an important element in user involvement and it is possible for both the designer and user to learn in this process, which can help reduce the semantic gap between the two sides.

Lastly, users' potential for involvement in system design differs according to their capabilities. Engler (1996) provides a step-by-step approach for involving an appropriate user to represent all users in the implementation project: 1) identify the correct user, 2) involve that particular user early and often, 3) create and maintain a quality relationship between this representative of the other users and the design team and 4) make changes to practices easy. By following these steps the designer should be able to ensure that the user representative continues to want to make progress in the implementation of the innovation, that feedback is continuous, that commitment holds during the system's entire life cycle and, among other things, that the designer can learn the user's language.

Failure and Success

The final literature to consider is that on success and failure and one first overall observation by Rad (2003) is that the failure or success of a project is often a matter of perception that is in turn influenced by people having different backgrounds and experiences.

Turning to actual measures of success, DeLone and McLean (1992) have a measure of information system success that has also been used to measure the success of an implementation process itself. The measure includes a model with six components in it: system quality, information quality, use, user satisfaction, individual impact and organisational impact. I will make use of this when evaluating the project at the end of the chapter.

We need to be aware that project failure rates can exceed 80 percent in information technology projects (Furton, 2003) and this can occur for many reasons. This failure can be caused by resistance or else the new system can differ too much from the assumptions made by and the requirements of the owner. Failure can relate to changes in project personnel and project objectives during the system development life cycle. The competence of the designer is also an issue – one difficult to evaluate. And in general incompetence can be found in unprofessional work, in unqualified personnel and in improper processes (Furton, 2003).

Burns et al. (1991) add several further explanations of why an implementation fails. The authors think that the reasons are connected with 1) a lack of understanding concerning the implementation process within the organisation, 2) the management of the organisation having difficulties in understanding the size of the implementation project, 3) underestimating the need for organisational change during implementation and 4) responsible project managers having no previous experience of implementing complicated information systems.

Furton (2003) goes on to remind us that any information technology project has to overcome many risks. These can come from the user's or customer's side, or from changes in priorities within the organisation. Changing requirements often emerge in projects where users are involved and where they become more active once the project is progressing. Problems are especially visible in projects where users cannot specify what they actually want (Halonen, 2005).

Then we have to consider the question of how to manage problems when they start to emerge. When carrying on any project various writers argue that the project manager should be able to judge the atmosphere among the people and stakeholders involved (for example, Nikander and Eloranta, 1997). There are so-called weak signals that indicate when something is going in the wrong direction. Examples of these weak signals include ever growing difficulties in arranging a suitable time for meetings about the new information system or people simply losing interest in the innovation. Weak signals tend to become stronger with the passing of time. Hence, those trying to manage the implementation process should be concerned about them at an early stage when the signals are still weak.

Griffith et al. (1999) offer a three-step process to aid the success of any implementation when issues arise:

1. Reframe expectations. The aim of this is to make the background of the implementation project clearer.
2. Create small gains. This entails generating small examples of evidence that the implementation is succeeding and can help to ensure executive support. It

also helps the organisation to understand that implementation is an ongoing, adaptive process that moves forward step by step.

3. Reduce conflicts of interest. If the new technology must be embedded in the existing organisational setting, it can meet problems if the existing organisation was not designed to function with the new technology.

Griffith et al. (1999) make the link between resistance and failure, noting that end-users often resist implementation because the technology conflicts with their personal interests. Hence, referring back to the literature at the start of this chapter, user involvement in developing an information system is a critical component in the success of any implementation project (Newman and Noble, 1990; Jiang et al., 2002).

Background of the Case Study

The organisation studied was a designer and a manufacturer of cables that were supplied to the global telecommunications sector and industry. In the organisation there was a department where the cables were coated. This coating was executed by large, noisy cable covering machines located in an industrial hall. In the hall, there were several machines serving different cable lines like copper cable, optical cable, cellular cable and data cable lines. The coating process was somewhat dirty and noisy and there were pauses in the work process when workers used to have a smoke or a cup of coffee while waiting for the cable for coating to arrive or waiting for the coating to be finished. If there were problems in the cable covering machine, a red lamp lit up, a siren howled and the workers went to adjust the cable, to add coating material or to insert new parameters into the machine. The workers needed to be strong since the cable material reels had to be changed when they were empty and replacement cable reels had to be moved when they were full. The coating phase could last several hours, during which shifts changed. Some coating phases were shorter, some longer than the others. Information about the coating process was updated by workers during the previous shift so that the next shift knew what coating had taken place – for example, who the customer was, what kind of cable type was coated, what the coating parameters were, if there had been any problems – before they came to work.

The customer organisations ordered cables according to their needs. The interval between orders from the same customer could vary from weeks to months or even to years. There were a limited number of customers around the world and the workers used to know which kind of cable was meant for a specific customer. All the necessary information was written down on papers that were kept in paper files on shelves and on tables. When the certain cable type was changed the information written on paper concerning that cable type was crossed out and coating parameters were re-written with a thicker pencil. Sometimes the workers wrote down some extra information about a certain coating time. In practice, the information was almost impossible to retrieve when needed, but the workers themselves did not see any need for a new information system. They were used to the messy A4 sheets and they knew how to coat cables.

The workers were middle-aged factory workers who had not had any previous experiences of PCs. Some of them had a PC at home, but it was mainly used by the children and for playing purposes only. The education level of these workers was quite low, mostly vocational training or comprehensive school. Coating was a task that could be learned only by doing it.

The need for the new information system became a topic when some customers started to ask for quality reports and information about the cable manufacturing process. At the same time there were changes in the organisation itself and a new manager also thought that it important to have knowledge about the coating process. This meant that information about all the parameters and materials that had been used in any one coating process had to be available. The manager also required higher levels of quality to be maintained in the industrial hall in terms of keeping the cable cover machines more tidy.

Implementation

The new coating information system commenced with design and specification phases, where the prospective users also participated. Because the factory environment was not familiar to the designer she needed a good deal of help from the workers who were experienced in coating cables. The designer visited the industrial hall several times, interviewing workers and becoming acquainted with the coating stage. The workers were very helpful and satisfied with a situation where somebody showed an interest in what they were doing. The requirement specification was developed by the combined efforts of the system specialist of the factory, one foreman, one worker and the designer. In addition, many necessary features became evident as the designer followed the coating process and the routines taking place in the hall.

At the beginning there were problems in understanding all the phases that were needed in the coating process. The workers chose some examples of the paper sheets that included the coating information. These were to be the basis for the new information system. However, the papers were difficult to be read because some of them were already many years old and consisted of dirty A4 sheets. The designer needed a considerable amount of help to understand the markings on the paper because they were made by handwriting and some of them were in the margins of the paper.

The first prototype of the coating information system helped the users and the designer to understand each other. It was very difficult to appreciate the specific importance of the many phases in the coating process and to understand all the parameters that had to be considered to coat a particular type of cable. The prototype was demonstrated on the designer's workstation and the workers were asked to give their impressions and ask questions freely of other users in the industrial hall. The prototype needed a lot of changes until the first pilot version was ready.

At the very beginning of the development project the need for this new information system in general was already questioned. A new workstation was installed by the side of the cable coating machine. The keyboard was covered with transparent plastic to keep it clean. But during the testing phase resistance was already so great that some of the workers refused to even test the system.

The first pilot versions were ready for these users on time. Before piloting, some screens on the new information system were shown to the key users who had participated in the design process. This took place at the designer's workplace. Several discussions were held and measures taken to get the application to function properly. These discussions were also fruitful in terms of overcoming language problems, because there had been situations where the designer and the workers had not been able to understand each other fully. There were terms relating to coating that the designer could not understand and there were buttons and menus on the new application that the workers could not understand.

The designer trained the users two at a time because there was no space for any more people. Since the training took place by the workstation near the cable coating machine it was sometimes very noisy and there many disturbances. The pilot database included fictitious parameters, customer names and cable types like ABC123, Donald Duck and Thick Cable. At times the workers could not concentrate on the user interface and on the functionality of the application because they were arguing that 'there is no such cable type' or 'no cable can be so thick'. The designer could not make it clear to them that she did not know all the right parameters for a certain cable type. During this phase strong resistance was perceived.

The information system was Windows-based and the user interface needed the user to use a mouse. The difficulty was that the interface was quite unfamiliar to the workers and some of them had major problems using the device. This increased the degree of difficulty so much that a few workers even refused to participate in the pilot. The electronic form on the screen resembled the A4 sheets as much as possible. Here, the problem was that it had not been possible to fit all the information needed onto one screen. Hence, users of the new system had to change page when inserting the information. According to the requirements, the user interface included all the information that had previously been written on separate A4 sheets. If there was specific information concerning a certain coating time it had to be inserted into the system afresh every time that coating was taking place. Under the old paper system, that information could already be seen on the A4 sheet and the men had tacit knowledge about which coating time it concerned.

There were many reasons for resistance. The most important reason was that the computer as a tool was too unfamiliar to the workers. In this respect, the situation improved somewhat when the game of Patience was installed into the coating line workstation in order to get the workers accustomed to the use of the mouse. Hence, the workers could play Patience when there were pauses in the coating process. Some of the men were very satisfied with the game and their resistance to and fear of computers seemed to decrease. Another reason for the resistance was the workers' opinion about the very need for this information system: they saw no reason for introducing the new system. They thought that it took up too much of their time and that it was useless because information about the coatings already existed in paper form. They also had difficulties deciding who was to enter the information into the software application because there were several men working together on the same cable coating machine. As the coating progressed they had to enter more parameters into the machine and after that insert that same information into the software application. The game of Patience was removed at one point because the foremen thought that it took up too much time. In addition, workers from other cable lines came to play on the workstation, which was not approved of by their foremen. But after new negotiations and more detailed arguments the game was reinstalled.

After the piloting phase, the application was given some minor enhancements according to the wishes of the users. The application was then installed on the workstation and more workers were trained to use the interface and the application. There were certain main users in every shift and they in turn trained the other workers to use the new system. The designer was available during office hours and visited the industrial hall every now and then to see how the application was used and to find out if there were any problems in the functioning of the software. On several of these occasions it was clear that the application was not in use and the workers had gone back to using the old paper sheets instead. After reminding the workers of the need to use the new application they sometimes started to insert the coating information into the database. But frequently they left the task to be done by the next shift.

According to the specified requirements, all the old data from the unofficial coating information that had been registered in the paper files were written into the new information system via the system's user interface. The designer spent some time entering these data but most of the data were entered by a hired student. Part of the information was so messy and inaccurate that it could not be entered into the database. It meant that the workers themselves had to insert all this information, including tens of parameters, into the information system. This seemed to them to be time-consuming and difficult. The cable types had complicated names and when digitised they had to be written correctly in order to be located the next time.

The implementation project lasted six months from the specification phase until the user training phase after installation. The industrial hall was cleaned and remained much cleaner than several months earlier. As noted earlier, this was to be part of the quality improvement in the coating phase. Use of the final version of the information system gradually declined until it was completely unused, cable by cable and shift by shift. By this time the designer had left the organisation.

The information system was brought back slowly into use again as new workers were employed and when it was later re-implemented new features had been added to the system. The features of the information system had by then been modified and new ones added to meet the changes in the coating function and new requirements. However, this new situation lies outside the scope of this case study.

Discussion

This chapter has discussed resistance to change among these particular factory workers in relation to the literature outlined at the start of the chapter. One overall conclusion is that resistance can be forceful and cannot always be overcome.

Was the coating information system a success or a failure? When assessed according to DeLone's and McLean's (1992) measure it seems, on the one hand, that the system quality and the information quality criteria were satisfied and they met the requirements. However, in terms of use the implementation did not pass this test, neither did it in terms of user satisfaction. The individual impact was poor and that meant that the organisational impact was also low. Measured by DeLone's and McLean's measurer the coating information system was undoubtedly a failure.

Next we turn to Engler's (1996) four-step approach to involving users. In this case study, the workers showed a willingness to participate and they were contacted very often at the beginning to give the designer an idea of their perspectives. In line with Engler's scheme, the several meetings and discussions with the users helped both the designer and the users to understand the language that was used. For example, when using the Windows interface it was falsely assumed that certain terms and tools would be understood by the workers – like 'space bar', 'window', 'field', 'menu', 'tab-key'. Conversely, when coating cables, there were working phrases that were specific to the coating process that were not commonly known to the designer. The discussions were productive and helped the designer to use the right coating terms and understand the whole process of coating.

The users were then encouraged to provide their knowledge during the development phase (Cairns and Beech, 1991). They were also able to participate in the design phase, as Markus (1983) proposes in her article.

The initiative for this whole project came from the managerial level, which gave its full support to the process. However, one key lesson is that even considerable user involvement alone may not ultimately be enough to reduce user resistance (despite the positive outcomes of such involvement, as discussed in Loos' chapter in this book). The new information system was more technical than its predecessor because it used a microcomputer instead of a pencil and paper. It is obvious that this was one key reason for user resistance. The users considered the new system not to be 'user friendly' because they did not like it at all and this increased their resistance (Markus, 1983). The workers were used to doing their job in their own traditional way and did not want to change. Finally, the idea for the new information system came from the managerial level to serve their quality purposes. Running against the principle proposed by Keefe (2003), the workers did not perceive any benefit to themselves from doing this extra work, learning the Windows user interface and entering the information about the coating (Effron, 2004). They felt that it was time-consuming and in vain from their point of view. Their main purpose was to coat cable and they were on the whole not interested in the development or use of this information system. This brings us back to the question of the culture of work and learning capabilities within the organisation (Ayas and Zeniuk, 2001).

Developing the prototype helped the designer a good deal in terms of actually learning the requirements of the information system. The workers were not used to specifying what they actually wanted (Jiang et al., 2002; Halonen, 2006) and with the prototype they could see what the computerised information system actually meant, what kind of information it needed and how the information about the cable types that in the past had been written could be retrieved from the database. However, there were drawbacks. To retrieve information the users had to be able to specify exactly the key information that was to be used when finding the cable type. Previously they had been able to browse through the paper files or else search the A4 sheets from the tables. Moreover, using the paper system they had been able to see the whole sheet at a glance.

Table 8.1 lists the most obvious reasons of resistance seen in the case and the actions or remedies taken to alleviate them.

Table 8.1   Reasons for resistance

Reason for resistance	Remedy	Reaction
Unknown user interface	Playing, training	Decrease in resistance to change
General unwillingness to change	Discussions	No change in resistance
New system too complicated	Training, information	Decrease in resistance to change
Lack of motivation	Discussions	No change in resistance
New system difficult to use	System development, training	Decrease in resistance to change
New system seen as being useless	Attitude training, information	No change in resistance

The unknown interface was the easiest barrier to overcome and playing the game also led to a positive atmosphere among the workers. In the beginning the new information system seemed more complicated than it was, because the sheet shown onscreen included all the different A4 sheets with the information that was gathered from coating different cable types.

The users seemed to be unwilling to change in general: certainly they did not use the new information system until they had to. It was as if the technology conflicted with the user's personal interests (referring back to Griffith et al., 1999). The users were hired to coat cable, not to develop information technology. It is difficult to say if the discussions helped the situation or not. Certainly by the end of the implementation project, use of the system was not as frequent as it could have been.

As regards difficulty of use, in the beginning the new system seemed to be complicated because the users had to choose the cable type using some key information from the database in order to get the parameters for the cable type they were currently using. This meant that the new application actually made it more difficult to find the current coating information. This problem was overcome by training and afterwards the users were satisfied with the parameters they could get from the database.

The last reason for resistance listed above, the fact that they did not appreciate the value of the system compared to the paper, was the most difficult to eliminate because it was substantial. Attitude training and information did not seem to provide a solution to this problem. Keefe (2003) refers to such problems in motivation and in this coating case no motivation was found.

In sum, while some reasons for resistance could be successfully addressed, some of the resistance can come from factors that cannot be influenced. The author believes that there will continue to be information system implementations that will fail because of such resistance.

References

Ayas, K. and Zeniuk, N. (2001), 'Project-based Learning: Building Communities of Reflective Practitioners', *Management Learning* 32, 61–76.

Burns, O.M., Turnipseed, D. and Riggs, W.E. (1991), 'Critical success factors in manufacturing resource planning in implementation', *International Journal of Operation & Production Management* 11, 5–19.

Cairns, G. and Beech, N. (1999), 'User involvement in organisational decision making', *Management Decision* 37, 14–23.

Davis, G.B. and Olson, M.H. (1985), 'Development, Implementation, and Management of Information System Resources', in Davis, G.B. and Olson, M.H. (1985), *Management Information Systems: Conceptual Foundations, Structure and Development*: 561–601 (New York: McGraw-Hill).

DeLone, W.H. and McLean, E.R. (1992), 'Information Systems Success: The Quest for the Dependent Variable', *Information Systems Research* 3, 60–95.

Effron, M.S. (2004), 'Knowledge Management Involves Neither Knowledge nor Management', in Goldsmith, M., Morgan, H. and Ogg, A.J. (eds), *Leading Organizational Learning* (San Francisco: Jossey-Bass).

Engler, N. (1996), 'Obtaining user involvement: A step-by-step approach', *Computerworld* 30, 71.

Furton, M.T. (2003), 'Discovering the true cause of failure in custom software development projects', *Computer and Internet Lawyer* 20, 1–3.

Griffith, T.L., Zammuto, R.F. and Aiman-Smith, L. (1999), 'Why new technologies fail', *Industrial Management* 41, 29–34.

Halonen, R. (2005), 'Changing user requirements in an inter-organisational information system', in Soliman, K.S. (eds), *Internet and Information Technology in Modern Organizations: Challenges & Answers. Electronic proceedings of the 5th IBIMA Conference Cairo*, 13–15 December 2005, 717–24.

Halonen, R. (2006), 'Digitizing Information Management', in Pit. Pichappan, Abraham, A., Chbeir, R, Badr, Y., El-Qawasmeh E., Gross-Amblard, D. and Safar, M. (eds), *Proceedings of the First IEEE International Conference on Digital Information Management*, 6–8 December 2006, Bangalore, India, 351–58.

Hevner, R., March, S.T., Park, J. and Ram, S. (2004), 'Design science in information systems research', *MIS Quarterly* 28, 75–105.

Jiang, J.J, Chen, E. and Klein, G. (2002), 'The importance of building a foundation for user involvement in information system projects', *Project Management Journal* 33, 20–26.

Keefe, P. (2003), 'The way to win', *Computerworld* 37, 24.

Lines, R. (2004), 'Influence of participation in strategic change: resistance, organizational commitment and change goal achievement', *Journal of Change Management* 4, 193–215.

Markus, M.L. (1983), 'Power, Politics, and MIS Implementation', *Communication of the ACM* 26, 430–44.

Newman, M. and Noble, R. (1990), 'User Involvement as an Interaction Process: A Case Study', *Information Systems Research* 1, 89–113.

Nikander, I.O. and Eloranta, E. (1997), 'Preliminary signals and early warnings in industrial investment projects', *International Journal of Project Management* 15, 371–76.

Rad, P.F. (2003), 'Project success attributes', *Cost Engineering* 45, 23–29.

Sahay, S. and Robey, D. (1996), 'Organizational Context, Social Interpretation, and the Implementation and Consequences of Geographic Information Systems', *Accounting, Management & Information Technology* 6, 255–82.

Schön, D. (1983), *The Reflective Practitioner, How Professionals Think in Action* (New York: Basic Books).

Stake, R.E. (2000), 'Case studies', in Denzin, N.K. and Lincoln, Y.S. (eds), *Handbook of Qualitative Research* (London: Sage).

Chapter 9

Using ICT in Human Service Organisations: An Enabling Constraint? Social Workers, New Technology and their Organisation

Eugène Loos

Introduction

The Hawthorne experiments (Mayo, 1933) at the beginning of the twentieth century investigated the impact of industrialisation on human behaviour in organisations. In the new millennium we need to continue such empirical research organisational settings, but this time looking at the implications of ICTs for the behaviour of their users (see also the Introduction of this book and Haddon et al., 2005). This chapter presents a case study focussing on the use of new media in a specific setting: a human service organisation (Hasenfeld, 1983; Gastelaars, 2005).

Before turning to the details of this case study, it is necessary to clarify the two types of effect that the introduction of ICTs in organisations could bring about. I will make use of Sproull and Kiesler (1991) in order to distinguish between the first-level (direct) and second-level (indirect) effects of technologies. Then, I will present the results of a case study that I conducted at Casita,[1] a social services institution in the Netherlands. The goal is to examine how the social workers in this organisation perceived the use of an intranet that was about to be imposed on them by their management and how they thought this obligatory use would affect their professional practices. I examine the ways that these actors evaluated the possible constraints and/or opportunities ('enabling constraint', Giddens, 1984) related to its use in order to gain more insight into second-level effects. Like Winograd and Flores (1986: 177), I am concerned with

> what happens when new devices are created, and with how possibilities arise. There is a circularity here: the world determines what we can do and what we do determines our world.

The first research question to be answered in this chapter is:
1. *How did the social workers in Casita, who were most of the time working individually with their clients, visualise their own organisation?* Asking respondents

---

1 The name of the organisation is a pseudonym in order to guarantee anonymity.

to draw the organisation to which they belonged and to focus on their own position within this organisational setting allowed me to examine self-representations of the social services institution where they worked (see Gergen and Whitney, 1996: 334–336 for more information about self-representation in organisations). These self-representations made it clear in which settings the participants themselves considered their professional activities to take place, which is important background information if we want to understand how they felt they would experience the obligatory use of the intranet in their organisation.

This brings us to the second research question:

2. *How did they experience the imminent and obligatory use of an intranet in their organisation? Were they afraid that the introduction of this new medium would inhibit their professional activities or did they instead consider the intranet to be a possible tool that could facilitate their work?*

As a research method I used focus groups (see also Jensen et al., Chapter 4 in this book), a research technique that collects data through group interaction on a specific topic (Morgan, 1997) allowing the social workers at the social services institution to discuss the possible consequences of the new medium for their work practices. Conducting empirical research in this way enabled me to gain an insight into the ways in which professionals make sense of the introduction of new technology within their organisation.

Second-level Effects in Human Service Organisations

Hasenfeld (1983: 1–3) argues that the relationships between citizens and the welfare state are mediated by human service organisations such as hospitals and municipalities, which register and respond to citizens' claims. Although he focuses on service delivery in the public sector, his work can also be applied to the human service organisations that can be found in the private sector, such as banks, insurance companies or restaurants, where services delivered to customers are an essential component of their business (see also Gastelaars, 2005). The social services institution Casita, where I conducted the case study, is another example of just such a human service organisation.

In order to examine how the imminent introduction of a new medium like an intranet was perceived by the social workers in Casita it is necessary to first define the effects related to the introduction of ICTs in organisations. Sproull and Kiesler (1991: 2) distinguish between the first-level and second-level effects of technologies. First-level effects are defined as direct effects; they are the reason why these technologies are introduced, for example to improve the efficiency of the organisation. Second-level effects are defined as social system effects; indirect consequences and often unexpected effects on organisational relations and communication patterns (as explored in depth by Rintala in the next chapter). The main objective of my empirical research is not to develop a tool to improve organisational efficiency but to gain some insight into the ways in which employees in an organisation perceive the introduction of a new medium related to the consequences for their professional activities. Therefore, I focus on second-level effects.

The Case Study: Professional Practices at a Social Services Institution

Casita was a private Dutch social services institution where 110 social workers helped employees to cope with stress and to improve their well-being. The headquarters were located in the north of the Netherlands. Most social workers only visited this location once, when they were interviewed for their job. Being employed by Casita meant being paid by the headquarters for professional activities that were executed to a large extent in the field at the client's organisation. Social workers are professionals who are acting rather individually and autonomously. In order to bind them to Casita, the management divided the Netherlands into 19 areas and asked a social worker in each of them to organise monthly meetings with the other social workers in his or her area so that experiences can be shared.

At the time of the study, management had decided to develop an internal website (an intranet) for the social workers, and asked me to examine their needs relating to the use of this new channel of communication. I proposed to focus not only on this new medium but also to contextualise this by asking their opinion about the use of other media. This would allow the management to develop a communications policy that was better adapted to the more general preferences of users working in the field. The management agreed and we decided that I would contact the coordinators of the 19 areas in different parts of the country. All of them were willing to cooperate. I visited 8 areas (those which were about to have their monthly meeting). In this way I was able to have discussions with 45 social workers (about 40 per cent of all the professionals working at Casita). To stimulate the discussion as much as possible I decided to organise focus groups. This qualitative research method uses group interviews to gather data in an effective way by focusing on a specific topic, in this case the use of favourite old and/or new media for internal communication. When using this approach the participants react to each other's opinions. This in turn promotes a dynamic discussion and allows us to get a better insight into the ways in which the social workers perceive the introduction of a new medium in their organisation:

> The comparative advantage of focus groups as an interview technique lies in their ability to observe interaction on a topic. Group discussions provide direct evidence about similarities and differences in the participants' opinions and experiences as opposed to reaching such conclusions from post hoc analyses of separate statements of each interviewee. (Morgan, 1997: 10)

The time spent with the focus groups was divided into three activities:
1. I wanted to get the discussion started in a creative way and to understand how the participants positioned themselves within the social services institution where they worked. Hence I asked them to draw a picture that represented their relationship as a social worker to Casita and then to discuss this picture with their colleagues.
2. I distributed ten yellow self-stick notes to each participant and asked them to stick them on one or more of several media (letter, bulletin, 'face-to-face', phone, e-mail, intranet, other media to be mentioned by themselves) that were indicated on a white board. In this way they could make clear which medium/media they preferred to use

for internal communication. After having done this they discussed their choices with each other.

3. Finally, I asked the participants to fill in a questionnaire in order to express their expectations related to the planned intranet. The aim was to get some feedback about how they thought they would be able to carry out their work as a professional adequately using the system. For this goal I used a 'multiple-item scale' based on Servqual, an instrument to measure the quality of services, which was developed by Parasuraman et al. (1988). Servqual was designed to gain insight into service quality at service encounters, by comparing the expectations and experiences of customers. I adapted the instrument for my empirical research in two ways. First of all I focused on expectations, because the social workers had not yet actually used the intranet since it was at the time only under development. Secondly, a Servqual item called Tangibles (covering physical facilities, equipment, and appearance of personnel) was useful for measuring the quality of services delivered by 'face-to-face' communication at service encounters. However, it was not as useful for measuring services delivered electronically by intranet (website and e-mail). It is for these two reasons that I designed a new 'multiple-item scale' in order to gain some insight into the expectations of employees who were about to use Casita's intranet. The following items are part of this scale: Reliability, Speed, Design, Empathy and User friendliness. The participants were asked to indicate how important (on a scale from 1 [not important at all] to 10 [very important]) they considered each item[2] to be for the future intranet in their organisation.

Participants' Representations of the Organisation and their Relationship to it

Table 9.1　　Visualising the organisation

Four main categories of drawings can be distinguished:
1. landscape (30%)
2. organism (19%)
3. person(s) (19%)
4. building (8%)
The remaining 24% of the social workers did not draw a picture. They told me and their colleagues that they could not form a clear mental picture of Casita and therefore were not able to visualise their organisation.

It was striking that most participants (30 per cent) drew pictures of landscapes where they depicted themselves as being located at a considerable distance from Casita's headquarters, reflecting the fact that the social workers' professional

---

2 See also the appendix for more information about the elements of which each item is composed.

activities took place to a large extent in the field, at the client's organisation with which they identified rather more than with their own organisation, symbolised by the headquarters. Other colleagues (19 per cent) used images of plants and trees to represent their organisation, visualizing themselves as being a leaf or a branch, thus symbolising themselves as being an integrated part of such an organism. A third group (also 19 per cent) used another image to symbolise the interdependency in the organisation: they represented their organisation by drawing persons connected by lines. Eight per cent of the social workers drew buildings, which usually included the headquarters (facilitating their work, as they explained) and the clients' organisation (where they spent most of their time, as they told me and their colleagues).

Though all the pictures focused on different aspects of the relationship between the social worker and his or her organisation, they all had one thing in common: they showed, in one way or another, the fact that the social workers perceived their professional activities as being embedded in an organisational setting that provided them with a link to their colleagues and/or to the headquarters. Let us now focus on the role that the imminent introduction of the intranet could play in relation to the professional activities of these social workers as perceived in their own eyes.

Favourite Media for Internal Communication

As explained above, yellow self-stick notes were distributed to the 44 participants in the 8 areas that were to be used to indicate their favourite internal medium/media. For practical reasons, focus groups from area 1 and 2 were combined. Table 9.2 shows the results.

It is clear that letters were not seen as being an appropriate internal communications medium by the social workers. They had a strong preference for e-mail and face-to-face communication, with the intranet occupying third position. Some participants mentioned the mobile phone and fax as other media to be used. During the discussion in the focus groups many participants complained about Casita's headquarters sending too much mail to their homes and instead proposed that making such information available on the intranet could be a solution to this problem.

Expectations Regarding the Use of the Intranet

Having focused on their favourite internal media I then asked the participants to use a questionnaire to express their expectations with regard to how they would be able to carry out their work as a professional adequately using the planned intranet. As explained earlier, the questionnaire consisted of a 'multiple-item scale'. Let us now have a look at Table 9.3 to see the social workers' expectations regarding the use of intranet in their organisation.

What strikes one is that in all areas the participants considered Design (a well-organised internal website, pictures, sound) to be the least important item. Empathy (an intranet that is oriented towards the user's questions, towards frequently asked questions and which has good search facilities) and Speed (meaning quick navigation and quick links) were considered to be the most important items.

Table 9.2   Favourite internal media

Area	N	Medium: letter	bulletin	face-to-face	phone	e-mail	intranet	other media
1+2	12	*5 [4.2%]*	13 [10.8%]	**29 [24.2%]**	14 [11.7%]	**29 [24.2%]**	21 [17.5%]	9 [7.5%]
3	4	*2 [5.0%]*	9 [22.5%]	**9 [22.5%]**	7 [17.5%]	8 [20%]	5 [12.5%]	-
4	6	*2 [3.3%]*	6 [10%]	11 [18.3%]	4 [6.6%]	**20 [33.3%]**	17 [28.3%]	-
5	6	*2 [3.3%]*	8 [13.3%]	8 [13.3%]	**13 [21.6%]**	17 [18.3%]	9 [15%]	3 [5%]
6	6	*4 [6.6%]*	6 [10%]	**13 [21.6%]**	12 [20%]	**13 [21.6%]**	10 [16.6%]	2 [3.3%]
7	4	-	2 [5%]	8 [20%]	4 [10%]	9 [22.5%]	**11 [27.5%]**	6 [15%]
8	6	*1 [1.6%]*	6 [10%]	**15 [25%]**	5 [8.3%]	**15 [25%]**	10 [16.6%]	8 [13.3%]
Total N	44							
Number of stickers and %		*16 [3.6%]*	50 [11.4%]	93 [21.13%]	59 [13.4%]	**111 [25.2%]**	83 [18.9%]	28 [6.4%]

N = number of participants (ten yellow self-stick notes for each participant)
% rounded off to one decimal point
bold: highest score
italic: lowest score

After they had completed the questionnaire the participants were asked to discuss the functions that the future intranet would have to fulfil for them.

The social workers underlined the fact that an intranet could play an important role by facilitating the sharing of professional knowledge. Being in the field with clients most of the time, visiting the headquarters rarely and meeting the colleagues in their area just once a month, they could appreciate having a medium at their disposal that would allow them to share knowledge with each other quickly and easily.

Finally, the focus groups discussed the conditions that the intranet would have to fulfil in order to facilitate their professional activities.

Though most of the participants had Internet access at home, they admitted almost unanimously in the focus groups that they only used the Internet for e-mail

Table 9.3   Using the intranet – expectations

Average score (on a scale from 1 [not important at all] to 10 [very important]) for each item

		Item				
		Reliability	Speed	Design	Empathy	User friendliness
	N					
Area						
1+2	12	8.8	**9.3**	*6.3*	8.5	8.4
3	4	**9.0**	8.5	*5.0*	8.7	8.0
4	6	**8.9**	7.9	*4.9*	7.8	7.8
5	7	7.7	**8.9**	*6.4*	**8.9**	**8.9**
6	6	9.2	**9.3**	*6.4*	9.0	8.5
7	4	8.3	8.3	*6.9*	**8.9**	8.4
8	6	8.8	8.0	*6.5*	**9.2**	8.5
Total N	45					
Total average score for each item		8.7	9.0	*6.1*	**9.1**	8.4

N = number of participants
Average score rounded off to one decimal point
bold: highest score
italic: lowest score

Table 9.4   Intranet's functions

In all areas, the following functions were mentioned:
1. enable them to share professional knowledge (by using the internal website and e-mail);
2. enable them to find information (eg. names and addresses of other social workers, information relating to the Human Resources department);
3. allow them to register the results of their professional activities;
4. allow them to put in their expenses.

Table 9.5   Conditions facilitating intranet use for professional activities

The participants mentioned the following three conditions:
1. training in how to use this new medium;
2. a helpdesk to provide support in case there were problems using the system;
3. keeping the intrtanet up-to-date.

and not for accessing Casita's website. If the management wanted the future intranet to become a success, the conditions mentioned above would have to be fulfilled.

Evaluation

The results of the empirical research allowed me to answer the questions presented in the introduction. How did the social workers visualise their organisation? The pictures of landscapes, organisms like plants and trees, persons connected by lines, and buildings showed, one way or another, how they perceived their professional activities as being embedded in an organisational setting that provided them with a link to their colleagues and/or to the headquarters.

The second research question concerned the social workers' expectations of the imminent and obligatory use of an intranet in their organisation. In fact, the results of the empirical research clearly showed that the social workers were not afraid that the introduction of the intranet would inhibit their professional activities. On the contrary, they were hopeful that the intranet was going to fulfil a variety of functions. They thought that it could enable them to share professional knowledge (by using the internal website and e-mail). It could help them to find information (for example, names and addresses of other social workers, information relating to the Human Resources department). Lastly, it could provide a means of registering the results of their professional activities as well as putting in their expense claims.

The social workers underlined the fact that the intranet could play an important role by facilitating the sharing of professional knowledge. Given the limited contact with HQ and colleagues, they could appreciate the value of having a medium at their disposal that would allow them to share knowledge with each other both quickly and easily. This explains their positive attitude towards the introduction of this new medium. Being a member of a professional network meant that in certain senses their organisation was already a virtual organisation (see also Handy, 1995: 41–42). From this viewpoint, the introduction of the intranet had the potential to support their work rather than constrain it, assuming that certain conditions were fulfilled (as regards the training, helpdesk and access to up-to-date information). This was clearly good news for the management of their organisation which was proposing this innovation. However, those managers would also have to be aware that by promoting the use of more ICTs in their organisation there are always potential consequences (as illustrated in Rintala's chapter in this book). In the Casita case study, extending the capabilities of their professional workers might result in less centralised control over the social workers' activities, as noted by previous writers in the field:

> Face-to-face representation is gradually replaced by visual or graphic constructions of organisational reality and by electronically disseminated discourses. This shift is accompanied by profound losses in management's capacity to direct or compel forms of everyday activity. (Gergen and Whitney, 1996: 331)

And as Handy (1995: 42) puts it:

Like it or not, the economics and technology mean that more and more of us will be spending time in virtual space – out of sight, if not out of touch. No longer will our colleagues be down the corridor, available for an unscheduled meeting or a quick progress check.

Using a new medium like an intranet in their organisation can be considered to be an 'enabling constraint' from the perspective of managers. Expressed in more theoretical terms:

> The constitution of agents and structures are not two independently given sets of phenomena, a dualism, but represent a duality. According to the notion of the duality of structure, the structural properties of social systems are both the medium and outcome of the practices they recursively organise. Structure is not "external" to individuals: as memory traces, and as instantiated in social practices, it is in a certain sense more "internal" than exterior to their activities in a Durkheimian sense. Structure is not to be equated with constraint but is always constraining and enabling. (Giddens, 1984: 25)

The introduction of this new medium is both constraining (creating the danger of managers losing control of their professional workers) and enabling (allowing those same professionals to communicate easily and quickly).

Implications

The results presented above already provided the basis for some clear practical recommendations for Casita, the organisation where the case study was conducted:

1. social workers should be offered some training in order to use the intranet as effectively as possible;
2. a helpdesk should be created to answer the questions from those social workers who have problems when dealing with the intranet;
3. one colleague should be made responsible for keeping the intranet up-to-date.

The professional social workers greatly appreciated the fact that their opinion was sought before the intranet was actually developed. One recommendation from this research was that once the intranet started functioning at Casita it would be advisable to monitor users' actual experiences of the services delivered. It was further suggested that the items of the questionnaire used for the empirical research can also be used for this monitoring process. This would allow managers to be kept informed of their professionals' experiences and expectations.

Moving beyond the particular experiences of this human services institution, there are wider implications. In the previous chapter we saw how a dialogue with the workforce did not ultimately guarantee the successful implementation of new ICTs in an organisation (Halonen). However, apart from the fact that these social workers saw the innovation as being intrinsically more useful than did the cable-coating workers in the previous chapter, in this study of Casita we can see that there can be positive consequences of consulting the end users, and indeed having a continuous dialogue between all members within the organisation. Moreover, both new and old media can be used to facilitate such an ongoing dialogue even after the implementation of the new technology. This is because, for example, communication by intranet (such as by e-mail) does not replace but instead supplements face-to-face encounters at a specific location (such as Casita's monthly meetings):

> A sense of place is as important to most of us as a sense of purpose. E-mail and voice mail have many attractions, including immediacy, but are not the same as watching the eyes of others. (…) Paradoxically, the more virtual an organisation becomes, the more its people need to meet in person. (Handy, 1995: 42, 46)

Finally, Handy proposes that if we want organisations to be 'more than a mere broker or a box of contracts' (1995: 50) the concept of membership could be a solution: 'a sense of belonging to a community, even if that community were a largely virtual one' (1995: 48–49). The broad lesson is that new ICTs need to be introduced carefully in organisations. As the case study presented in this chapter shows, if management decides to use ways of fostering involvement such as focus groups in order to ask its employees how they wish to use the intranet, it can actually gain some support for such a new medium through this very process. This is true even if these employees are critical professionals who work almost all the time with their clients at a considerable distance from the headquarters and want to be as autonomous as possible. Managers introducing ICTs in such a way have a better chance of succeeding in terms of extending human capabilities, awareness and spheres of action.

References

Gastelaars, M. (2005), *Excuses voor het ongemak. De vele gevolgen van klantgericht organiseren* (Amsterdam: SWP).

Gergen, K. and Whitney, D. (1996), 'Technologies of Representation in the Global Corporation: Power and Polyphony', in Boje, D.M., Gephart Jr, R.P. and Tatchenkery, T.J. (eds), *Postmodern Management and Organization Theory* (London: Sage).

Giddens, A. (1984), *The Constitution of Society: Outline of the Theory of Structuration* (Cambridge: Polity Press).

Haddon, L., Mante, E.A., Sapio, B., Kommonen, K.-H., Fortunati, L. and Kant, A. (eds) (2005), *Everyday Innovators: Researching the Role of Users in Shaping ICTs* (Dordrecht: Springer).

Handy, C. (1995), 'Trust and the Virtual Organization', *Harvard Business Review*, 40–50.

Hasenfeld, Y. (1983), *Human Service Organizations* (Englewood Cliffs: Prentice-Hall).

Mayo, E. (1933), *The Human Problems of an Industrial Civilization* (New York: Macmillan).

Morgan, D. (1997), *Focus Groups as Qualitative Research* (London: Sage).

Parasuraman, A., Zeithaml, V.A. and Berry, L.L. (1988), 'Servqual: A Multiple-Item Scale for Measuring Consumer Perceptions of Service Quality', *Journal of Retailing*, 64 (1), 12–37.

Sproull, L. and Kiesler, S. (1991), *New Ways of Working in the Networked Organization* (Cambridge: MIT Press).

Winograd, T. and Flores, F. (1986), *Understanding Computers and Cognition: A New Foundation for Design* (Reading: Addison-Wesley).

APPENDIX

Questionnaire: Future Use of an Intranet

Instruction

Please be so kind as to indicate for each of the following items how important you consider this is for the intranet that Casita is going to develop:

I. Reliability
II. Speed
III. Design
IV. Empathy
V. User friendliness

Each item is composed of different aspects. The more important an aspect is for you as a future user, the higher your score should be (between 1 [not important at all] and 10 [very important]).

I. RELIABILITY

1. Reliable information

| 1 | 2 | 3 | 4 | 5 | 6 | 7 | 8 | 9 | 10 |

2. Complete information

| 1 | 2 | 3 | 4 | 5 | 6 | 7 | 8 | 9 | 10 |

3. Up-to-date information

| 1 | 2 | 3 | 4 | 5 | 6 | 7 | 8 | 9 | 10 |

4. One person is responsible for the information

| 1 | 2 | 3 | 4 | 5 | 6 | 7 | 8 | 9 | 10 |

II. SPEED

5. Quick navigation

| 1 | 2 | 3 | 4 | 5 | 6 | 7 | 8 | 9 | 10 |

6. Quick links

| 1 | 2 | 3 | 4 | 5 | 6 | 7 | 8 | 9 | 10 |

III. DESIGN

7. A well-organised internal website

| 1 | 2 | 3 | 4 | 5 | 6 | 7 | 8 | 9 | 10 |

8. Pictures

| 1 | 2 | 3 | 4 | 5 | 6 | 7 | 8 | 9 | 10 |

9. Sound

| 1 | 2 | 3 | 4 | 5 | 6 | 7 | 8 | 9 | 10 |

IV. EMPATHY

10. Intranet is oriented towards the user's questions

| 1 | 2 | 3 | 4 | 5 | 6 | 7 | 8 | 9 | 10 |

11. Frequently asked questions

| 1 | 2 | 3 | 4 | 5 | 6 | 7 | 8 | 9 | 10 |

12. Good search facilities

| 1 | 2 | 3 | 4 | 5 | 6 | 7 | 8 | 9 | 10 |

V. USER FRIENDLINESS

13. Easy navigation

| 1 | 2 | 3 | 4 | 5 | 6 | 7 | 8 | 9 | 10 |

14. Possible to get information from the HR department

| 1 | 2 | 3 | 4 | 5 | 6 | 7 | 8 | 9 | 10 |

15. Possible to pose questions to the headquarters

| 1 | 2 | 3 | 4 | 5 | 6 | 7 | 8 | 9 | 10 |

16. Possible to communicate with colleagues using an electronic bulletin board

| 1 | 2 | 3 | 4 | 5 | 6 | 7 | 8 | 9 | 10 |

17. Possible to communicate with colleagues using a chat box

| 1 | 2 | 3 | 4 | 5 | 6 | 7 | 8 | 9 | 10 |

18. Possible to use the organisation's online library

| 1 | 2 | 3 | 4 | 5 | 6 | 7 | 8 | 9 | 10 |

19. Possible to use PROBIS (a system used by Casita to register clients) online

| 1 | 2 | 3 | 4 | 5 | 6 | 7 | 8 | 9 | 10 |

20. Guarantee that personal data are protected

| 1 | 2 | 3 | 4 | 5 | 6 | 7 | 8 | 9 | 10 |

Chapter 10

The Impact of ICT Implementations on Social Interaction in Work Communities

Niina Rintala

Introduction

The implementation of an ICT in work organisations is often justified by considerations such as enhancing the productivity of work and improving working conditions ('first-level effects', as described by Loos in the previous chapter). Technological developments in the office have indeed made work more efficient and promoted the quality of working life in many ways. However, the implementation of new ICTs is still often accompanied by unanticipated, or even undesirable, impacts upon work communities (the 'second-level effects' referred to by Loos), especially if the social dynamics of workplaces are not sufficiently addressed during the implementation process.

This chapter looks at the introduction of a new ICT from a social interaction perspective that here refers mainly to face-to-face interaction as opposed to technology-mediated interaction. The chapter presents a case study of the introduction of a new ICT in which face-to-face social interaction decreased but the technology was not able to replace human communication. In addition, the degree of collective innovation within the work communities decreased and workplace interaction became more functional. The requirement to develop new competences caused social tension and conflicts. On the other hand, the introduction of this ICT created a new need for more collective, informal problem-solving, which was elicited in an ad hoc manner and took place mainly in evolving, but in some cases also stable, social networks. In this case, the ICT had both positive and negative effects on work, working conditions and social dynamics. Thus, this ICT turned out to be both a tool and a curse.

Technological Development and the Nature of Office Work

Technological development in the workplace has changed the nature of work and working conditions in all industries. Mechanisation was first applied to the processing of industrial products, but spread to the office in the second half of the nineteenth century in the form of telephones, dictating machines and typewriters (Giuliano, 1991). With the development of microelectronics and the introduction of new technology to offices, generally referred to as 'office automation', work in offices became so-called 'information work', using sophisticated technological tools (Wainwright and Francis, 1984: 13).

The first office computers were crude and designed to serve a single purpose, for example to prepare text, to access stock-market data or to make air-travel reservations. Thus, the first terminals served as complete workstations only for those people who were engaged in more-or-less repetitive tasks. Thereafter, the capabilities of workstations were extended by developments in information processing technology, in communications and by enhancements of the software, as a result of which a variety of resources and functions became accessible from a single workstation (Giuliano, 1991). In addition, the number of computers rose dramatically in the early 1970s from one computer per organisation to a situation where nearly all clerical employees had access to a workstation (Feldberg and Nakano Glenn, 1987).

Throughout the 1980s, computing in offices consisted of two major forms: computer-based information systems, with which transaction-level data was entered and retrieved, and word-processing systems (Iacono and Kling, 1987). In the 1990s we witnessed the emergence of networked communication technologies, which again radically shaped the nature and dynamics of office work. Developments in ICT have changed office work from information work to knowledge work, which is non-routine and complex, requiring both individual and external knowledge to produce outputs characterised by information content (Järvenpää and Eloranta, 2001). Technology-mediated social interaction has become a cornerstone for knowledge work – it is almost impossible to accomplish any work task in isolation or 'offline'. We are constantly interacting with each other in different technological surroundings. Technology enables us to work remotely in different locations but still in the same virtual place, as well as to work asynchronously while still being able to share information with others.

As problems with divided times and places have been solved at a technical level, one might ask whether they are also solved socially or culturally? More specifically, how do implementations of new technologies change the nature of workplace interaction, as technology becomes an extension of face-to-face communication? This chapter focuses on the social consequences of implementing a new ICT in offices and presents the results from a case study that examined the changes in social interaction in two work communities due to the introduction of a new ICT.

The Role of Social Interaction in the Twenty-First Century Workplace: Three Perspectives

First we examine findings from previous studies concerning the role and importance of social interaction in work communities. These are examined from the perspectives of (1) working with ICTs, (2) knowledge work and (3) implementing new ICT in the workplace, as depicted in Figure 10.1 which compares the form and type of social interaction before and after the ICT implementation in the work communities that were studied.

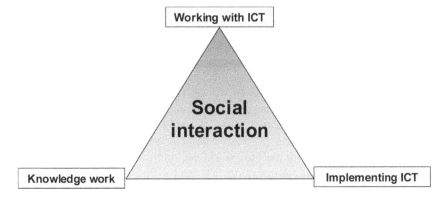

Figure 10.1   Three perspectives from previous studies on the role of social interaction in work communities

(1) Social face-to-face interaction is significant when working with ICTs

Although technology facilitates knowledge transfer and enables the extension of social networks both within and across organisations, in some previous studies technology has been found to reduce face-to-face social interaction: employees interact increasingly with the computer, not with the other members of the work community (Mark and Wulf, 1999; Bradley, 2000; Paulsson and Sundin, 2000). From a perspective concerned with issues of social support and feedback, this leads to a situation in which contact with work colleagues is reduced and made more impersonal (Paulsson and Sundin, 2000). Thus, such contact can become a less frequent and less satisfying component of the work life of employees. In other words, the decrease in traditional forms of communication is experienced as negative in terms of the quality of working life (Kraut et al., 1989; Bradley, 2000).

It has been found that with the decrease in face-to-face social interaction, the level of social support and trust also decrease, because communication is highly mediated by technology and there are fewer opportunities to pose questions in order to clarify ambiguities and misunderstandings. The instrumental, as well as emotional, support from managers and colleagues is also reduced (Mikkelsen et al., 2002). As a result, coping with stress becomes more difficult from the viewpoint of the worker. The lack of face-to-face social interaction may also lead to a reduced level of trust among workers. When characterised by low levels of trust, organisations are not able to implement and use ICT in an optimal way (Hossain and Wigand, 2004). Traditionally it has been thought that social support is mobilised whenever strains are encountered at work. However, more recent studies show that social support actually reduces the level of stressors in the first place rather than that support being mobilised after stressors are experienced (Viswesvaran et al., 1999). That is to say, existing social networks and their corresponding communication and social support act, in practice, as a shield against stress, and should therefore be actively created and maintained within organisations. The problem is that as a new ICT is implemented, studies have also found that channels of communication with other people may become restricted and opportunities to develop such strong social support networks may be denied due to employees being restricted to their workstations (Sutherland and Cooper, 2000).

Direct and face-to-face social interaction is also significant from a perspective looking at feedback, job performance and work motivation. Without social interaction and communication, workers receive less feedback about the degree to which their work performance is successful. Therefore, workers may lack motivation and rewards, leading to their decreased well-being and, once again, greater experience of stress. However, technostress or ICT stress is caused not only by a lack of communication but can also be caused by a range of other factors as well, for example, too much communication or too much or too little workload, information, flexibility, and too many or too few opportunities for development and training (Bradley, 2000, 2001).

(2) Social interaction has a special importance in knowledge work

The ability to create, refine and utilise knowledge has become critical in determining the competitiveness of companies (Tobin, 1998). Organisations have to be able to form and maintain social networks in which new knowledge is created, then disseminated and combined, and later refined into new knowledge. And social interaction is the key element in turning the organisation into a 'learning organisation'. According to Argyris and Schön (1996), a learning organisation is able to bind and store knowledge both in humans and in physical artefacts as well as to create distinctive social routines and ways of action, thereby making knowledge an inherent characteristic of the organisation. This remains an organisational capability despite the turnover of particular employees. In addition, Senge (1990) emphasises the role of social dynamics in organisational learning and states that shared language as well as open and collective problem-solving are essential for developing a culture of social learning. Even if learning occurs individually and can be thought of as self-development, the impetus to learn comes from the (social) environment, in which the learner is situated at the time. Thus, the nature of 'learning' in a learning organisation is always social and requires social interaction.

The learning organisation and the social dimension of learning are similar to and overlapping with the concept of the knowledge-creating organisation from Nonaka and Takeuchi (1995). Knowledge creation is based on the interplay between individual, tacit knowledge and social, explicit knowledge – as well as the conversion of knowledge within and across the spheres of tacit and explicit knowledge. In order to support knowledge creation, an organisation should enable social interaction so that workers can learn from each other, access existing data and knowledge, construct new routines and behaviours as well as adopt and internalise knowledge. Thus, an organisation should be able to create opportunities and arenas for both formal and informal dialogue as well as for observation, imitation and socialisation among workers.

(3) Social interaction is one of the key factors determining the success of ICT implementations

The degree to which the social environment in which an ICT is implemented is taken into account seems to be critical in terms of the success of ICT adoption and use. Studies of information systems reveal that implementations often fail if the implementers treat technology solely as being a technical issue, ignoring the organisational structure, corporate culture and human resource policies within which the application must operate (Mahmood et al., 2000). The successful implementation of technological change requires those managing that change to consider both adapting the appropriate technology to the organisational environment and adapting the organisational environment to the appropriate use of the technology (as noted also in the earlier chapter by Halonen). From a socio-technical perspective, implementations do not occur in isolation, but are accompanied by changes in the social construction and dynamics of the workplace. Other key factors in the introduction of new ICTs include the degree of participation of workers in those implementation projects (Karasek and Theorell, 1990; Korunka et al., 1993; Carayon and Karsh, 2000; Halonen and Loos in this book), the degree of legitimacy that the new technology has in the organisation (Mahmood et al., 2000; Mikkelsen et al., 2002; and we saw an example of how this was lacking in the Halonen chapter) as well as the individual thoughts, beliefs and expectations of the workers (Haddad 1996; Mahmood et al., 2000; documented also in the Loos chapter). Thus organisational, rather than technical, factors emerge as the most salient predictors of degree to which ICT implementations succeed.

The Material and Methods of the Case Study

This chapter of the book contributes to the following research question: *How does the implementation of ICT change social interaction in work communities, looking at the context of office work?*

The chapter reports results from a study conducted within a media company in 2001–2002 during the process of digitalizing the technology for producing radio and television programmes. The study examines how the ICT implementation affected job descriptions and competencies and how the implementation was experienced in terms of the quality of working life. In the study, employee experiences were examined using an open-ended qualitative theory-building research approach. This approach was chosen because it has been argued that pre-designed and structured methods of study, such as surveys. often blind the researcher to what is really happening onsite, leaving the most important phenomena overlooked or misrepresented. Moreover, such methods are often stripped of any context in order to make their results universal, uniform and comparable (Miles and Huberman, 1994). In this study it was expected that, using qualitative open-ended data-gathering methods, it would be possible to become better acquainted with the reality of the interviewees: to study employee experiences as well as examine processes related to the ICT implementation more successfully than by using a quantitative method (see, for example, Lehto, 1996).

Hence this study was carried out as a cross-sectional, inductive qualitative case study. The case study research strategy was used deliberately in order to cover contextual conditions that are relevant to the phenomenon being studied (Eisenhardt, 1989; Yin, 1994). The case study design can be used in theory-building research since it can lead to new insights and development of new theory (Voss et al., 2002).

Furthermore, it has been argued that the most reliable knowledge concerning the specific social consequences of technological implementations comes from field studies of specific technological systems conducted in specific social and organisational settings (King, 1986), since such implementations have inconsistent influences upon the quality of working life, both positive and negative at the same time (Kraut et al., 1989). Furthermore, by using the case study design, it was possible to locate the feedback from individual and separate interviews within a larger activity system (Eisenhardt, 1989; Mäkitalo, 1997), that is, the case unit in question.

Multiple criteria were used in data selection, in which the researchers and managers cooperated. Three cases were selected for examination, one from radio and two from television programme production (television case 1 has a focus on documentaries and television case 2 has a focus on news and topical programmes). The subjects that were selected for the study represented professions that were highly involved in programme production and were affected by the implementation of the new ICT. The subjects represented both genders, different age groups, employees with different occupational statuses and people with different work experience.

The main data were thematic interviews conducted with 32 employees. By using an open approach rather than conducting all the interviews in the same, strictly structured pattern, it was possible for the interviewees to define the key concepts, such as 'social interaction' and 'communication' for themselves. The thematic interview also provides insights into social processes, the motivations of workers and the consequences of the implementation. The themes of the interviews covered jobs, job redesign, skill requirements, changes in skill requirements and the quality of working life. The interviews were recorded, transcribed and read through several times before beginning the analysis.

The data were examined by means of a qualitative content analysis, aiming to construct models representing the studied phenomenon in a summarised form. As a result of the analysis, categories, concepts, hierarchies of concepts and models could be produced. The analysis began by conducting within-case analyses to uncover the unique patterns of each case before the researchers generalised patterns across cases (Eisenhardt, 1989). The within-case analyses were conducted inductively by (1) reducing the data (coding), (2) grouping codes, (3) elaborating code hierarchies and (4) writing the analysis (Kyngäs and Vanhanen, 1999) Thereafter, a cross-case analysis was performed in which similarities and differences between the categories of the within-cases analyses were evaluated and explicated.

The data and the analyses were validated by sending the results to three interviewees at their request. As the analysis required no considerable changes after this process it was assumed to be valid. Further validation was achieved as the results were reported to the case units. Interactive reporting sessions were organised both for the managers and for the personnel. Results were also reported to various interest groups in the company, for example to the industrial safety commission, the equality commission and the cooperation consultative committee of the organisation as well as to the executive group of the research project. Moreover, further validation of the data, the analysis and the findings occurred as the researchers discussed the results with individual representatives of the company, for example with a work psychologist, a trainer and a personnel manager. The feedback received from these different audiences was used for eliminating misunderstandings and specifying the terms used in the reporting of the data.

In terms of social interaction, it was expected that the ICT implementation would change the social construction of the work. Based on previous theoretical findings outlined earlier, it was expected that the degree of face-to-face interaction would decrease, which might result in a decrease in the level of work-related well-being and/or an increase in the level of stress.

Results: Social Interaction Decreased but New Forms of Collaboration Emerged

The introduction of this new ICT changed the jobs in all the case units. Traditionally, work processes had been divided into separate functional phases, which were carried out by different professional groups. Journalists produced the content of the programme. The production of the radio programme often included interviews, discussions or sound effects. These were recorded by sound editors. The production of the television programme consisted of video material, which was filmed by cameramen. After being produced and collected, the material for the programme was edited: audio material by sound editors and video material by video editors, who also engineered the sound for the video material. When finished, the programme was broadcast. In radio programme production, broadcasting was managed by sound editors, who were responsible for the technical quality of the broadcast audio programmes, and by announcers, who hosted the radio broadcasts. In television programme production, programmes were broadcast by a broadcasting team, including representatives from several professional groups: for example, a director, a script girl, an audio editor, a video mixer, cameramen and a video broadcaster.

Alongside the ICT implementation – which consisted of the transfer from analogue to digital programme production technology – job descriptions were also changed. In the radio case, journalists, in addition to their traditional tasks of designing and producing the content for the programmes, began to edit the sound, previously the job of sound editors. It was planned that announcers, in addition to hosting the broadcasts, would also be responsible for the technical quality of the broadcast sound without the involvement of sound editors. Thus the jobs of the journalists and announcers were enriched, whereas the job of sound editors was narrowed down as editing tasks were transferred to journalists and broadcasting tasks to announcers. At the time of the study, training sound editors to be journalists was not planned. In the television case 1, similar changes had occurred as journalists had begun to record and edit video material. The job of journalists was supplemented by new tasks of a technical nature, while, simultaneously, the workload of editors and cameramen was in danger of being reduced. In the television case 2, the changes in jobs were of a different nature. A new job description for media journalists was created. This work consisted of several job descriptions previously associated with analogue production, mainly the contributions of editors, graphic artists and directors. Media journalists worked in three shifts with tasks relating to editing, producing graphics and also directing and broadcasting. The boundaries between the job of the media journalists (who had tasks similar to those of audio and video editors under the old analogue system of production) and journalists had changed somewhat, as the task of searching for appropriate video material from archives was transferred from journalists to media journalists. According to the interviewees, the aim of the job redesign was, or at least had been, to train all journalists to be media journalists, capable of not only producing content but also of recording, editing and broadcasting material autonomously. Some professionals in the television cases did not experience changes in their job descriptions, for example, the job of television producers had not yet changed and, in contrast, some separate, specialised jobs and professions had always been entirely linked to digital production, such as an Internet producer, for example. Figure 10.2 illustrates the changes in job descriptions due to the implementation of the ICT.

With the changes in job descriptions, *the autonomy of work increased*, which the interviewees experienced as contributing positively to the quality of their working life. In the case of radio, the journalists could produce programmes in a more independent and autonomous way and the announcers began to broadcast programmes by themselves, without the technical support of the sound editors. A journalist described the increase in the autonomy of work in the following way: *'When I worked with c-tapes I had to make a tape chart and go to the studio and work with a sound editor. The change, which is solely positive, is that I get to do the entire programme by myself from the beginning to the end and I have a sound editor for the work, which I consider to take time unnecessarily and excessively from my other tasks, such as this finishing. But all the editing, which I can do in my office, I feel as a plus, as positive without a doubt.'* (A radio journalist, aged 37)

In the television case 2, the work of media journalists (whose equivalent job description under the previous analogue organisation of work had been mainly editorial) became more autonomous, as they could search for video clips themselves

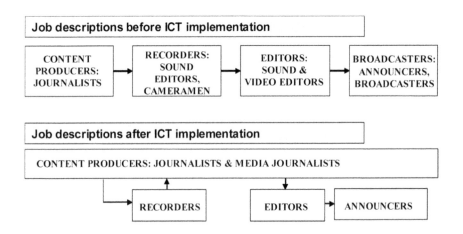

Figure 10.2   Changes in job descriptions due to the implementation of the new ICT

before editing the appropriate material. In the television case 1, allowing journalists to film made the journalistic work more autonomous and less dependent on the schedules of professional cameramen. The editing of sound and video material by journalists also made the journalistic work more flexible because the journalist could pre-edit the programme and the professional editor could thereafter do the final editing. A journalist described the new possibilities for editing in a very positive way: '*This digital editing is a fantastic revolution (...) I don't know how any journalist can oppose it (...) and it doesn't change the fact that you can take your material to a professional editor, because he sees things differently, but the editing is more profound as I know the material so well.*' (A television journalist, aged 54)

Some interviewees expressed the opinion that after the implementation *traditional cooperation between different professionals had been reduced*. The interviewees felt that, due to the introduction of the ICT, accompanied by the more independent job descriptions, the degree of social face-to-face interaction had decreased and work had become lonelier. This induced stress and feelings of isolation. In the case of radio, there was less cooperation between journalists, between journalists and sound editors, and between sound editors and announcers. Social contacts in the work community decreased. As the amount of direct social interaction diminished, journalists received less feedback about their work and felt that they were performing in increasing isolation, as described by one participant: '*And you should really have a work group with which you communicate. There is a danger, which I recognise as well, that you bury yourself too deeply in what you do and there should be social communication and dialogue (...) because just by concentrating on your own tasks you go blind.*' (A radio journalist, aged 38)

In television case 1, the social interaction between the journalists, editors and recorders also diminished. Moreover, some television journalists had began working as web journalists. Their work had become lonelier as making appointments and conducting interviews were no longer included in their jobs. In television case 2, no views were expressed about work becoming lonelier or about there being less social interaction.

It was also felt that collective innovation decreased within the organisation, as journalists interacted less with their colleagues and with sound editors. Thus, as the jobs became more separated and individualised, workplace interaction became more functional, as the employees communicated mainly when sound or video material was passed over to another expert, for example from journalists to sound editors and from sound editors to announcers. As a qualification, not all work processes went this direction. One unit had actually implemented a Lotus Notes based collaboration tool that enabled the employees to share information – for example, relating to the status of programme production – in a new, more informative way.

Moreover, the interviewees said that the diminished cooperation had the effect of *increasing demands on their concentration*, which in turn created stress. As tasks were added to the job descriptions of journalists, media journalists and announcers, causing cooperation to decrease, these employees had to take on more responsibility for the work process. Some interviewees experienced this as being stressful, since the responsibility that some employees now had to take on was experienced as being excessive. The interviewees felt incapable of controlling their work. Excessive demands for concentration were experienced in the case of radio by announcers who were beginning to manage broadcasting by themselves, in television case 1 by journalists who were beginning to film video material and in television case 2 by journalists who were beginning to edit material and by journalists learning to use the new equipment. One announcer said that the increase in responsibility resulted from not being able to double check with a colleague that work tasks were carried out correctly: '*I feel that it is a pity because broadcasting goes well if there is co-operation between a sound editor and an announcer. (...) [With the implementation of the new system] a backup is lost. When both the announcer and the sound editor are conducting the broadcast one or the other always ensures that work tasks are done correctly and asks if he does not know how tasks ought to be carried out.*' (An announcer, aged 37)

However, the stressful experiences due to decreased cooperation and increased loneliness were partly replaced by *new forms of collaborating*. Some interviewees stated that the ICT implementation created a new need for cooperation, which led to the emergence of new kinds of informal interaction. For example, the unreliability of the technology itself required collective problem solving within work units. As there were only a few technicians, employees turned to their colleagues for help when facing new technical problems. For example, it was not unusual for a group of employees to be gathered around a computer, trying to think of a solution to a malfunction. According to the interviews, some employees made new social contacts and relationships as they asked for advice from someone technically more experienced. New unofficial and autonomous learning groups were created ad hoc for each problem situation. Some of these learning and coaching relationships formed into more stable relationships over time. Certain employees who were especially competent with the new digital technology were likely to become central and more stable actors in these informal networks. In the case of radio, knowledge was shared in these kinds of unofficial ways between journalists, between journalists and sound editors, and between sound editors. In the television case 2, some interviewees built informal relationships and 'networks' in order to cope collectively with technical problems. This type of knowledge sharing interconnected the work units of the radio case and television case 2 in a new fashion and resulted in new social relationships. A sound editor described technical problems as having brought sound editors together, but the issues that initiated these new forms of cooperation were usually themselves negative: '*Rushing and technical problems have brought people together (...) when something happens, everyone gathers around to see and then we all go and ask someone, if (s)he knows what to do (...) But the things that bring us together are usually negative.*' (A sound editor, aged 35)

At the time of the study, the changeover to the new ICT had not progressed far in television case 1, which could explain why reference to informal learning groups did not come up in the interviews. The need to share knowledge in general across professional and age groups was, however, expressed by some interviewees even in this unit.

Some interviewees saw that the work had also become *more fragmented* due to new technical opportunities, such as compiling different versions of the original audio or video material into different programmes, producing programmes and material for different media (such as radio, television, the Internet and teletext) and different channels, consulting with technological experts in the organisation, as well as using both analogue and digital technological formats simultaneously. Some interviewees felt that the fragmentation of work actually resulted in an increase in the sheer number of contacts necessary to carry out the work process. But the problem was that these contacts were more superficial than in the case of the previous cooperation that they had had with editors. The new contacts were often brief and mediated by technology. Thus, even if the quantity of social contacts increased for some individuals the quality of social contacts actually decreased.

The changes in jobs made some skills obsolete while at the same time giving rise to new skill requirements. Changes in skill requirements resulted in reorganised work and altered work roles, which had negative effects on the work community in both television cases. A new work unit was formed for television case 2 due to the ICT implementation, which lead to stress among the employees and had a negative influence on the atmosphere of the work community. In the television case 1, technical skills were valued more after the ICT implementation. This led to changes in the division of tasks and status structures and disrupted the social dynamics within this work community. One television programme producer observed: '*And then I come from another organisation outside and my task is to reorganise the entire unit. And then everything is turned upside down because of it.*'

In the case of radio, such social conflicts did not occur. This might be due to the radio case being a well-established work unit whereas the television cases experienced more extensive changes in personnel during the change to the new technical system. Figure 10.3 illustrates the changes in social interaction and communication due to the implementation of the new ICT.

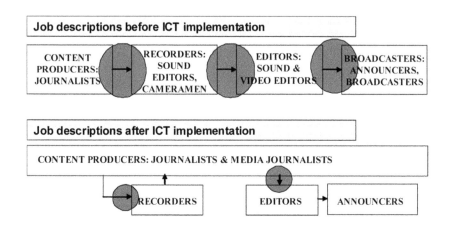

Figure 10.3   Changes in social interaction due to the implementation of the new ICT

Conclusions

This chapter has focused upon the impacts of ICT implementations on social interaction within work communities. The case study revealed that the ICT implementation had direct effects on social interaction but also indirect effects through changing jobs, task divisions and forms of cooperation. Overall, jobs became more independent and autonomous, which had some positive influences on the quality of working life. Employees were able to schedule, organise and control their work more freely. Yet, at the same time, traditional cooperation diminished and work was experienced as becoming lonelier. The level and quality of social contacts and feedback decreased, even though the number of social contacts for some individuals actually increased. We saw earlier in the chapter how Mikkelsen et al. (2002) had noticed the same phenomenon: as communication is mediated by ICT, there are fewer opportunities to pose questions to clarify ambiguities, reducing instrumental, as well as emotional, support from managers and colleagues. In this study, the decrease in managerial support and communication did not come up as an issue, but the decline in communication between co-workers was highlighted in the interviews. It is worth bearing in mind that any decrease in social interaction may also have implications for decision-making within the work communities. If the decision-making processes become informal and based on dialogue rather than bureaucratic and structured (Symon, 2000), there might be a consistent decrease in the opportunities for employees to take part in those decision-making processes if they do not have sufficient contact with their colleagues.

To compensate for the forms of cooperation that had declined, new informal forms of cooperation emerged, especially due to technological uncertainties and malfunctions. Other research has shown that the emergence of such informal networks may also result from organisational units becoming leaner and job descriptions becoming less structured (Shamir, 1999; Symon, 2000) or from the inability of formal links to support the work (Heckscher, 1994).

While interviewees from some units mentioned an increase in the loneliness of work, this did not occur in the television case 2. This might be due to the nature of this programme production (since news production requires intensive information sharing and cooperation), due to the type of workspace (as the personnel worked physically close to each other in an open-plan office), due to fact that there were only minor changes in job descriptions (as the number of entirely new job descriptions created and of tasks transferred from one job to another were minimal) and due to the average age of the interviewees (the average age was seven years younger than in other case studies).

Some journalists mentioned the fact that their work had become more fragmented, as well as more independent. While this fragmentation led to somewhat increased social contacts the quality of these was not sufficient to replace the previous level of cooperation that they had had with editors.

Overall, the results support the previous findings outlined at the start of this chapter whereby work can become more socially isolated due the increase in technology-mediated communication (Mark and Wulf, 1999; Bradley, 2000; Paulsson and Sundin, 2000). We saw that social interaction decreased as employees interacted increasingly with the computer rather than with their colleagues. Technology was not a sufficient extension of human communication, since the decrease in social interaction had negative impacts on the quality of working life that was experienced. The decrease in social interaction resulted in employees being provided with less social support and feedback from their colleagues and managers. In addition, the degree of collective innovation within the work communities decreased and the workplace interaction became more functional, as the employees communicated with their colleagues only on issues related to handing over material from one contact point to another and mainly via technological interfaces. Moreover, the diminished social support and cooperation increased demands on their concentration, which in turn induced feelings of stress and helplessness. The changes in jobs made some skill sets obsolete and lead to other new skill requirements, which reorganised work and altered work roles, thereby spreading a negative atmosphere and causing social conflicts within the work communities.

On the other hand, we saw how the decrease in cooperation and the increased loneliness were compensated for by new forms of collaborating. The ICT implementation itself created a demand for collective, informal problem solving that was elicited ad hoc and carried out mainly in evolving, but in some cases also stable, social networks created around a technologically competent employee. The employees shared their experiences as regards the ways to operate and manage new equipment. Thus, the type of social interaction changed from interaction between individuals to interaction in groups and from formal interaction required by the job descriptions to informal interaction brought about on the basis of a new need. However, we saw how the stimulus for such interactions was usually negative and that in general the situation remained stressful.

Table 10.1   The form and types of social interaction before and after the ICT implementation

Before ICT Implementation	After ICT Implementation
Interaction with colleagues	Interaction with ICT
Constant interaction	Functional interaction
Clear social status and roles	Social conflicts
Formal interaction	Informal interaction
Planned interaction	Need-basis interaction
Information sharing	Problem solving, knowledge creation
Stabile networks	Varying networks
Individual interaction	Social interaction
Positive or neutral stimulus for interaction	Negative stimulus for interaction

Lastly, we can reflect on the implications from the viewpoint of the organisation. The implementation of this ICT resulted in increased collective problem solving and social learning within the work communities. Workers sharing (tacit) knowledge and learning from each other is characteristic of a learning organisation (Nonaka and Takeuchi, 1995; Senge, 1990). Thus after the implementation of ICT the organisation seemed to resemble a learning organisation more than before the implementation.

Discussion

The impact that the introduction of a new ICT has on social interaction is, of course, closely linked to the type of technology being implemented as well as to the managerial actions taken during that implementation. It can be presumed that implementing simple automation that renders some routine tasks obsolete is less likely to affect social interaction, whereas an ICT that changes work processes and jobs radically is more likely to have profound effects on social interaction and dynamics. Selecting the appropriate ICT to be implemented, planning and conducting the implementation project as well as redesigning jobs, task divisions and roles are all dependent on managerial decision-making.

How should we then implement a new ICT, taking account of social interaction in work communities? Firstly, we need to acknowledge and understand the role of social interaction from the perspective of individual workers (for example, in terms of dealing with stress) and from the perspective of work communities (for example, in terms of corporate culture, emotional and social support, managerial practices and routines). Social interaction helps new recruits to integrate into the organisation and adopt its values. It also creates a sense of belonging and commitment. In addition, face-to-face social interaction seems to support technology-mediated interaction since sending e-mails or attending virtual meetings may be easier and more efficient if based upon a personal relationship between colleagues. Receiving feedback from colleagues and managers in face-to-face situations can improve work motivation. Thus, even though nearly all social interaction and communication *could* be technology-mediated, it does not mean that it *should* be.

The implementation of an ICT may be accompanied by radical changes in personnel, job descriptions and roles as well as power and status structures. The social dimension of ICT implementations should already be taken into account at the planning stage. How can we justify and explain the need and importance of the implementation to the employees? What kind of resistance can we expect and from whom? How do the changes in personnel, job descriptions and roles affect individual career paths? What kind of training and support are needed? How should teams/work units be organised (in terms of size, competencies and personalities) to best support the work? These are some of the questions that should be answered before launching a new ICT implementation project.

As a result of the implementation of new systems, new forms of social interaction may appear. These may be critical substitutes for more traditional types of social interaction, which may become technology-mediated due to the implementation of the new ICT. For example, face-to-face interaction between certain professionals may decrease due to the implementation of an ICT as specific tasks and operations are digitalised. This may lead to decreased emotional and social support from colleagues and less feedback, simply because the professionals have fewer opportunities to engage in direct social interaction with their peers. As a result, these workers may seek new opportunities to interact with their colleagues. In this study, face-to-face interaction was reduced between journalists and editors who compensated for the reduction by interacting with each other in new, more informal situations (for example when confronted with technical difficulties) and more on a need basis. These new forms of interaction can be critical in terms of the quality of working life experienced by workers, as face-to-face social interaction plays an important role in terms of social support, work motivation and work stress.

It is important to be aware of new manifestations of social interaction and to create opportunities for employees to engage in them. In the case study presented in this chapter, social interaction was transformed into informal interaction that was elicited on need basis and resided in varying networks formed by colleagues within and across professional groups. In order to support human networks, an organisation has to be flexible in the way that it allows the construction and reconstruction of social structures within the work communities.

References

Argyris, C. and Schön, D.A. (1996), *Organizational Learning II: Theory, Method and Practice* (Reading: Addison-Wesley).

Bradley, G. (2000), 'The Information and Communication Society: How People Will Live and Work in the New Millennium', *Ergonomics*, 43, 844–57.

Bradley, G. (2001), 'Information and Communication Technology (ICT) and Humans: How We Will Live, Learn and Work', in Bradley, G. (ed.), *Humans on the Net: Information and Communication Technology (ICT), Work Organization and Human Beings* (Stockholm: Prevent).

Carayon, P. and Karsh, B-T. (2000), 'Sociotechnical Issues in the Implementation of Imaging Technology', *Behaviour and Information Technology* 19 (4), 247–62.

Eisenhardt, K. (1989), 'Building Theories From Case Study Research', *Academy of Management Review* 14 (4), 532–50.

Feldberg, R.L. and Nakano Glenn, E. (1987), 'Technology and the Transformation of Clerical Work', in Kraut, R.E. (ed.), *Technology and the Transformation of White-Collar Work* (New Jersey: Lawrence Erlbaum Associates).

Giuliano, V.E. (1991), 'The Mechanization of Office Work', in Dunlop, C. and Kling, R. (eds), *Computerization and Controversy: Value Conflicts and Social Choices* (San Diego: Academic Press).

Haddad, C.J. (1996), 'Employee Attitudes Toward New Technology in a Unionized Manufacturing Plant', *Journal of Engineering and Technology Management* 13, 145–62.

Heckscher, C. (1994), 'Defining the Post-Bureaucratic Type', in Heckscher, C. and Donnellon, A. (eds), *The Post-Bureaucratic Organization. New Perspectives on Organizational Change* (London: Sage).

Hossain, L. and Wigand, R.T. (2004), 'ICT Enabled Virtual Collaboration through Trust', *Journal of Computer-Mediated Communication* 10, Article 8.

Iacono, S and Kling, R. (1987), 'Changing Office Technologies and Transformations of Clerical Jobs: A Historical Perspective', in Kraut, R.E. (ed.), *Technology and the Transformation of White-Collar Work* (New Jersey: Lawrence Erlbaum Associates).

Järvenpää, E. and Eloranta, E. (2001), 'Information and Communication Technologies and Quality of Working Life: Implications for Competencies and Well-Being', in Bradley, G. (ed.), *Humans on the Net: Information and Communication Technology (ICT), Work Organization and Human Beings* (Stockholm: Prevent).

Karasek, R. and Theorell, T. (1990), *Healthy Work: Stress Productivity and the Reconstruction of Working Life* (New York: Basic Books).

King, R. (1986), 'The Social Dimensions of Computerization', in Mantei, M. and Orbeton, P. (eds), *CHI/GI 1987 Conference Proceedings on Human Factors in Computing Systems and Graphics Interface* (New York: ACM Press).

Korunka, C., Weiss, A. and Karetta, B. (1993), 'Effects of New Technologies with Special Regard for the Implementation Process per se', *Journal of Organizational Behavior* 14, 331–48.

Kraut, R., Dumais, S. and Koch, S. (1989), 'Computerization, Productivity and Quality of Work Life', *Communications of the ACM* 32 (2), 220–38.

Kyngäs, H. and Vanhanen, L. (1999), Content Analysis (In Finnish: Sisällönanalyysi), *Hoitotiede* 11 (1), 3–12.

Lehto, A-M. (1996), *Työolot tutkimuskohteena. Työolotutkimusten sisällöllistä ja menetelmällistä arviointia yhteiskuntatieteen ja naistutkimuksen näkökulmasta* (Work Conditions as a Research Subject. The Content and Methodological Evaluation of Work Condition Research from the Point of View of Social and Women Studies) (in Finnish) (Rep. No. 222) (Helsinki: Statistics Finland).

Mahmood, M.A., Burn, J.M., Gomoets, L.A. and Jacquez, C. (2000), 'Variables Affecting Information Technology End-User Satisfaction: A Meta-Analysis of the Empirical Literature', *International Journal of Human-Computer Studies* 52, 751–71.

Mäkitalo, J. (1997), *How to Study Work-Related Well-Being?* University of Helsinki, Department of Education, Center for Activity Theory and Developmental Work Research, Vol. 1, Working paper number 9/1997.

Mark, G. and Wulf, V. (1999), 'Changing Interpersonal Communication Through Groupware Use', *Behavior and Information Technology*, 18 (5), 385–95.

Mikkelsen, A., Øgaard, T., Lindøe, P.H. and Olsen, O.E. (2002), 'Job Characteristics and Computer Anxiety in the Production Industry', *Computers in Human Behavior* 18, 223–39.

Miles, M.B. and Huberman, M. (1994), *Qualitative Data Analysis: An Expanded Sourcebook* (London: Sage).

Nonaka, I. and Takeuchi, H. (1995), *The Knowledge-Creating Company* (Oxford: Oxford University Press).

Paulsson, K. and Sundin, L. (2000), 'Learning at Work – A Combination of Experience-Based Learning and Theoretical Education', *Behaviour and Information Technology*, 19 (3), 181–88.

Senge, P.M. (1990), *The Fifth Discipline: The Art and Practice of the Learning Organization* (New York: Currency Doubleday).

Shamir, B. (1999), 'Leadership in Boundaryless Organizations: Disposable or Indispensable?', *European Journal of Work and Organizational Psychology* 8 (1), 49–71.

Sutherland, V.J. and Cooper, C.L. (2000), *Strategic Stress Management: An Organizational Approach* (New York: MacMillan Press).

Symon, G. (2000), 'Information and Communication Technologies and Network Organization: A Critical Analysis', *Journal of Occupational and Organizational Psychology*, 73 (4), 389–415.

Tobin, D.R. (1998), *The Knowledge-Enabled Organization* (New York: Amacom).

Viswesvaran, C., Sanchez, J.I. and Fisher, J. (1999), 'The Role of Social Support in the Process of Work Stress: A Meta-Analysis', *Journal of Vocational Behavior* 54, 314–34.

Voss, C., Tsikriktsis, N. and Frohlich, M. (2002), 'Case Research in Operations Management', *International Journal of Operations and Production Management* 22 (2), 195–219.

Wainwright, J. and Francis, A. (1984), *Office Automation, Organisation and the Nature of Work* (Hampshire: Gower Publishing Company).

Yin, R.K. (1994), *Case Study Research: Design and Methods* (London: Sage).

PART IV
The Future: The Boundaries between Work and Non-work Life

There is no Business like Small Business: The Use and Meaning of ICTs for Micro-enterprises

Jo Pierson

Introduction

The aim of this chapter is to illustrate the blurring boundaries between professional and private life in the context of the use of ICTs in a small business. Despite their preponderance in society and the economy, there are still relatively few exact figures concerning these small and very small businesses as well as a substantial lack of understanding of their characteristics in relation to ICTs. Our assumption is that in order to fully grasp the role, meaning and significance of ICTs in a small business setting, we need to consider additional factors going beyond typical parameters in business economics. This implies complementing the 'economic dynamics' of the business company with the 'social dynamics' of the business entrepreneur. The latter refers to characteristics like the type of professional work that is involved as well as to the entrepreneur's private life.

In order to tackle the issue of social dynamics in relation to ICT use in small businesses we need to identify the main characteristics that help to explain their experience of ICTs. For this an analytical framework is used, based on former qualitative research, which incorporates relevant economic and social factors relating to the meaning and significance of ICT for the owner of a micro-enterprise (Pierson, 2000). The value of these factors for small businesses in Flanders (Belgium) is measured by way of a number of specific parameters within a quantitative telephone survey. The focus is on the computer in the office, looking at three key indicators: the presence of a computer in the business, the frequency of use by the self-employed owner and the self-assessed computer knowledge of the latter. However, key figures on other ICTs are also included.

Based on these indicators we find a digital divide among micro-enterprises that takes shape along the lines of both the industry sector and the private characteristics of the self-employed owners. This complements the approach in traditional economic and organisational studies regarding ICT implementation in companies, where the focus is on technological and organisational explanations.

Scope of Research

In the course of the transition in techno-economic paradigm from a (post-) industrial to an information society, ICTs, and broadband in particular, become increasingly embedded within the socio-economic system (Perez, 2002). ICTs are seen as major tools with the potential to fundamentally change business behaviour and company strategies (European Commission, 2001b). However, until recently the role of the Small and Medium-sized Enterprises (SMEs) in these developments has been ignored in policy-making and research to some extent. It is only over the last decade that policy makers and ICT companies have become interested in the role of SMEs in the information economy. Figures showed that company size is one of the significant factors influencing ICT adoption and use. International organisations, European authorities and national governments began to realise that these SMEs could not be left out of new technological developments. This has led to a multitude of stimulation programmes aimed at smaller companies. In addition, the private ICT sector saw a chance for extending its client base by incorporating the SME market. These developments support the idea of including this business-level into research on the digital divide. Moreover, this fits in with the broad OECD definition as proposed in its report 'Understanding the digital divide':

> The term 'digital divide' refers to the gap between individuals, households, businesses and geographic areas at different socio-economic levels with regard both to their opportunities to access information and communication technologies (ICTs) and to their use of the internet for a wide variety of activities. (OECD, 2001: 5)

This raises the question of the extent to which existing enterprises have adopted computer technologies. In general most European companies have, indeed, incorporated ICTs into their organisations to a large extent (DTI, 2004; European Commission, 2006). However, an additional effort is still needed for Small and Medium-sized Enterprises (SMEs) to achieve this, which is important given that they represent 99.7 per cent of all enterprises and are therefore the backbone of the European economy (European Commission, 2003). Earlier research had shown that SMEs in particular lagged behind in the usage of ICTs in comparison to larger enterprises (Eurostat, 2002; DTI, 2004; European Commission, 2006). Furthermore, micro-enterprises (SMEs with less than 10 employees) are, in particular, on the wrong side of the digital divide (Arbore and Ordanini, 2006). Therefore public and private institutions are heavily stressing the importance of 'SME-oriented' R&D policy and innovation strategies (for example, EU i2010 strategy, Competitiveness and Innovation Programme).

To fill in the notion of 'SME-oriented', we need to define SMEs and to identify the characteristics that help to explain the obstacles to adopting ICTs that are embedded in small business. An SME is still defined very differently depending on the country, the kind of research or the organisation doing the research. According to European regulations an SME is a company with less than 250 employees.[1] However the

---

1 On 6 May 2003 the Commission adopted the Recommendation 2003/361/EC which defines SMEs on the basis of the number of employees (less than 250), then annual turnover

common Belgian definition sees SMEs as companies with less than 50 employees. In our study we discuss the disadvantaged position of the micro-enterprises, the very small enterprises with less than 10 employees.[2] They represent 93 per cent of all enterprises in Europe. More than half of the European micro-enterprises (54 per cent) have no employees, thus providing employment and income only for the self-employed and family workers (i.e. they are self-employers) (European Commission, 2001a).

The majority of research concerning ICT implementation in small businesses starts from a generic approach and thereby fails to expose the significant differences between companies. First, these studies often concentrate on medium sized and large businesses. Up-to-date figures on ICTs in small enterprises are increasingly available, but still less common. Second, research to date often pays little or no attention to the diversity of sectors and the types of professional activities, even though these aspects may have a significant influence on ICT usage. The few studies that have been done in this regard demonstrate that the industry sector seems to be as significant, or possibly even more significant, a factor than the size of the enterprise (Pierson, 2003; Barrett and Rainnie, 2005). Finally, in contrast to large companies, the behaviour of small companies' business owners is not only determined by economic motives, but also by social ones. Previous studies often ignore these socio-professional factors that on a micro level influence the ICT decisions of entrepreneurs. However, studies have shown that these factors play an essential role in the case of very small businesses or micro-enterprises (Pierson, 2005).

Social Dynamics of (Very) Small Businesses

Within social-theoretical knowledge there is still a lack of assessment concerning the capacity of SMEs and micro-enterprises to incorporate ICTs into their work praxis. Generally, the point of departure in the literature is a technological or economic logic, which we could characterise as the 'technological or economic dynamics'. The factors shaping the success and failure of ICTs within large organisations are then usually extrapolated to the context of small enterprises. However, our assumption is that we are dealing with different worlds of experience, which in the case of micro-enterprises resembles to a large degree the home context where non-economic aspects play an essential role.

Decision-making in these (very) small businesses is mostly centred on one person, the self-employed owner, director or entrepreneur himself or herself. This can be a business manager, petty shopkeeper, craftsman or any other person in charge of the commercial activity. As a consequence, the business owner in a micro-

---

(not exceeding 50 million Euro) or balance sheet (not exceeding 43 million Euro), and finally economic independence. However the non-personnel criteria are hard to cover in aggregate statistics and therefore are not taken into account in this study.

2 On 6 May 2003 the Commission adopted the Recommendation 2003/361/EC which defines micro-enterprises on the basis of the number of employees (less than 10), then annual turnover (not exceeding 2 million Euro) or balance sheet (exceeding 2 million Euro), and finally economic independence. However these extra criteria are hard to cover in aggregate statistics and therefore are not taken into account in this study.

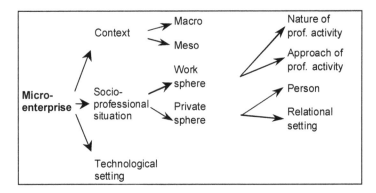

Figure 11.1   A framework regarding the social dynamics of ICT adoption and use by micro-enterprises

enterprise has maximum autonomy (Frissen, 1999). Here, personal motives, besides work-related motives, can have more impact in comparison to larger enterprises. These motives are in a sense the 'social dynamics' of small business behaviour. In larger firms decisions regarding ICT adoption more often pass through different (hierarchical) levels, which makes them less dependent on one key person. ICT decisions are based more on consultation and power differences. Hence, we usually find explanations of this kind of process in organisation theory and in the literature concerning organisation communication and the management of technology.

In order to examine which characteristics configure ICT adoption and use among small businesses one must start from the perception of the business owner or entrepreneur. Taking this kind of user-oriented approach, incorporating features of the work as well as the private situation of the owner, will lead to a better understanding of ICTs in SMEs and micro-enterprises. Former research has identified the key factors enabling and constraining ICT adoption and use being situated on different levels (Pierson, 2000). We distinguish three major levels: (1) the wider context level, (2) the socio-professional user level and (3) the technology level.

The framework used in analysis uses qualitative research among micro-enterprises in very different sectors (accountants, fruit farmers, booksellers, journalists, real estate agents, building contractors) (Pierson, 1999). This framework is itself based upon a social-constructivist approach, in the tradition of the social construction and the social shaping of technology (Lievrouw, 2002). Basically, the framework serves as an analytical checklist for exploring the techno-economic and social dynamics of the interaction between the ICTs and the micro-enterprise context. It indicates the factors and the characteristics that play a part in the adoption and use of an ICT, as seen from the perspective of the self-employer or the key person in the small enterprise. The different levels are now exemplified briefly.

Table 11.1   The proportion of enterprises having internet access and broadband connection in 2005 (%)

		EU25	EU15	BE	CZ	DK	DE	EE	EL	ES	FR	IE	IT	CY	LV	LT	LU	HU	MT	NL	AT	PL	PT	SI	SK	FI	SE	UK	IS	NO
All enterprises	broadband	63	65	78	52	82	62	67	44	76	:	48	57	40	48	57	64	48	:	71	61	43	:	74	48	81	83	65	:	78
	Internet	91	92	95	92	97	94	90	92	90	:	92	92	85	75	86	92	78	:	91	95	87	:	96	92	98	96	90	:	93
Large	broadband	92	93	93	81	97	95	91	77	93	:	86	93	91	73	72	85	83	:	92	94	90	:	96	66	96	98	90	:	98
	Internet	99	99	98	100	100	99	95	100	98	:	100	99	100	98	100	100	99	:	97	100	99	:	100	98	100	100	100	:	100
Medium	broadband	79	83	89	65	91	82	79	59	86	:	62	79	60	60	67	77	66	:	84	81	65	:	88	60	90	94	84	:	91
	Internet	98	98	99	98	100	99	96	98	96	:	98	98	99	93	98	98	100	:	96	99	98	:	98	98	99	100	99	:	98
Small	broadband	59	61	75	48	80	57	63	41	74	:	43	54	36	45	54	61	43	:	68	56	36	:	69	45	78	80	61	:	76
	Internet	90	91	94	91	97	93	88	90	89	:	90	91	82	71	83	91	74	:	89	94	84	:	95	91	98	95	88	:	92

Source: Eurostat, Community survey on ICT usage in enterprises.
N.B.: Data not available for FR, MT, PT, IS.
EU or EU-25 (European Union, comprising 25 Member States); BE (Belgium), CZ (Czech Republic), DK (Denmark), DE (Germany), EE (Estonia), EL (Greece), ES (Spain), FR (France), IE (Ireland), IT (Italy), CY (Cyprus), LV (Latvia), LT (Lithuania), LU (Luxembourg), MT (Malta), NL (Netherlands), AT (Austria), PL (Poland), PT (Portugal), SI (Slovenia), SK (Slovakia), FI (Finland), SE (Sweden), UK (United Kingdom); BG (Bulgaria), RO (Romania), TR (Turkey); IS (Iceland), NO Norway).

(1) Wider context

The wider social-economic context in which business affairs are conducted, divided into macro and meso levels, plays a crucial role. The macro level refers to the general socio-economic situation as well as to the policy and regulation that govern the design and use of ICTs. This becomes apparent when comparing, for example, Internet and broadband use by small, medium and large enterprises in Europe in different countries and cultures. Consider for example the striking difference between Sweden and Denmark where 80 per cent of small enterprises have broadband Internet access compared to those in Greece where only 41 per cent have broadband connectivity.

Especially when dealing with the self-employed and the very small businesses, ICT appropriation is often also contingent upon the meso level. This refers to the attitudes and initiatives of (inter) professional organisations (deontological restrictions on advertising for liberal professions, general innovativeness, etc.), training and support initiatives and the behaviour of competitors and collaborators. Another essential factor with regard to the wider context on this meso level is the kind of profession and the sort of industry sector. We will look at these contextual characteristics as they are experienced by the self-employed.

(2) Socio-professional situation

The socio-professional situation (i.e. micro level) takes into account the mix of professional and private (domestic) characteristics. Given that micro-enterprises often work within or close to the domestic space, the 'blurring of boundaries' between work and home is prevalent. The work sphere has two dimensions. On the one hand, this refers to the business-level or the nature of the professional activity, which is characterised by the legal status of the entity, the kind of product/service, turnover, etc. – i.e. structural components. On the other hand, the work sphere relates to the entrepreneur-level or the approach of the entrepreneur to the professional activity, including typical management style of the self-employed owner (degree to which he/she is expansion-oriented, degree of experience, degree of independence etc.) – i.e. the action component. The private sphere is also two-dimensional, including both personal characteristics (for example knowledge, attitudes and lifestyle) and relational networks (for example family, friends and acquaintances).

(3) Technological setting

We also situate the micro-enterprise within an informational and technological setting. To do this we investigate how technologies and applications that are already available themselves serve as a condition or impulse for the adoption and use of other ICTs. Certain technologies can be a prerequisite for other technologies, like a network connection for the Internet or a web browser for an online banking application. However, the technological setting also refers to the availability, quality and pricing of the network infrastructure, platforms and services for the sector or profession in question. How this is perceived and evaluated by the self-employed person in question is especially important. Another important criterion is the adequate supply of useful content, for example whether or not basic information about the job can be consulted via ICT applications.

A further central feature is the 'technological culture' of the small business and the owner. This refers to the mode of living in which the social and economic relations are reflected in the way people deal with technological artefacts for example whether the culture is very open to technological innovations leading to a kind of ICT accumulation – or possibly the opposite (Punie, 2000).

Small Business Survey

Research design

The general purpose of the study is to investigate the role of social dynamics in relation to ICT adoption, use and knowledge in a small business. The research results reported in this chapter are based on telephone interviews conducted with 550 randomly selected small businesses having less than 10 employees in the Flemish region of Belgium. First, a letter was sent to announce that they would be called by phone to take part in an interview. Next, the same respondents were called, with a maximum of five attempts, before replacing the respondent by a similar respondent. The interviewing took place between 6 December and 21 December 2000 and was done by means of a CATI (Computer Assisted Telephone Interviewing) system. There is some difference between the sample and the population. In the sample the businesses with no employees as well as the sectors of 'producer services' are somewhat underrepresented. There is an overrepresentation of companies with one to four employees and businesses in the sector of 'agriculture'. The overall target population was the 411,000 micro-enterprises in Flanders. Non-commercial activities, like governments and schools, were excluded because the focus is on the self-employed and those commercial businesses working for themselves. We aimed to discern different work activities based on a European classification of individual industries (European Commission, 2000: 48–53).[3]

Social dynamics in relation to ICT presence, use and knowledge[4]

Our research assumption was that besides the traditional business traits, other characteristics also play a major role in configuring ICT adoption, use and knowledge among micro-enterprises. This is indicated in the framework regarding micro-enterprises described earlier, broadly labelled as social dynamics (see Figure 11.1). We now investigate the explicative value of the different variables in the framework by looking for significant associations between specific parameters of these variables and computer presence and frequency of use in the workplace. The latter scale is summarised as daily, non-daily and never. To give an indication of people's capabilities, respondents' self-assessment of their computer knowledge was measured on a scale from one to five. In some cases the scale is summarised as low (1–2), average (3) and high (4–5).[5]

Wider Context

Macro level

The *economic situation* is one parameter of the wider macro context. Given our user-oriented approach, it is important to know how businesses themselves perceive the economic environment. When a substantial share of the respondents labels the situation as 'good' to 'very good', there is a considerable chance that the sector is also doing well in the economy – and vice versa if the situation is perceived to be

---

3 Agriculture; Extraction (not included because there are almost no micro-enterprises in this field); Manufacturing; Construction; Wholesale trade; Retail distribution; Transport & Communication; Producer services (i.e. all kind of financial and business services like accountancy, real estate agents, rental or informatics); Personal services (i.e. all kind of services delivered directly to the customer, often involving face-to-face contact, like hotels, restaurants, cafés, hairdressers or recreation).

4 The main goal of this survey research is to find underlying patterns and general trends that can explain (the lack of) ICT adoption and use in micro-enterprises. Therefore, although some of these figures can look outdated, the general findings are time-independent and thus still relevant.

5 For our analysis of the statistical results we maintain a significance level (alpha) of 0.05. This means there is a 5 per cent chance of mistakenly rejecting the null hypothesis. In addition, the chi-square (X^2) is calculated, as well as the Spearman Correlation (Rs), the Mann-Whitney test (MW) and the Kruskall-Wallis test (KW) if appropriate.

bad. In the survey we asked for an assessment of the current economic situation in their sector on a five-points-scale from very good to very bad. At the time of questioning, all the micro-enterprises taken together appeared to be slightly more positive about the general economic situation, with 49 per cent answering 'good' to 'very good'. More than a quarter (28 per cent) perceived the situation as average, while just under a quarter were more negative (23 per cent).

We found that this wider context factor correlated with a computer at the workplace[6] and, to a larger degree, with actual use.[7] When the economic situation was perceived to be more negative there was a significantly smaller chance of adoption and of use. Even when the computer was present, the degree of actual use was also linked with the perceived economic condition. But the latter was to a large extent itself related to computer knowledge.[8] The more they saw the economic environment as positive, the more they knew about computers.

Meso level

One of the main elements that characterises the meso level adequately is the kind of industry or *sector* in which respondents operate. The figures clearly demonstrate how the latter determines the digital divide among micro-enterprises. First we observe a notable statistical relation as regards the adoption of all ICTs examined in the survey.[9] This is clear in the figure below, which shows how the various ICTs are distributed very unequally over the different sectors.

When focusing only on the computer, the nature of the sector also offered a significant explanation for differences in use[10] and in knowledge.[11] Business managers working in the sectors of producer services and of transport and communication were the most frequent computer users and they had the most computer knowledge. At the other end of the scale we found agriculture and personal services as the least frequent users and the least-informed sectors. The largest discrepancies were found between agriculture on the one hand and producer services on the other.[12]

The table shows that more than half of the agricultural micro-enterprises did not have a computer compared to only one in twenty businesses delivering producer

---

6 $X^2 = 14.244 \rightarrow p = 0.001$ / $CC = 0.160 \rightarrow p = 0.001$ (df = 2; n = 543).

7 $X^2 = 12.608 \rightarrow p = 0.013$ / $CC = 0.184 \rightarrow p = 0.013$ (df = 4; n = 358).

8 $X^2 = 44.835 \rightarrow p = 0.000$ / $CC = 0.276 \rightarrow p = 0.000$ (df = 16; n = 544) / $R_s = -0.194$ $\rightarrow p = 0.000$ (n = 544).

9 Computer: $X^2 = 69.384 \rightarrow p = 0.000$ / $CC = 0.333 \rightarrow p = 0.000$ (df = 7; n = 558); Internet: $X^2 = 52.278 \rightarrow p = 0.000$ / $CC = 0.294 \rightarrow p = 0.000$ (df = 7; n = 554); Mobile phone: $X^2 = 62.474 \rightarrow p = 0.000$ / $CC = 0.317 \rightarrow p = 0.000$ (df = 7; n = 559); Fax: $X^2 = 76.376 \rightarrow p = 0.000$ / $CC = 0.347 \rightarrow p = 0.000$ (df = 7; n = 558); ISDN: $X^2 = 45.815 \rightarrow p = 0.000$ / $CC = 0.275 \rightarrow p = 0.000$ (df = 7; n = 559).

10 $X^2 = 38.293 \rightarrow p = 0.000$ / $CC = 0.306 \rightarrow p = 0.000$ (df = 14; n = 371) / $KW = 34.580$ $\rightarrow p = 0.000$ (df = 7; n = 370).

11 $X^2 = 56.448 \rightarrow p = 0.040$ / $CC = 0.303 \rightarrow p = 0.000$ (df = 14; n = 559) / $KW = 52.216$ $\rightarrow p = 0.000$ (df = 7; n = 559).

12 Producer services consist of all kind of financial and business services like accountancy, real estate agents, rental or informatics.

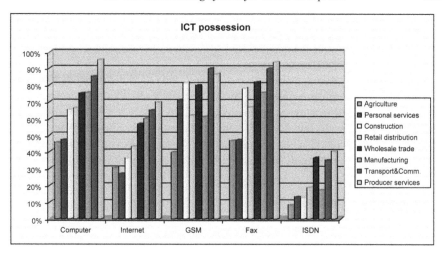

Figure 11.2   ICT adoption in different sectors

services. Even when there was a PC at work, many business owners working in agriculture did not use it themselves. In addition, the share of respondents working in agriculture who had a low to very low knowledge of computers was twice as large as that of those working in producer services.

These findings on sectors correspond with results from more recent studies. In our online survey among 966 Belgian enterprises with less than 50 employees at the beginning of 2006 we also found that agriculture and industry on the one hand and producer services on the other hand were each others' opposite with regard to ICT intensity (Baelden et al., 2006; Pierson et al., 2006).[13] Another confirmation of our first survey in 2000 can be found in the latest 'e-Business W@tch Survey 2006' (European Commission, 2006), being one of the few large-scale studies taking a sectoral approach with regard to ICTs. This study demonstrated sector-specific discrepancies concerning involvement with ICTs. Yet here, the construction sector was lagging behind on different parameters. According to the e-Business W@tch study, only 27 per cent of the construction companies used e-invoices, whilst 64 per

Table 11.2   A comparison of computer use in the workplace

Computer at work	Agriculture	Producer services
Not present	54.5%	5%
Present but not used	22.5%	6%
Least-informed	78%	38%

13 Under the authority of the Belgian Ministry of Economy VUB-SMIT, in co-operation with FUNDP-CITA, investigated the optimal approach to stimulating ICT adoption by small firms based on sector specificity. This research took place in the period from November 2005 to July 2006.

cent of hospitals had already integrated this application into their daily management practices. These numbers corresponded to a great extent to the results of our 2006 online survey (27 per cent in construction SMEs and 63 per cent in personal service SMEs).

Finally, when comparing macro and meso levels, the very noticeable link between the kind of sector and the assessment of the economic situation should be taken into account.[14] People's work or professional activity not only explains computer adoption and use directly, but also indirectly via the economic situation in the sector concerned. Yet the latter also has an independent effect. For example, when looking at the work activities separately, the economic situation was still influential.[15]

Socio-professional Situation

Besides the wider context discussed above, the second kind of explanation for ICT adoption is the socio-professional situation. This refers to the micro factors incorporating both work characteristics, but also, as indicated in the framework above, social or private traits. Both need to be examined in order to be able to understand the spread of ICTs among micro-enterprises. First, we discuss some essential indicators within the work sphere.

Work sphere

Characteristics belonging to the professional sphere are subdivided into the nature of the firm (business-level) and the owner's approach to his/her professional activity (entrepreneur-level). The first refers to characteristics like size and turnover, while the owner's desire for expansion provides an example of an entrepreneur-level factor.

The *turnover*, as a typical economic parameter, explained the presence[16] and, even more, the use of computers.[17] When looking at the adoption rate, we found a significant differentiation between SMEs with different sizes of turnover. Taking 62,000 Euro[18] as the dividing line, we found that below this threshold 59 per cent of the respondents had a computer and 60 per cent of these used it daily, whereas this increased to 83 per cent and 74 per cent respectively for those with a turnover above this level. However, turnover was not decisively linked to the computer knowledge of the business owner.[19]

---

14 $X^2 = 123.253 \to p = 0.000 / CC = 0.427 \to p = 0.000$ (df = 14; n = 553)/ $KW = 81.673 \to p = 0.000$ (df = 7; n = 553).

15 For example In fruit farming sector: computer possession & economic situation: $X^2 = 8.762 \to p = 0.013 / CC = 0.283 \to p = 0.013$ (df = 2; n = 101) / $MW = 870.500 \to p = 0.005$ (n = 101).

16 $X^2 = 16.112 \to p = 0.000 / CC = 0.250 \to p = 0.000$ (df = 1; n = 241).

17 $X^2 = 9.698 \to p = 0.008 / CC = 0.224 \to p = 0.008$ (df = 2; n = 184) / $KW = 1.671 \to p = 0.643$ (df = ; n = 184).

18 The exact turnover figure is 2.5 million Bfr. or 61,973 Euro.

19 $X^2 = 8.086 \to p = 0.232 / CC = 0.180 \to p = 0.232$ (df = 6; n = 241) / $R_s = 0.071 \to p = 0.269$ (n = 241).

The situation is less distinct, but still significant, as regards the *size of the business*. In particular, businesses with no employees were generally much less equipped with information technologies such as the computer.[20] They also assessed themselves as being lower on the knowledge scale. [21]

In order to measure the *desire for expansion*, the respondents were asked to what extent they were satisfied with their current business size in terms of the number of personnel. Besides its link to the general economic environment, this also indicated the attitude of the owner or the company style. Again there was an association with the presence of a computer.[22] Of the self-employed longing for some expansion, 88 per cent had a computer, compared to only 62 per cent for those satisfied with the current number of personnel in the firm. The degree of computer knowledge also had a weak link with the desire for expansion.[23]

Private sphere

The most decisive factors explaining computer adoption, use and knowledge – besides sector – relate to the private or domestic sphere. The owner's education was especially crucial and age played a role to a lesser degree.

Educational level appears to be one of the strongest characteristics explaining computer adoption, use and knowledge. We see that possession[24] as well as frequency of use[25] were very much related to the kind of schooling that respondents had had. The higher the education level, the greater the chance that a computer was present in the business and also the more it was used. The greatest difference was between those with only a primary school education, only 12 per cent of whom had a computer, and those with a higher education, among whom there was more than 90 per cent computer penetration. We found an even stronger correlation regarding knowledge.[26] The main dividing line was whether or not one had a higher education degree. Almost one third (31 per cent) of the self-employed having a higher education degree labelled themselves as being 'much' to 'very much' informed about computers, while less than a tenth (8.5 per cent) of the other self-employed said this. Computer illiterates (having little or no computer knowledge) represented only 37 per cent of the business owners who had higher education degree, versus 78 per cent of the other group.

---

20 $X^2 = 21.822 \rightarrow p = 0.000$ / **CC** $= 0.196 \rightarrow p = 0.000$ (df = 2; n = 549).

21 $X^2 = 16.437 \rightarrow p = 0.002$ / **CC** $= 0.170 \rightarrow p = 0.002$ (df = 4; n = 550) / **MW** $= 32612.000 \rightarrow p = 0.007$ (n = 550).

22 $X^2 = 19.414 \rightarrow p = 0.000$ / **CC** $= 0.185 \rightarrow p = 0.000$ (df = 1; n = 546).

23 $X^2 = 16.992 \rightarrow p = 0.000$ / **CC** $= 0.174 \rightarrow p = 0.000$ (df = 2; n = 547) / **KW** $= 23.285 \rightarrow p = 0.000$ (df = 2; n = 547).

24 $X^2 = 98.219 \rightarrow p = 0.000$ / **CC** $= 0.393 \rightarrow p = 0.000$ (df = 4; n = 539).

25 $X^2 = 35.582 \rightarrow p = 0.000$ / **CC** $= 0.312 \rightarrow p = 0.000$ (df = 6; n = 357) / $\mathbf{R}_s = -0.279 \rightarrow p = 0.000$ (n = 357).

26 $X^2 = 113.969 \rightarrow p = 0.000$ / **CC** $= 0.417 \rightarrow p = 0.000$ (df = 12; n = 540) / $\mathbf{R}_s = 0.424 \rightarrow p = 0.000$ (n = 540).

Other private characteristics also had a significant influence. Although *gender* difference is a typical socio-demographic trait, this classical factor turned out to be less predictive than perhaps expected. A computer's presence in the business[27] as well as knowledge[28] did depend on the gender of the business manager, but this was less pronounced than other private characteristics. *Age,* for example, provided a strong predictor of computer ownership in the business.[29] Not surprisingly, computer knowledge was inversely proportional to age, such that the age category of 30–39 year olds seemed to be the most informed.[30] Having a computer in the workplace[31] and knowing about it[32] was also significantly linked to the personal trait of perceiving computer use as being a *hobby.*

Technological Setting

Besides external and internal economic and social characteristics, we also found that technological features configured ICT adoption and use in general. First, the figures showed a kind of technological accumulation whereby the presence of one ICT often went together with the presence and use of other ICTs. Second, we looked at characteristics explaining Internet adoption and use since this is generally taken together with the computer when analysing the information society. One cannot talk about electronic business and micro-enterprises without including the Internet. However, we found that Internet adoption and use were not influenced by those same private characteristics that explained computer adoption and use.

General technological accumulation

The results indicated that appropriating one kind of communication technology often coincided with the appropriation of other ICTs. Especially (not) having 'old' fax technology in the workplace provided a very good indication of the possession of and knowledge about the computer, and the same applies to other ICTs. Therefore, an ICT often needs to be seen in combination with other ICTs. This kind of technological accumulation fits within the idea of a 'technological culture' (Punie, 2000) that was mentioned earlier. Apparently, the self-employed who were open to one kind of ICT were more eager to adopt other ICTs. This disposition, however, also had the effect of intensifying the digital divide among different micro-enterprises. It led to an unequal situation with, on the one side, enterprises having almost no advanced means of

---

27 $X^2 = 9.036 \rightarrow p = 0.003$ / $CC = 0.127 \rightarrow p = 0.003$ (df = 1; n = 549).

28 $X^2 = 9.634 \rightarrow p = 0.047$ / $CC = 0.131 \rightarrow p = 0.047$ (df = 4; n = 550) / $MW = 23666.500 \rightarrow p = 0.003$ (n = 550).

29 $X^2 = 45.894 \rightarrow p = 0.000$ / $CC = 0.278 \rightarrow p = 0.000$ (df = 5; n = 549).

30 $X^2 = 44.914 \rightarrow p = 0.000$ / $CC = 0.275 \rightarrow p = 0.000$ (df = 16; n = 550) / $R_s = -0.168 \rightarrow p = 0.000$ (n = 550).

31 $X^2 = 20.508 \rightarrow p = 0.000$ / $CC = 0.190 \rightarrow p = 0.000$ (df = 1; n = 546).

32 $X^2 = 92.200 \rightarrow p = 0.000$ / $CC = 0.380 \rightarrow p = 0.000$ (df = 4; n = 547) / $MW = 6372.000 \rightarrow p = 0.000$ (n = 547).

technological communication (not even a fax) and, on the other side, businesses that were fully equipped and much more involved with ICT developments.

If we take the computer at work as the subject of investigation again, apparently when the self-employed possessed an ISDN telephone line,[33] a fax machine[34] or a mobile phone,[35] they were very also likely to have a computer in the workplace. The latter was the case with 94 per cent of the ISDN owners, 80 per cent of the fax owners and 75 per cent of the mobile phone owners. The survey results also showed that the frequency of computer use correlated with the presence of ISDN,[36] fax[37] and to a minor degree mobile phone.[38] In particular, when an ISDN connection or a fax was present in the micro-enterprise, the computer was used much more on a daily basis. And finally, computer capabilities also differed significantly along the lines of the possession of ISDN,[39] fax[40] or mobile phone.[41] It is not surprising that those self-employed who had none of those ICTs evaluated themselves as being very low in terms of knowledge of computers.

Internet adoption and use

When looking at the presence and the use of an Internet connection among micro-enterprises with a computer, none of the private characteristics discussed earlier (for example education, gender, age) seemed to have a significant correlation. More or less the same was true for the wider context factors on the macro and meso levels. Yet the story is different when we look at work characteristics.

Surprisingly, then, none of the wider context factors, nor the private traits, are linked to Internet adoption by computer-owners. Hence, businesses delivering producer services and having a computer were, for example, not significantly more connected to the Internet than construction businesses which had a computer. The same was true for business owners with a university degree compared to those with only secondary education. The situation was different as regards professional attributes. Those striving for expansion of personnel were more connected to the Internet.[42]

---

33 $X^2 = 49.715 \rightarrow p = 0.000$ / **CC** $= 0.288 \rightarrow p = 0.000$ (df = 1; n = 549).

34 $X^2 = 105.414 \rightarrow p = 0.000$ / **CC** $= 0.402 \rightarrow p = 0.000$ (df = 1; n = 548).

35 $X^2 = 42.713 \rightarrow p = 0.000$ / **CC** $= 0.269 \rightarrow p = 0.000$ (df = 1; n = 549).

36 $X^2 = 13.702 \rightarrow p = 0.001$ / **CC** $= 0.191 \rightarrow p = 0.001$ (df = 2; n = 362) / **MW** $= 11175.000 \rightarrow p = 0.002$ (n = 362).

37 $X^2 = 14.196 \rightarrow p = 0.001$ / **CC** $= 0.194 \rightarrow p = 0.001$ (df = 2; n = 362) / **MW** $= 7035.000 \rightarrow p = 0.000$ (n = 362).

38 $X^2 = 5.563 \rightarrow p = 0.062$ / **CC** $= 0.123 \rightarrow p = 0.062$ (df = 2; n = 362) / **MW** $= 9732.500 \rightarrow p = 0.026$ (n = 362).

39 $X^2 = 39.219 \rightarrow p = 0.000$ / **CC** $= 0.258 \rightarrow p = 0.000$ (df = 4; n = 550) / **MW** $= 15806.000 \rightarrow p = 0.000$ (n = 550).

40 $X^2 = 85.773 \rightarrow p = 0.000$ / **CC** $= 0.368 \rightarrow p = 0.000$ (df = 4; n = 549) / **MW** $= 18542.000 \rightarrow p = 0.000$ (n = 549).

41 $X^2 = 43.178 \rightarrow p = 0.000$ / **CC** $= 0.270 \rightarrow p = 0.000$ (df = 4; n = 550) / **MW** $= 22075.000 \rightarrow p = 0.000$ (n = 550).

42 $X^2 = 4.213 \rightarrow p = 0.040$ / **CC** $= 0.108 \rightarrow p = 0.040$ (df = 1; n = 355) / **MW** $= 12393.000 \rightarrow p = 0.036$ (n = 355).

In addition, the business size mattered.[43] In particular, those micro-enterprises with five or more employees differed significantly, with 84 per cent having online access as against only 66 per cent of the smaller firms. But the most decisive factor for online access was turnover.[44] Eighty-seven per cent of the businesses with a turnover of more than 500,000 Euro[45] had an Internet subscription via their work computer, while this figure dropped to 65 per cent for the other enterprises.

However, the professional characteristics outlined above were not linked to the actual frequency of Internet use. Only the meso setting, made explicit by the sector, was related to the latter.[46] The most frequent use of the Internet was found in producer services where 60 per cent used the Internet on a daily basis. In agriculture this group represented only one fifth (20 per cent) of the computer owners.

Finally, the technological setting, i.e. the influence of technological accumulation, had a strong link with Internet adoption and use. Having an ISDN line,[47] a fax machine[48] or a mobile phone[49] led to a greater probability of having an Internet connection at the workplace. The figures also showed a slight tendency whereby having an ISDN connection,[50] a fax[51] or a mobile phone[52] also went together with more Internet use.

Conclusion

Characteristics for explaining ICT prominence in small businesses

We analysed the characteristics that can configure unequal adoption, use and knowledge with regard to ICTs, in particular the computer, among small businesses and micro-enterprises. For this we used a framework based on former qualitative research conducted among these kinds of small-scale professional users. The framework identifies the different variables relating to the social dynamics of the business owner. As assumed, the survey results did indeed reveal that the unequal ICT and computer adoption by micro-enterprises takes shape to a very large extent along lines other than economic characteristics.

---

43 $X^2 = 6.680 \rightarrow p = 0.035$ / $CC = 0.136 \rightarrow p = 0.035$ (df = 2; n = 356) / $MW = 11883.000 \rightarrow p = 0.019$ (n = 356).

44 $X^2 = 9.616 \rightarrow p = 0.022$ / $CC = 0.226 \rightarrow p = 0.022$ (df = 3; n = 179) / $MW = 2536.500 \rightarrow p = 0.016$ (n = 179).

45 The exact turnover figure is 20 million Bfr. or 495,787 Euro.

46 $X^2 = 16.864 \rightarrow p = 0.018$ / $CC = 0.271 \rightarrow p = 0.018$ (df = 7; n = 213) / $KW = 11.924 \rightarrow p = 0.103$ (df = 7; n = 213).

47 $X^2 = 9.889 \rightarrow p = 0.002$ / $CC = 0.164 \rightarrow p = 0.002$ (df = 1; n = 356).

48 $X^2 = 5.583 \rightarrow p = 0.018$ / $CC = 0.124 \rightarrow p = 0.018$ (df = 1; n = 356).

49 $X^2 = 6.262 \rightarrow p = 0.012$ / $CC = 0.131 \rightarrow p = 0.012$ (df = 1; n = 356).

50 $X^2 = 5.303 \rightarrow p = 0.071$ / $CC = 0.158 \rightarrow p = 0.071$ (df = 2; n = 208) / $MW = 4192.000 \rightarrow p = 0.022$ (n = 208).

51 $X^2 = 4.694 \rightarrow p = 0.096$ / $CC = 0.149 \rightarrow p = 0.096$ (df = 2; n = 208) / $MW = 1405.500 \rightarrow p = 0.047$ (n = 208).

52 $X^2 = 4.254 \rightarrow p = 0.119$ / $CC = 0.142 \rightarrow p = 0.119$ (df = 2; n = 208) / $MW = 2084.500 \rightarrow p = 0.040$ (n = 208).

A first set of variables was situated at the private level of the self-employed entrepreneurs. In particular, when the business owner had a higher education degree, the chances of a having a computer in the micro-enterprise, using it and knowing more about it were much higher. This private trait outweighed professional characteristics like turnover, size of business or the need for expansion. It even outweighed the influence of the macro and meso situation, although factors such as education and the industry sector were themselves also closely related to it.

The meso context on its own, indicated here by the kind of sector or work, was, however, also important for explaining computer adoption, use and knowledge. Professionals in some sectors in comparison to others seemed to experience ICTs as being much less useful. Two sectors seem to be each others' opposite in this regard, i.e. agriculture versus producer services.

We also examined linkages with the technological setting. In our study the latter refers to – besides the computer and the internet – having an ISDN connection, a fax machine and a mobile phone. The most striking fact was the confirmation of technological accumulation. In particular, the presence of a fax machine was a statistical 'predictor' of the adoption, the use of and the knowledge of other ICTs. The micro-enterprise possessing a fax significantly correlated with the presence, the frequency of use of and the knowledge of IDSN, mobile phone, and computers as well as of the Internet. This technological accumulation could lead to an intensified digital divide between those micro-enterprises having almost no communication technologies and the 'innovators' and 'early adopters' who have an extensive choice of different means for digital business communication and information exchange.

With regard to an Internet connection, the divide between micro-enterprises seemed to be linked predominantly with business characteristics. So contrary to our presupposition, having and using the Internet was not related to the typical private characteristics that were found to influence having and using the computer. It would seem that having a computer with online access was more a matter of specific professional characteristics, at least at the time of the study. It was mainly business dimensions, as indicated by the number of employees as well as turnover, that seemed to play a major part. Larger firms – with at least five employees and a turnover exceeding 500,000 Euro – had significantly more online access. This means that having an Internet connection was linked to business size, independently of the kind of business and the kind of business owner. This again stresses the possible digital exclusion of (very) small micro-enterprises with regard to electronic business.

Policy and research implications

Different implications can be derived from the survey results. First, policy makers and researchers should become aware that for many micro-enterprises, ICTs are of little significance because they experience them as being irrelevant for their everyday working life. In order to understand this situation, a sector-oriented point of view is needed. This implies a differentiated sector approach instead of a generalised SME-approach, taking into account the working practices linked to the different sector or their professional activities. This requires more qualitative research into business owners and their workplace in order to understand better the meaning of ICTs in their sector.

Within the different sectors, the typical orientation in the literature towards business economics, such as turnover, needs to be supplemented by a consideration of the private characteristics of the business owner, such as educational background. We saw how the survey showed, for instance, that computer adoption, use and knowledge were more dependent upon private and domestic characteristics than upon business-related features. So when looking at small businesses, traditional explanations deriving from organisational studies of ICT adoption and use need to be supplemented by a social constructivist and interpretative viewpoint, based on ethnographic research into the everyday life and work of the entrepreneur. Only then will the 'social embeddedness' of ICT adoption and use by small businesses be appreciated. However, when focusing only on Internet adoption among computer-owners, the private features seem to be less relevant.

Finally the study showed that the process of technological accumulation could possibly lead to a deepening of the digital divide. Some businesses had an extensive set of 'information society tools', while others even went without a fax machine. Therefore, policy efforts to strengthen the economic fabric by promoting technological innovation in regional and local economic development cannot adopt a purely economically inspired 'one-size-fits-all' approach to these small businesses. The research showed that factors influencing ICT adoption and use by micro-enterprises were contingent upon the wider context and socio-professional setting as well as on the technology itself. Therefore in order to further economic and social sustainability, technological innovation policy and research needs to complement the current views on 'economic dynamics' with insights into 'social dynamics'. This implies new ways of investigating and interpreting the role and meaning of ICTs in small businesses.

References

Arbore, A. and Ordanini, A. (2006), 'Broadband divide among SMEs', *International Small Business Journal* 24 (1), 83–99.

Baelden, D., Pierson, J., Lievens, B., Lobet-Maris, C. and Marsigny, C. (2006), *Stimuleringsbeleid voor ICT-gebruik bij KMO's: onderzoeksverslag en input voor sensibiliseringscampagne* (Brussels: Federale Overheidsdienst Economie, KMO, Middenstand en Energie), 153.

Barrett, R. and Rainnie, A. (2005), 'Editorial: small firms and new technology', *New Technology, Work and Employment* 20 (3), 184–219.

DTI (2004), *Business in the Information Age: The International Benchmarking Study 2004* (London: Department of Trade and Industry).

European Commission (2000), *The European Observatory for SMEs: Sixth Report* (Luxembourg: ENSR – KPMG Consulting – EIM).

European Commission (2001a), *Enterprises in Europe (Sixth Report): Data 1987– 97* (Luxembourg: Eurostat, 1999).

European Commission (2001b), *The Impact of the e-Economy on European Enterprises: Economic Analysis and Policy Implications* – Communication from the Commission to the Council and the European Parliament, COM (2001), Brussels Consultancy.

European Commission, (2003), *Observatory for European SMEs 2003: No.8 – Highlights from the 2003 Survey* (Luxembourg: ENSR – KPMG – EIM).

European Commission (2006), *A Pocketbook of e-Business Indicators: A Portrait of e-Business in 10 sectors of the EU Economy (e-business w@tch)* (Luxembourg: DG Enterprise).

Eurostat (2002), *Statistics in Focus – Industry, Trade and Services: Enterprises in Europe – Does Size Matter?* Theme 4 - 3/2002, 7.

Frissen, V. (1999), *ICT en arbeid in het dagelijks leven (Werkdocument 71)* (Den Haag: Rathenau Instituut).

Lievrouw, L.A. (2002) 'Determination and contingency in new media development: diffusion of innovations and social shaping of technology perspectives', in Lievrouw, L.A. and Livingstone, S. (eds), *The Handbook of the New Media* (London: Sage).

OECD (2001), *Understanding the Digital Divide* (Paris: Organisation for Economic Cooperation and Development).

Perez, C. (2002) *Technological Revolutions and Financial Capital: The Dynamics of Bubbles and Golden Ages* (Cheltenham: Elgar).

Pierson, J. (1999), 'Acceptance and use of ICT by Small Office & Home Office (SOHO): analysing the appropriation of transaction-oriented and knowledge-oriented applications', *Conference Proceedings of the International Conference on Uses of Services and Telecommunications (ICUST)* (Bordeaux: SEE, IREST & ADERA), 376–87.

Pierson, J. (2000), 'ICT appropriation by small businesses: an interplay between home and work', in Sloane, A. and Rijn, F. van (eds), *Home Informatics and Telematics: Information, Technology and Society* (Boston: Kluwer Academic Publishers).

Pierson, J. (2003), *De (on)verenigbaarheid van informatie- en communicatietechnologie en zelfstandige ondernemers: Een gebruikersgericht en innovatiestrategisch onderzoek naar adoptie, gebruik en betekenis van ICT voor zaakvoerders van micro-ondernemingen* (The (in)compatibility between information and communication technology and self-employed entrepreneurs: User-oriented and innovation-strategic research on adoption, use and meaning of ICT for business owners of micro-enterprises). Unpublished PhD thesis (Brussels: Vrije Universiteit Brussel).

Pierson, J. (2005), 'Domestication at work in small businesses', in Berker, T., Hartmann, M., Punie, Y. and Ward, K. (eds), *Domestication of Media and Technology* (Berkshire: Open University Press).

Pierson, J., Baelden, D., Lievens, B. and Marsigny, C. (2006), 'Understanding sector specificity regarding ICT and broadband usage by SMEs in Belgium', paper presented at *BroadBand Europe 2006 Conference*, 11–14 December 2006, Geneva.

Punie, Y. (2000), *Domesticatie van Informatie- en Communicatietechnologie. Adoptie, gebruik en betekenis van media in het dagelijkse leven: Continue beperking of discontinue bevrijding?* (Brussels: Vrije Universiteit Brussel).

Chapter 12

Teleworking Behind the Front Door: The Patterns and Meaning of Telework in the Everyday Lives of Workers

Arjan de Jong and Enid Mante-Meijer

Introduction

One of the great expectations of technologists and policy makers is that ICTs will completely change the boundaries between work and non-work life. With modern technology work could be done at any time and in any place. Working patterns will completely change, whilst the office as such will become nothing more than a meeting place, where employees drop in for social contacts and in order to keep in touch with their organisation (Toffler, 1981). The home, not the office, will be the base from where all work activities would be conducted. One problem is that not much attention has been paid to how the blurring of the two spheres will affect the daily lives of people.

Jack Nilles, one of the founding fathers of the concept of telecommuting, observed in an interview for Network World that although at the moment the necessary technology is in place, developments in the direction predicted by Toffler are actually happening at an even slower pace than he had anticipated in the 1970s (Mears, 2007). In fact, in this respect Pierson's study (Chapter 11 in this book) shows how the adoption and use of ICT in small private business firms turns out to be far from self-evident. Beyond the mere availability of ICTs, social dynamics and circumstances like the pressures from the work and the home sphere are important factors shaping the use of information technology in small enterprises based in the home of the entrepreneur.

Pierson researched single owners of small enterprises and their use and perception of telecommunication as a tool to conduct their business. This brings us to the question of how much larger organisations cope with the phenomenon of office work at home in the form of so-called telework. This is the subject of this chapter, which is based on the outcomes of a small qualitative research project that aimed to explore in more depth the blurring of boundaries between the work sphere and home sphere in the case of teleworking. The goal of the project was not to provide a complete overview of how and when people work outside their office, nor to explore the much discussed potential benefits of telework. Instead, the aim was to present a realistic picture of how people engage with the possibility of working outside the office, how they actually make use of that possibility. Part of this intention was to gain some insight into how the social dynamics of the organisation and of the home interact to shape actual patterns of telework. This small qualitative study may form a basis for a more extended discussion of how telework can be made useful for organisations. The results of this research will also provide insight into the issues that teleworkers consider important with regard to the management of their everyday lives and the choices they have to make.

The notion of telework – literally far-work, or working at a distance – has existed since the 1970s. The general assumption was and is that telework will benefit workers and organisations in multiple ways. It could contribute to the reduction of traffic jams and increase the productivity of workers. On the other hand, critics of telework emphasise potential dangers, such as the lack of supervision of work circumstances and the chance of it leading to excessive working hours that could enhance the risks of repetitive strain injury (RSI) or burnout.

In spite of much research on the subject, the precise status of telework is still unclear. Research and project evaluations show, over and over again, that in many organisations teleworking is not accepted as a normal way of working, or else it is only accepted with restrictions. Employees telework on a relatively modest scale. This was the case when the study was conducted in 2002 and it is still the case in 2007.[1] Studies by Van de Wijngaert (2001, 2004) showed that the percentage of people doing some kind of telework from home was rising slowly, but that this still only covers a small part of the labour market. This is so despite the development of broadband technology as an enabler of quick and easy connections.

The gap between the expectations that people have of telework as a concept and the actual practice of telework raises the question of how much this work at home connects with employee's general working patterns. By investigating how workers find a place to telework in their everyday lives, we wanted in the research project to reveal the meaning of this way of working within the more general pattern of daily working practices. Our special attention was focused on the problem of the blurring of the work and the private sphere. The goals of the research project were to gain an insight into:

1. the ways in which workers give teleworking a place in their everyday lives and the extent to which general patterns can be recognised in this process;
2. how workers search for a balance between their work sphere and private sphere;
3. the extent to which the possibilities of ICT-applications fit in with the ways in which workers (want to) do their work;
4. the role that the interaction between organisation and employee plays in the practice of telework.

---

1 For example, although telework is seen in the Netherlands as a solution for the growing traffic problems and the problems of climate change and global warming, the market for new office buildings is still growing (*NRC Handelsblad*, July 11, 2007).

The central question we posed is: *how do workers experience teleworking and what patterns can be recognised?* In this chapter we first review the spread of telework, present an overview of the literature in this field and identify some gaps in the research. We then outline our own project, briefly clarifying the concept of teleworking being used here, the assumptions on which we based our research and the methods we used for the fieldwork before turning to the results of our analysis. Finally, we present our conclusions.

Assumptions and Frame of Reference

We start with some observations about the prevalence of telework. A study by the Social Cultural Planning Agency (SCP) in the Netherlands in 2006 (Steyaart and De Haan, 2007) mentioned that The Netherlands was currently taking the lead in teleworking in Europe, with about 20 per cent of the working population doing some office work from the home. The mean for Europe was only 7 per cent. Other countries with a relatively high occurrence of telework were Denmark with 18 per cent and Finland with 16 per cent.

Nevertheless, it is rare to find organisations where telework is implemented as a normal way of working for every worker. In organisations where teleworking is officially allowed, it is seldom used as a standard strategy but more as a form of crisis management in order to be able to cope with time pressure and workload (Steyaart and De Haan, 2007). In most organisations it is allowed under specific conditions and not open to everyone. A reason for this reserved attitude is the supposed loss of control by management. And, although many workers claim that they would like to telework, in practice only a minority really does, even when given the opportunity. Moreover, many employees claim that teleworking does not actually suit their work situation. Research by Vermaas and Van de Wijngaert (2007) outlined the reasons that people (with an ADSL access) do not telework. The most often mentioned reasons, apart from '*I do not use a computer at my work*' (38 per cent) were:

- '*My work cannot be done at home*' (34 per cent)
- '*No access to company network*' (16 per cent)
- '*My employer does not allow it*' (11 per cent)
- '*Costs are not covered by my employer*' (7 per cent)
- '*No suitable workspace at home*' (11 per cent)

In addition, people declared that they were afraid that teleworking would reduce their chances of a promotion. This reflects the fact that the office plays an important role by enabling social networking.

If we now take a look at the teleworking literature, since Toffler first introduced his vision on the future in *The Third Wave* – concerning the disappearing office and the full integration of the work sphere and the private sphere – numerous publications on teleworking have been published. Roughly speaking, the publications can be divided into three categories.

The first category is connected with extensive discussions, like Toffler's, about the progression from an industrial society towards a network society. This network society places totally different demands on labour and the organisation of labour. In these publications, problems involving individualisation and increased mobility play an important part, as do the solutions to these problems that technology could offer. These types of studies usually focus not only on teleworking, but also on the 'informatisation' of society in general (Mante-Meijer and Van der Loo, 1997; Jones, 2001).

The publications in a second category bring the managerial aspects of telework into focus. They are often very practical and deal with costs and benefits, legal aspects and do's and don'ts. (Van der Wielen and Tailleu, 1992, 1995; Ovum, 1993; Zegveld et al., 1995; Weijers, 1995).

A third category contains publications that are generally based on empirical research on teleworking. These research projects evaluate pilot projects and compare different aspects of teleworking (Huws et al., 1993; Haddon and Lewis, 1994; van Reisen, 1997). Frequent topics within the above sets of publications on teleworking include social and organisational obstructions and requirements, the perceptions and experiences of managers and colleagues, the perceptions and (dis)satisfaction of the teleworker, preconditions, costs and working conditions.

In contrast to the actual figures about the take up of teleworking outlined earlier, the recommendation of most of the research is that telework should be allowed, that employees want it and that it has major benefits for the employee, as well as for the organisation. The main obstacles are recognised as lying in the spheres of management and leadership. One problem with this research is that most studies dealing with telework as such focus on the teleworker. Little attention is paid to the workers who do not make use of the option of teleworking. Nor has much attention been paid to what goes on behind the front door when people telework at home. The EURESCOM-research project 'Telework and Quality of Life' (Jones, 2001) showed that individual factors play an important role in determining how people telework and how they experience teleworking as a part of their lifestyle. The EURESCOM-research project 'ICT uses in everyday life' (Mante and Haddon, 2001) also showed that the adoption and usage of ICTs is connected to very specific situations in an individual's everyday life. The use of telework is related to people's life phase, type of work and personality. The fit that people try to find between work and private life is an important issue.

Information about the actual practice of teleworking can provide insights into the possibilities and limitations of teleworking as a way of working compared to, or instead of, working in the office. This may help management in organisations to make better use of the option of teleworking. For example, a more realistic understanding of necessary, or advisable, technical implementations and supports could be developed.

Research Concepts, Implementation and Methods

There is no single unambiguous definition of telework. In 1973 Nilles et al. introduced the notion of 'telecommuting', which in Europe became better known as teleworking (Mears, 2007). This concept relates to 'work that is done outside the normal organisational boundaries of time and place and for which computer and information technology is often used'. In our research project the concept of teleworking was operationalised as 'working outside the office environment'. Three types of teleworking could then be distinguished:

Mobile working: workers have the means to work in many different places (office, home, clients' office, etc.)

Fixed teleworking: workers structurally work a fixed part of the working week at home.

Flexible teleworking: workers have a fully equipped place to telework at home, but they only use it as a back up when incidents occur or to enable them to extend their working week.

We found that all the organisations we investigated drew this distinction.

As the budget for the research was small and we wanted to get in-depth insights into the actual use of telework under different work regimes, we decided to make a selection of four large organisations that could be seen as representing the most common types of environment for office work: a department within a government office, a large banking firm, a consultancy bureau and a software company. In each of these organisations we conducted interviews both with the management and with employees.

Contextual Mapping

In order to be able to register how people find a place for telework in their everyday lives we used a research method that combined observation and interview techniques: contextual mapping. This qualitative research method had been developed as an item in their marketing programme by KPN Research in the Netherlands (Tax, 1998). Contextual mapping offers the researcher the possibility to map the wishes and needs of workers in their real life working environment. This method is in practice a simulation of the observation technique. Using real life examples, the researcher tries, together with the respondent, to explore combinations of situations (contexts), tasks, means and aims. In addition, the method gives the respondent the opportunity to talk about possible and desired improvements, as well as about (dis)satisfactions.

Contextual mapping starts by paying attention to the more general context within which a respondent uses technology (contextual inquiry) and then moves on to visualise more specific situations within this wider context in which technology is used (cognitive mapping). Contextual mapping uses hexagons: hexagonal, re-writable cards in different colours. Each hexagon represents a context, respectively situations, tasks and needs, which together form clusters that can be connected. Hence the map that can be drawn with the use of these hexagons provides precise information about the context in which a respondent uses an ICT application, the exact needs he/she perceives within that context and the means he/she uses to fulfil that need. By visualising information concerning these aspects (situations, tasks, means, etc.) with the aid of hexagons, a systematic and a pretty complete overview can be generated that goes from the general to the (very) specific. This provides reasonably in-depth information about why and how the respondent uses the ICT-application and about various aspects of the respondent's behaviour in that particular situation.

The approach to cognitive mapping is often used to study behaviour in relation to technology. In this research project, we focused not only on the role of technology for teleworking but also, more generally, on the place that telework occupied in people's everyday lives. For us, contextual mapping provided insights into the extent to which different contextual factors fitted the actual needs of teleworkers. In the interviews, we did not start from one specific context, but from a recent full (teleworking) day, within which several contexts could be recognised. On the basis of this outline, we then asked questions about wider experiences and the background factors influencing the specific choices that the respondent had made.

Using this method, we interviewed 20 employees from four different organisations mentioned before: a consultancy agency, a banking firm, a Dutch government office and a software company. These organisations were selected because of the following characteristics:

– a concrete policy on telework had been developed;
– teleworking was, in principle, accessible for all employees;
– a long term experience of teleworking had been built up.

The way that people incorporated telework into their everyday lives cannot be seen separately from the organisation's telework policy. Therefore, we also interviewed policy-makers in all four organisations and studied (policy) documents. We asked our contact persons in the organisations to make a random selection of teleworkers for the interviews but we also specifically requested them to differentiate in their selection between task, position, age, sex and marital status.

Although teleworking can be carried out at home, in a clients' office, on the road or elsewhere, it is common to telework in places other than at home, as a necessary part of a job or for a specific task. However, since in this research project we were mainly interested in the meaning telework had for teleworkers in their everyday life situation and the choices they made we focused mainly on teleworking (of whatever kind) when it was taking place at home, behind the front door.

First, we looked at the ways in which respondents actually conducted their work at home. The main topics were the specific activities, the use of technology and the time and place of (tele)work. Starting from a recent actual day (preferable yesterday or the day before) when the respondent had been teleworking, we asked the respondents questions about their behaviour, the meaning of that behaviour and their experiences of telework. We looked respectively at activities undertaken, means used, the perceived relationship between the office and home as a base for doing the job, the time devoted to telework, the meaning of telework to the worker and the perception of the blurring of work and private spheres.

Lastly it is worth noting the scope of this research project. It was an explorative study on ways in which people from our four different types of organisations incorporated telework in their everyday lives. The outcome was not representative for teleworkers in general. The sample of organisations we investigated was too small and the number of respondents too few. What the results of our inventory do provide, however, is an insight into the issues teleworkers relate to teleworking, as well as their considerations and reflections. The results should not be interpreted as final conclusions, but rather as a starting point for a more extended discussion on the role that teleworking plays or could play in organisations, separate from the expectations that people have had since the 1970s. Our research provides insight into meanings of telework for both teleworkers and organisations.

The Organisation of Telework

Activities: Tasks that require concentration, peace and quiet

All the teleworkers (mobile, fixed and flexible) performed especially those tasks at home that required concentration and a peaceful and quiet work environment. Some teleworkers did their thinking at home, most of them wrote and/or read there. Examples of specific tasks that were done at home included writing a report, writing a project plan, studying in-depth information or literature, preparing a presentation or writing a letter. Teleworkers preferred to do such tasks at home, although timetabling problems and meetings did not always allow it. Obviously, at the office these people did not find enough peace. Also, the people interviewed said that they felt more comfortable in their own environment, which was less formal and more flexible.

Most respondents checked their email regularly at night or at the weekends from home. Much incidental telework boiled down to this. After a course, a conference or a day at a client's office, employees acquainted themselves with what had been going on at their own office during their absence, so that they would not be confronted with any surprises the next day. The teleworkers we interviewed appreciated being informed of any developments relating to their work.

Technology: Simple ICTs are often sufficient

Some teleworkers, especially mobile workers, had the possibility to work with technically advanced, but demanding, applications. Making efficient use of these was not always easy. The teleworkers saw themselves as being confronted with time-consuming and sometimes complicated tasks such as making back-ups, downloading, synchronising a laptop and PDA, dealing with firewalls, finding an internet-connection at the clients' office, charging the laptop battery, protecting the laptop from theft, etc.

Teleworkers had two ways of dealing with these technical difficulties. Some saw them as being challenges and emphasised the added value of using advanced ICT applications. Others indicated that it was not always enjoyable, but that it was part of the job. If advanced technology was not necessary to complete the job in hand, they often made use of more simple applications.

One surprising consequence of this was that many teleworkers, especially ICT experts, made use of an old fashioned analogue line to connect to their organisation's network. The respondents were indeed familiar with the faster network connection possibilities, but rarely took the initiative in terms of urging their employer to provide them with one. Probably, the kind of activities people did at home did not demand a continuous and/or fast connection The lack of need for a faster connection was one of the barriers to adopting the (at that time) more expensive broadband technology. If they had to download large files, people could do it at the office.[2]

Place: The office as operating base

Our respondents worked at home for between half a day and a day and a half per week at most.[3] In fact, most respondents would have preferred to work at home for one day a week or for a fixed period everyday. But in practice, that was not always possible. Employees often gave priority to a meeting or to an appointment at the office, or to their boss's request to be at the office. Many respondents also indicated that they would have liked to have worked at home more often than they did at the time, but that the work did not allow it. (Project)-management tasks, for example, demanded the presence of the manager. The interviews showed that people found it necessary to be at the office for at least two days a week. This allowed them to maintain their informal contacts and stay informed. Being up to date was important for doing the work properly, but also from a career perspective. It was hard to plan meetings if people worked at home for a good deal of the time, especially since many employees in service and government organisations had by then turned to a four day working week.

Only one or two (young) respondents said they would consider using their workplace at home as an operating base instead of the office. Most people valued having their

---

2 This situation has changed since the period when the research has been conducted. The incidence of DSL connections in the Netherlands, partly due to an active role of the Dutch Government and the competition between telecom companies, has risen considerably during the last few years. In 2005, 55 per cent of the Dutch households had a broadband connection, always on, speed and flat-fee being the most important triggers for adoption. However, the more recent research of Vermaas and Van de Wijngaert (2007) still show that the main use of teleworking at this time demand not ask for very advanced technology. Email is used by 89 per cent, followed by telephone (36 per cent), access to the company's network (34 per cent) and intranet (31 per cent). The use of more advanced technology as video conferencing and video communication is still very low (respectively 3 per cent and 11 per cent)

3 Recent research by Vermaas (2007) and Vermaas and Van de Wijngaert (2007) shows that this pattern has not changed: telework is still more or less done incidentally. The majority of their respondents did not use their ADSL connection more than a few times a week or less, 24 per cent used their connection at least once a day for telework. The duration of the session was often less than two hours.

own workplace at the office, although most of them realised that saving workspace by introducing flexible workplaces could be desirable for the organisation.

Time: Office hours are also standard at home

The flexibility that teleworking has to offer is being able to work anyplace, anytime. Our research, however, showed that in practice teleworkers were attached to fixed working patterns. The respondents made relatively little use of the possibilities they had open to them for working at different times and places. Most of them only worked during standard office hours unless the work made it necessary to do otherwise, for example because of a deadline or some kind of emergency situation. What people did appreciate was the possibility to work at home instead of at the office.

The teleworkers were generally knowledge and information workers. For them, it was essential that they were able to share information and knowledge. Therefore it was important to be reachable by colleagues and clients, something of which employees were well aware. After office hours, though, the need to be reachable was no longer felt. This was probably an important reason why people maintained working office hours, even when they worked at home. Teleworkers wanted limitations on the times when they had to be contactable.

Our research showed that life stage and life situation (which largely correlated with age) were important determinants shaping the way that people dealt with teleworking and filled in the days on which they teleworked. Roughly speaking, the teleworkers could be divided into three categories:

– age 25–35, single or living together, no children, largely 'career-driven'
– age 30–45, family, young children, 'rush-hour of life'
– age 45+, grown up children, 'settled'

In general, teleworking was considered to be a relief for people from the middle category, which covered most of the respondents we interviewed. The research did show that workers with young children used their teleworking facilities in order to be able to have breakfast/lunch with their children or take them to school. Some respondents in this category did the occasional domestic chore in between work. But the research did not show that people combined working at home with taking care of the children or housekeeping. Teleworkers did not – at least not structurally – shift work to evening hours or weekends in order to be able to do other things during office hours. Having a young family made it necessary to organise and arrange everyday life carefully. Obviously, a flexible attitude towards working times was not compatible with this necessity. On the contrary, these teleworkers planned their work carefully, often days in advance, and employed fixed patterns. Meanwhile employers generally did not allow workers to telework for reasons related to such personal circumstances. In addition, employees were expected to use their telework facilities only for work-related reasons. As described previously, our research showed that teleworkers did indeed give priority to work needs instead of home demands, when they had to decide where or when to work. Therefore, the alleged function of telework as the grease that oils the organisational machine of busy family life appears to be a myth.

Respondents from the first category (aged 25–35) could afford to work flexible hours. They did not have to take their children into account. If they had a partner he or she often also had a job. Therefore, the working day of these young employees was generally somewhat more fragmented in the sense that they more often took a break to do something else in between work (a small chore, a private telephone call, shopping, sport). These young teleworkers let their work and private sphere interfere with each other somewhat more and they employed less fixed working patterns. They indicated that they especially valued the autonomy that teleworking brought with it. Being able to plan their own time gave them a sense of freedom. In practice, though, just like the respondents from the other categories, they mainly used teleworking in order to be able to do their work well and efficiently. The young workers also seemed hesitant about working in the evening or at the weekend. They too preferred to maintain standard working office hours, probably also because of the need to be reachable by colleagues and clients during those hours. What the young teleworkers we interviewed did seem to like was working towards some concrete result. It gave them a clearly defined goal and grip on their time. If a deadline approached, some of them did not have a problem with working extra hours for a couple of weeks. Others carefully tried to plan their work within office hours. It depended on their character. Young workers seemed to be a bit more flexible than their older colleagues, but they did need a clear framework.

Employees in the third category (age 45+) had generally progressed to a job in which they could do what they wanted to a certain extent. Their position, experience and record of service sometimes allowed them to decide for themselves which tasks they took up and how they worked. Their career drive had decreased, but because the children (if they had them) had left home, work was still an important aspect of their lives. They too worked office hours when they worked at home, but teleworkers in this category more often worked at night or at the weekend for a couple of hours. They considered freedom of choice to be important in relation to their work. And they were well able to make those choices, because in the meantime they had built up enough experience and knowledge of their own capabilities. For them, teleworking allowed them a degree of freedom to organise their work.

Meaning of telework: A moment away from the hectic life of the office

The respondents indicated that at home they mainly did tasks that required peace and concentration. When we asked them why, many of them answered that in the office they often lacked the peace that they could have at home. They were reachable at home, as at the office, through e-mail or telephone – and they in fact did receive calls and e-mails at home. But in spite of this they had the feeling that at home they could work without being disturbed all the time. Apparently, interruptions that were of a social kind and had to do with face-to-face contact were more disturbing than work-related interruptions through the telephone or Internet.

When respondents did get interrupted at home it was almost always because of a work-related issue. Some respondents even indicated that they were actually more reachable at home than at the office, because they had no reason to leave their (tele)workplace at home, whereas in the office they felt that the need to get away once in a while. In general, though, people received fewer telephone calls when they worked at home than if they worked at the office.

In particular the number of telephone calls from colleagues decreased, because when colleagues checked the office diary or the workplace at the office and noticed that the employee worked at home on that day, they often preferred to postpone making contact, instead of using the phone or emails. Respondents apparently considered their home to be an oasis. At the office, people could drop in without being asked, which gave them the feeling that they had to stay continuously alert. Working at home gave them the opportunity to get away from that hectic working life for a moment.

Experiences: No blurring of work and private sphere

Traditionally, different locations for working and living guaranteed the maintenance of the boundary between work and the private sphere. If people work at home, this boundary is no longer automatically maintained. Our research showed that this does not mean that both spheres blur. Teleworkers established those same boundaries themselves, by employing fixed patterns in terms of working time and place. When teleworking, work did enter the private home, but the teleworkplace was often kept strictly separated from the rest of the house. Only the younger teleworkers sometimes crawled onto the couch in the living room with their laptop.

According to some respondents, working at home involved the danger that someone would work more than is good for him or her. Then, RSI or burnout may be a possible consequence. This danger was especially relevant for mobile workers, who worked relatively independent and individually. The mobile workers we interviewed indicated that a teleworker had to be capable of guarding his or her own boundaries.

Employees from bureaucratic organisations like the bank or the government office had a clearer framework, because they were subjected to numerous rules. In these organisations the workers were relatively more dependent on colleagues, and their work involved many meetings. The fixed and flexible teleworkers of these organisations saw the option to work at home as a bonus or even a right, within the normal working hours. The fixed teleworkers even indicated that their greater productivity on a telework day was enough reason for them to 'call it a day' after they had worked eight hours or sometimes even less. Several respondents saved specific tasks to do at home.

Some teleworkers had the feeling that they had to prove that they had been productive on their telework day. For example, some wrote a summary of tasks performed at the end of the day and emailed it to their bosses. Apparently, in their eyes, teleworking was not generally accepted as a normal way of working. Others, however, indicated that they did not feel this pressure to prove themselves at all. Many (mostly older) respondents still saw the traditional separation of work and the private sphere as their norm. An important factor in relation to this kind of perception was the attitude of the employer towards teleworking. The government office, for example, actively supported teleworking. Hence many employees (about 60 per cent) actually made use of teleworking facilities. At the banking firm, however, many managers were much more hesitant about letting their subordinates work at home. This attitude was mirrored by the fact that only 12 per cent of the employees made use of the (standard) teleworking facilities of the bank. Telework there could be characterised as being 'a favour'. The software company provided its employees with state-of-the-art ICT facilities, but mainly to enable them to work sixty hours a week. The employees were officially not allowed to work at home during office hours, but some of them sometimes did if they had a valid reason. Concrete personal goals and direct supervision by superiors formed a clear framework for these employees. Since they loved (to work with) ICT, they happily accepted these working conditions. They thought it was normal to use teleworking facilities to extend the regular working week.

Conclusions

The conclusions we present here will indicate which issues matter to teleworkers when they choose to use teleworking facilities in their everyday lives. They will also give an indication of the patterns that can be recognised in those choices and the role that the social dynamics in the home and organisational setting play in the perception and the realisation of telework.

With regard to the place that teleworkers give to teleworking in their everyday lives, we recognise patterns on three different levels:

(1) The character of telework depends largely on the characteristics of the work organisation

First of all, we conclude that the conditions under which teleworkers see themselves as being confronted with teleworking have a large influence on the way they perceive this practice. The telework policy and management style within the work organisation shape the opportunities for and boundaries around teleworking. Thus for the consultants we interviewed, teleworking was perceived as a *necessity* in order to be able to do the work. Assignments and clients determined the agenda to a large extent. Therefore, the type of work that consultants did mainly determined which part of their time they spent working at home, at the office, or at a client's office.

At the banking firm we studied, the situation was different. There, workers were committed to strict guidelines for teleworking and they did not have a choice in terms of the facilities they could use. They could only put in a request for a standard package of teleworking facilities. Teleworking had not been generally accepted, yet. Managers were hesitant about letting their subordinates work at home. Teleworking could be characterised as a *favour*. Therefore, teleworkers organised the way they worked at home according to this wider picture, within certain specific preconditions.

In the government office we studied, teleworking was seen as a normal phenomenon, which had turned into a *right*. Every employee who had a job for which teleworking could be useful had the option to work at home, whenever he or she wanted to. He/she received a fixed budget (about €25 per month) and could decide for him/herself which ICT applications he/she wanted to use. All employees in the office had the freedom to work at home according to the ways that they considered most appropriate for their job. Nevertheless, they were still conscious of a certain degree of social control as regards being engaged in non-work activities during office hours.

At the software company teleworking was an obvious instrument, a *tool*. Using this tool could be seen as a 'voluntary duty'. The company culture demanded from employees that they should work extra hours and the company enabled them to do that by providing excellent facilities for working at home. Teleworking for reasons of a personal nature was 'not allowed'. In practice, though, the way that people actually made use of teleworking depended to a certain extent on their life situation.

Table 12.1   Teleworking is ...

Organisation	Teleworking is a ...	and is being filled in relation to ...
consultancy agency	necessity	the type of work
bank	favour	formal agreements and procedures
government office	right	the individual workers' choices
software company	tool	the company culture

(2) One day a week is normal

Our research results showed that some encouraging as well as some discouraging forces affected the use of teleworking facilities. The average amount of time spent teleworking lay between half a day and one and a half days. Often teleworkers had the intention to work at home for one day a week. Factors that influenced the amount of working time spent at home were connected to the different choices a teleworker had to make. Those choices developed in relation to the social dynamics between the worker and his or her direct environment. Changing expectations, experiences and shared values of the teleworker and his or her family members, friends and colleagues influenced the flexibility of choices.

The fact that some people did work at home appears to be simply a product of the options they had. In some organisations, teleworking was an instrument used to organise things more effectively and efficiently. The need for peaceful and quiet moments to be able to do certain tasks that required concentration seemed to be the most important reason for people to work at home. Factors like job redefinition, the need to be reachable, the reduction of secretarial and administrative support, increasing labour productivity and the increasing amount of information and communication all led to a major increase in the dynamics of the knowledge worker's workplace. Many of these factors were related to the speed with which ICT developments took place. Many of our respondents indicated that they used

Table 12.2   Teleworking - encouraging and discouraging forces

Encouraging forces	Discouraging forces
Flexible teleworking connects with the 'zeitgeist' (the spirit of the times)	People do not always want to be confronted with work-related issues at home
Working at home is pleasant	Social interaction with colleagues in the office is positive and necessary for career opportunities
Working at home increases productivity	Managers and colleagues may distrust the output of homework
ICT offers many opportunities. Being reachable is necessary	The usage of ICT requires adjustments in work practices
Teleworking offers (a sense of) freedom and autonomy	Reachability of the office worker at home is supposed to be limited
Teleworking can save time and money	People need frameworks. Teleworking requires preparation and organisation

teleworking to flee from the changing dynamics of the workplace, rather than as a means to make their work more flexible. (Knowledge) workers seemed to find themselves captured in an ICT spiral: ICT developments increased work dynamics, but to be able to cope with this increase, people expected help from those same ICT innovations. These developments in ICTs apparently not only supported employees in their work, but also influenced how and when people worked.

(3) Patterns of telework depend on lifestyle and life stage

The third main conclusion that can be drawn from the research results is that the role of telework on an individual level influences the way people manage teleworking. This role may vary by worker, but it is generally connected to life stage and to personal characteristics like life experience, lifestyle and personality.

Based on our research results, the classic vision of telework as a means to cope flexibly with the demands that a busy family life imposes on a worker appears to be a myth. Teleworkers hardly ever used their time in a more flexible way than office workers. Instead, teleworking functioned mainly as a bridge between the work and the private sphere. Because they could work at home, teleworkers were able to take their children to school once in a while, or have lunch with them. Work remained the most important factor during office hours, but teleworking simply provided some degree of latitude. It is clear that, from the point of view of the employer, teleworking was not being perceived as being a system used to meet the personal needs of employees. Those remained the sole responsibility of the worker him-/herself. Therefore, if workers wanted to accommodate work to the demands of their private life sphere, working part-time would be a better solution than teleworking. Part-time working provides the opportunity to plan a day according to personal wants and needs, with fewer work-related restrictions or requirements. It provides independence in terms of using the time *and* place of work, whereas teleworking, in practice, mainly offers only independence in terms of choosing the place.

For young workers, the added value of teleworking was generally the sense of freedom it gave them. Flexibility appealed to them. They had not yet made all of life's important choices and liked the idea that options were always open: an *illusion of freedom*. Teleworking seemed to offer them the freedom to organise their work, but in fact that autonomy was limited. To a certain extent, young teleworkers could decide for themselves how they performed their tasks, but they generally could not influence which tasks they had to do. The option to work at home gave these young employees the opportunity to prove that they could handle responsibility. It gave them a sense of autonomy. Working part-time, however, would have given them an actual opportunity to spend time on self-development. Teleworking mainly only gave them the feeling that they were worth that opportunity.

For the workers in the third category (age 45+), teleworking had a different meaning from the ones in the first and second group. They had often reached a position with which they felt content. They did not feel an urgent need to pursue a major career anymore and they had work they liked and that suited them. For them, teleworking contributed to their autonomy. The workers from this category deliberately chose to work at home; being at the office had less intrinsic value to them. They were not very interested in social talk anymore, 'they had heard the stories before', and they did not have to be at the office as regularly in order to build or maintain a social network anymore. The children had left home to live on their own and therefore work had become once again an important part in the parents' lives. Working part-time would not have benefited these workers very much. That would have meant taking a step back in salary and/or job content, and it was much too early for that. Teleworking, on the other hand, provided a welcome contribution to their independence.

Table 12.3   Teleworking and life stage

Life stage	Function of teleworking	Function of working part-time
young (25–35)	Allows a feeling of independence	Allows self-development
family (30–45)	offers some latitude	provides a real solution to the demands of home life
settled (45+)	contributes to autonomy	constitutes a step back financially and in job content

Concluding Remarks

It is clear that for some time to come telework will not be the panacea for the problems of climate change, traffic jams, pollution, etc. that are on the front page of the newspapers and on radio and TV broadcasts nowadays. Working at an office has an intrinsic social and career value for people and the constant blurring of work sphere and private sphere is only attractive for certain personalities and in some professions. Even the younger workers we interviewed did not make much use of the flexible options that were open to them.

Although in the rush time of life the possibility to do (part of the) work at home means an alleviation of the pressures of family life for working couples with children, the requirement to do a job within an allotted time *and* the need to regulate the day according to social and family needs will put limits on the possibility of blurring home and work time.

In the previously mentioned interview, Jack Nilles pointed, rightly, to the attitude of employers who still ask for major changes before telework will be an accepted normal way of working. He came to the conclusion that there is still a long way to go. But apart from this, the established cultural ways in which people view their own home and work sphere will demand the creation of a creative equilibrium between what is possible and what is wanted. Old habits die hard and people's needs do not change quickly.

References

Haddon, L. and Lewis, A. (1994), 'The experience of teleworking: an annotated review', *International Journal of Human Resource Management* 5(1), 193–223.

Huws, U. (1993), *Teleworking in Britain* Research Series no. 18 (Sheffield: Employment Department).

Huws, U., Korte, E.W.B. and Robinson, S. (1990), *Telework towards the Exclusive Office* (Chichester: Wiley).

Jones, M. (ed.) (2001), *Telework and Quality of Life* (Heidelberg: Eurescom).

Mante, E.A. and Haddon, L. (eds) (2001), *ICT Uses in Everyday Life* (Heidelberg: Eurescom).

Mante, E.A. and Loo, H.R. van der (1997), *Blurring of Life Spheres, Flexibility and Teleworking* (Stockholm: Cost).

Mears, J. (2007), 'Father of telecommuting Jack Nilles says security, managing remote workers remain big hurdles', *Network World.* Available at <http://www.networkworld.com/news/2007/051507-telecommuting-nilles-security.html>.

Ovum (1993), *Flexible Working with Information Technology: the Business Opportunity*, Ovum Data Monitor. Available at: <www.Ovum.com>.

Reisen, F. van (1997), *Ruim Baan door Telewerken?* (Delft: Nederlandse Geografische Studies).

Steyaart, J. and Haan, J. de (eds) (2007), *Jaarboek ICT en samenleving, gewoon digitaal* (The Hague: Sociaal Cultureel Planbureau (SCP)).

Tax, S. (1998), *Contextual Mapping: An Interviewing Method that Uses Hexagons to Investigate Communication Needs* (Leidschendam: KPN Research).

Toffler, A. (1981), *The Third Wave* (New York: Bantam Books).

Vermaas, K. (2007), *Fast diffusion and broadening use: a research on residential adoption and usage of broadband internet in the Netherlands between 2001 and 2005.* [Dissertation Utrecht University, Department of Information and Computer Sciences, Center for Organization & Information].

Vermaas, K. and Wijngaert, L. van de (2007), 'A longitudinal study to investigate consumer/user adoption and use of broadband technology in the Netherlands', in Dwivedi, Y.K. (ed.), *Consumer Adoption and Usage of Broadband* (Hershey: Idea Group).

Weijers, T.C.M. (1995), 'De kosten en baten van telewerk voor de organisatie, telewerker en samenleving', in Zegveld, W., Weijers, Th., Maas, T. van der and Lith, W. van (eds), *Handboek Telewerken* (Assen: Van Gorcum).

Wielen, J.M.M. van der and Tailleu, T.C.B. (1992), 'Telewerk: een arbeidsvorm met een gespreid activiteitenpatroon', *Informatie en Informatiebeleid*, 10, 43–50.

Wielen, J.M.M. van der and Tailleu, T.C.B. (1995), 'Recent conceptual Developments', *Proceedings of the Organisational Management Group* (The Association of Management) 13 (2), 19–26.

Wielen, J.M.M. van der, Berg, P.T. van de and Diggelen, W. van (1995), *Telewerk, de organisatorische aspecten* (Deventer: Kluwer Bedrijfswetenschappen).

Wijngaert, L. van de (2001) 'Internet in Context: Fysieke en affectieve toegang, geschiktheid; vraag, aanbod en Context', in Bouwman, H. (ed.), *Communicatie in de Informatiesamenleving* (Utrecht: Lemma).

Wijngaert, L. van de (2004), 'Old and New Media: A Threshold Model of Technology Use', in Oostendorp, H. van, Breure, L. and Dillon, A. (eds), *Creation, Use and Deployment of Digital Information* (Mahwah: Erlbaum).

Zegveld, W., Weijers, Th.C.M., Maas, T. van der and Lith, W. van (eds) (1995), *Handboek telewerken* (Assen: Van Gorcum).

PART V
Future Developments

Chapter 13

Enabling Humans to Control the Ethical Behaviour of Persuasive Agents

Boldur Bărbat, Andrei Moiceanu, Hermina Anghelescu

Introduction

Given that even conventional ICTs fail to fulfil user expectations as regards questions of ethics,[1] it is all the more necessary to take into account the ethical dimensions of software agents as they increasingly penetrate innovations across all types of application. Moreover, it becomes urgent to examine ethical issues when the very purpose of such agents is to interact with humans as well as with other agents, since software agents consistently act with their own intentions – regardless of whether they are opponents (for example, in e-commerce) or partners (for example, in e-therapy). The key point is that they try to persuade. Writers on the ethics of design have noted that from ancient rhetoric to modern advertising:

> the power of persuasion introduces additional legal and ethical questions. (…) No simple list could empower agent designers to guide their agent development efforts ethically and legally. (Heckman and Wobbrock, 2000)

Accordingly, the objectives of this chapter are:

1. To show how ethics – regarded 'a rational, consistent system for determining right and wrong, usually in the context of specific actions or policies' (Berdichevsky and Neunschwander, 1999) – can be part of the general design-space for agent-oriented applications.
2. To substantiate the urgency of user-driven[2] ethical behaviour of self-aware agents (Moiceanu and Bărbat, 2007).

---

1 For example, the Internet generates a range of fears about various (un)ethical facets of information online. This is shown in debates about online content (censorship vs. human rights in relation to filtering what can be uploaded), online access (transparency vs. the protection of children in relation to filtering what can be downloaded) and control (security vs. privacy in relation to what online information can be processed). At the time of writing problems such as those encountered by Yahoo in China show that the Big Brother effect is a real concern.

2 Here 'user-driven' means the ethics chosen by the user in real time during the interaction, not a system of ethics programmed in advance by a team of developers who are not able to predict all the specific environment conditions that may arise.

3. To illustrate such behaviour through examining an ethically relevant application domain.
4. To propose an 'ethical potentiometer'[3] based on this perspective.

What the chapter does not do is to compare or suggest particular ethical behaviours, or appraise motivations.

Since intention involves moral responsibility, the behaviour of software agents must show a wise blend of ethical intransigence and pragmatic effectiveness. Therefore, the different elements of ethics required in the design process need to correspond to categories of ethics as a system, expressing various degrees of rigour. At one extremity, one has the strict deontological form of ethics (total intransigence: standards can never be broken, regardless of causing pain), at the other end one has Epicurean act-based pragmatism (the ethics that talks in terms of 'pros and cons'); and somewhere in between one can place rule-based utilitarianism (rules are set in place only if always following them proves to be beneficial) (Berdichevsky and Neunschwander, 1999).

To demonstrate how this works in practice, it is convenient to use the example of a controversial ethical issue relating to an ethically uncontroversial application within a sensitive domain: e-therapy. Suppose that an agent acting as a virtual therapist aims to persuade a smoker to quit this harmful habit. The 'ethical potentiometer' can indicate what we have called 'variable ethical rigour', i.e. enabling us to switch on a scale from one ethical level to another. The ethically divisive topic that we have chosen is the clandestine practice of sending a patient subliminal messages.

The rest of the chapter is organised as follows: after trying to clarify a few concepts, the second section indicates the premises, rationale and approach of the chapter. The third section examines ethics as design-space dimension. The next section focuses on the 'ethical potentiometer', while the last describes other generic architectural features suitable for providing a benchmark for ethical behaviour. The conclusions summarise our views on controlling ethics in agent-based applications.

Concepts, Premises and Approach

Concepts

In order to explain the approach, some key concepts need to be made clear up front for the following reasons (especially valid in sensitive matters like ethics):

1. Concepts are derived from a general perspective and often develop it further;
2. Since perspectives are sometimes vague or subconscious, they are mostly *implicit* and they can remain hidden, whereas concepts have to be dealt with, hence they must be *explicit*;

---

3 A potentiometer is an instrument for measuring or adjusting electrical potential.

3. These implicit, sometimes fuzzy, connotations associated with (especially new) concepts often result in confusions that can be harmful;
4. Using terms that are partially, and ambiguously, synonymous increases confusion and distorts any debate.

The first question of terminology is whether the term '*e*-ethics' is appropriate to describe the field under discussion here. The widespread prefix '*e-*' started as an abbreviation for '*electronic*'. Nowadays, it may be attached to anything that has moved from a traditional form to its ICT alternative (for example e-mail, e-commerce, e-business, e-government, e-learning, e-procurement). In other words, and possibly oversimplified, it refers to 'something available via the computer and the Internet'. The problem is that ambiguity appears when the prefix is used metaphorically (for instance, the term '*e*Europe' is confusing, since it is not an alternative, 'electronic Europe', as in the case of 'e-mail').

An alternative term that has been used in the literature is 'digital ethics'. But using 'digital' instead of '*e-*' deserves a detailed commentary, since this too is problematic even if reflecting on its connotations is revealing. The first technological connotations of 'digital' were 'a set of discrete, distinct levels' or (at most), 'a sequence of discrete, distinct steps enabling users to control an application or a device'. At a later stage in its semantic journey, 'digital' described electronic technology that encoded information in binary form (i.e. not as a continuous spectrum of values, as in analogue representations). Since in computers the information is processed in both *electronic* and *digital* form, the terms could be used interchangeably when referring to ICTs. Moreover, 'digital' is more accurate (semantically); therefore, old terms preserve the '*e*'– (for example e-mail), while new ones use 'digital' (for example digital divide).

However, further connotations of the word 'digital' reflect the subconscious influence of an 'anti-technology' mindset: whereas nature – humans included – has always been intrinsically analogue, the invading ICT has been digital and, until a decade ago, that technology was unable to interact with all its users through a totally analogue interface. While ICTs are now powerful enough to afford interfaces enabling users to interact with technology in their natural, ancestral, analogue manner, nearly forty years of manifestly digital ICT structures have induced the feeling that 'digital' involves a kind of Frankenstein-like unnatural and dangerous feature (the next contrasting pair is more than enlightening in this respect: *electronic processing* versus *digital manipulation*). As a result, bad circumstances are more likely to get the attribute 'digital', while more palatable ones are characterised as 'electronic'. The confusion reaches its pinnacle when old, amenable, common technologies progressed from an analogue form to a digital one, dramatically amplifying their performances. Now, 'digital' is used reasonably in *digital camera* (because it replaced the old one, based on analogue technology) and acceptably in *digital television* (for the same reason). On the other hand, using the 'digital' is debatable in *digital certificate*, ridiculous in *digital certificate authority*, or in *digital privacy* and mystifying – even deplorable, given its current connotation – in *digital ethics* (the matter is very accurately discussed in McDonald and McDonald, 2004).

In a nutshell, nowadays the phrase 'digital ethics' is faulty because, although it is not defined as such, it refers to *human* ethical behaviour when using *digital* devices (or, more generally, ICTs). On the other hand, it is appropriate to refer to '*e*Hippocrates' (in e-therapy) or to '*e*Machiavelli' (in e-commerce) as figurative alternatives to their historical counterparts. But the term '*e*-ethics' is definitely debatable since it is not – or, it should not be – another type of ethics, just because ICTs are involved.

The need for clarifying such concepts is underlined by the diverse use of the phrase 'agent-based approach' in many important fields:

> There are two basic approaches to integrating ethics in business: the action-based approach, and the agent-based approach. The traditional approach is action-based in that it focuses on developing rules or guidelines to constrain management's actions (…) the agent-based approach concerns the fundamental character and motivations of the individual agent. (Dobson, 2006).

Premises

The need to explore the ethical behaviour of software agents stems from the set of premises listed below. Two of them, regarding the *necessity* and the *urgency* of carrying out such a scrutiny of ethics in the design of agents, were noted in the introduction. Here the premises are ranked from general (valid for any technology) to specific (focusing on e-therapy):

- Technology *per se* can be neither ethical nor unethical because it acts as a lever. But its applications can certainly raise ethical issues.
- Like any amplifier, powerful technologies increase the impact of (macro-architectural) application features – including their previously unnoticed side effects – and, hence, the risk of ethical problems.
- Two such major, innovative and influential technologies are *broadband* (offering huge amounts of information) and *agents* (proposing new ways to process it). Their combined effect is that humans act in entirely new environments that are open, dynamic and uncertain. In this lawless jungle, the risk of ethical problems becomes huge.
- The corollary is that in the age of 'computing as interaction' and of increasing application complexity (AgentLink III, 2005), in 'technologically unmanageable' environments (which are expanding, changing, unsure and fuzzy) intentionality is not restricted to humans. Indeed, agents interact with humans and with their non-human environment in a way that is consistent with their own intentions. Hence, they must behave ethically too.
- The ethical facet of any medical act is of major significance, and persuasion broadens that significance.
- The act of persuasion distributes responsibility for subsequent actions and it certainly involves the persuader's moral liability (Andersen, 1971).
- Persuasion is commonplace in e-therapy, due to the major role it plays in therapeutics – no matter what technology is employed.

Therefore, although the day when computers will be able to hypnotise humans may be still far away, it seems neither excessive nor premature to look at the ethical dimension of *any* agent-oriented applications.

Approach

In this chapter we attempt to examine the ethical dimension of agent-based applications and to show, via an experimental model, how ways to control agent ethical behaviour are driven by, and filtered through, the following assumptions, criteria, and guidelines:

- Persuasion is considered, according to Fogg's definition, as being 'an attempt to shape, reinforce, or change behaviours, feelings, or thoughts about an issue, object, or action' (Fogg, 1999). Here the motivation behind the persuasive act is ignored as being irrelevant.
- Although behavioural changes may be caused by the side effects of other technologies that are non-persuasive, what we are interested in here is the case where 'an attempt to' influence, as defined above, implies *intentionality* (with the connotation of there being a 'planned effect').
- From a user viewpoint, intentionality depends on his or her stance in relation to the technology. If, due to the complexity of a system, the user finds it impossible to view the situation from a mechanistic or a functional stance, users may instead show empathy with the computer as an 'intentional system (…) whose behaviour can be predicted by the method of attributing belief, desires and rational acumen'.[4] (Bărbat and Crețulescu, 2003).
- Ethical questions mainly arise when humans interact with intentional entities – for the most part, agents.[5]
- Hence, it is legitimate to simplify the situation and consider agent intentions while ignoring developer ones.
- One the one hand, ethical behaviour may be eased through agents showing, at least a primitive form of, self-awareness since such agents will consider a wider range of possible initiatives they might take compared to agents that are unaware of themselves. However, that very awareness may mean more unpredictability and hence more (potentially) unethical behaviour. As a result, the role of ethical restrictions on such agents becomes paramount.
- The focus here is on endogenously persuasive applications, where a persuasive intent is endogenous if it comes from within the application. That is because the strategies or tactics used are actually embedded within the application.[6]
- Only basic persuasive strategies are taken into account (for example, positive or negative feedback, role-play, simulated experiences, surveillance, environments of discovery, personalising (King and Tester, 1999) not the

---

4 Details regarding the 'Dennett stances' in ICT context are given in Bărbat (2005).

5 In curative applications, e-therapists must interact directly with the humans they take care of.

6 Almost all medical applications fall in this category.

fields where theories come from (sociology, psychology, rhetoric, etc.).

– The huge diversity displayed by all kinds of users (for example, depending on personality, cultural background, current area of interest, age, socio-economic status, motivation, level of information, even previous exposure to information technology) is amplified further in sensitive situations such as those where persuasion is involved.[7]

– Coupled strongly with the previous dimension, but having its own clear-cut idiosyncratic dynamics,[8] many elements in people's personal history change only gradually.[9] The problems that arise because of gradual change and where this crosses (fuzzy) borders are hard to avoid – for example, between (respecting) someone's privacy and feeling a sense of (social) responsibility.

– Because 'persuaders have always stood on uneasy ethical ground' (Berdichevsky and Neunschwander, 1999), so as to prevent unintended outcomes, an agent's behaviour should be more strictly controlled. The application developers should use their 'demiurgic privilege' as the 'gods' creating the software to incorporate ethical values into their agents.

The approach taken here is first to propose a field for testing an experimental model of human-controlled self-aware interface agents, albeit one of reduced cognitive complexity (Bărbat and Moiceanu, 2007). On this basis, in some later version of this model the level of ethical rigour could, on the one hand, be raised by the 'ethically aware Hippocratic e-therapist' (by itself creating an improved version of the 'ethical potentiometer'). But it could be lowered only by the user (Bărbat and Moiceanu, 2007). In order to compare the results from this test, the same example – the conflict-ridden practice of subliminal messages (SM) – was considered in relation to a variety of different ethical levels.

Ethics in the Design Space

When designing requirements for the persuasion-related features in the application domain being considered, (for example, credibility, rhetoric, agent voice pitch, rise/fall of agent emotions) one has to separate out the relevant concerns, identify the more important dimensions of the design-space and after that delimit the different elements of the particular application in question. However, why should ethics be a dimension of the design-space? Moreover, why should the level and type of ethics involved be adjustable?

Especially when designing such requirements in medical applications it is both very difficult and very necessary to combine ethical firmness and pragmatic value

---

7 The stress of persuasion alone can be enough to magnify behavioural dissimilarities.

8 For example, consider the role of anamnesis, the ability of the patient to recall his or her medical history, in any therapy and even making a diagnosis.

9 For instance, the effect of aging on one's driving abilities is obviously gradual. When the decline in a person's visual ability because of, say, a cataract problem, exceeds a (fuzzy) threshold, an ophthalmologist has a definite ethical problem as regards delaying or insisting upon cataract surgery.

for two main reasons. The first is the '*primum non nocere*' principle. As in the case of its human counterpart, a Hippocratic agent has to decline to carry out a task if it believes that it could be harmful. The second is because of the 'therapeutic role of unawareness'.[10]

As a result, it seems unavoidable that one has to have what we have called 'variable rigour', being able to switch – for example in intensive care units, maybe in real time – between one ethical consideration and another.[11]

From a technical perspective, in a simplified manner, this feature is actually related to the principle of 'being open to inspection' that already exists in traditional expert systems. This 'openness' (with its undertone of 'frankness') is nevertheless implemented to various degrees in all intentional agents because their trustworthiness depends on it. Such 'honesty' becomes vital in the case of topics that are evidently ethically controversial, such as the ethical questions implied when using clandestine persuasive practices, for example in the debate relating to the use of subliminal messages.[12]

As a result, there are two ways to shape the design-space:

1. For rather simple applications, one can imagine two dimensions related to ethics (see also Figure 13.1). The first, *CE* (Categories of *E*thics), would have at least the following possibilities: strict deontological ethics, CE_1; rule-based utilitarianism, CE_2; act-based pragmatism CE_3. The second, *SEI* (*S*trategies with *E*thic *I*mpact) would have equivalent categories this time corresponding to the strategies being applied (for instance, a 'carrot and stick' persuasion strategy).
2. Sometimes, in practice, it is necessary to use a more complex solution, merging the two dimensions outlined above into a single one, *E* (*E*thics), with elements E_i on a scale covering both *CE* and *SEI*.[13]

The 'Ethical Potentiometer'

The metaphor of the 'potentiometer' suggests that end users can adjust the ethical behaviour of their agents (for example through a scrollbar or button on the screen),

---

10 To avoid distorted perceptions and biased assertions, the need for the patient to be unaware of what is happening is sometimes essential in medical diagnosis and testing (if one takes the 'placebo" as an example). But is often required in therapy too, primarily in modern therapeutics, where physician, patient, and family act on a team-work basis. Hence, a virtual therapist must be carefully guided by the human therapist in order to circumvent discussions about a topic that could mislead – and, thus, harm – a particular patient in a particular situation.

11 To what extent such a feature has to be under the control of the physician, nurse and/or patient is outside the scope of this chapter.

12 Due to ease with which they can be used in applications, the temptation to use subliminal messages is high.

13 If gradual positive and/or negative feedback is used within a 'carrot and stick' persuasive strategy, then some further persuasive strategies that would be unacceptable within

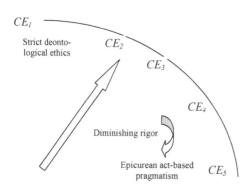

LEGEND

CE: Category of Ethics

CE_1:   avoid SM

CE_2:   if SM are allowed, then the user
         should be able to cut them off

CE_3:   else, at least to check them

CE_4:   when their matter must be hidden,
         the patient is warned that SM are used

CE_5:   SM are used without notice

Figure 13.1   'Ethical potentiometer' (variable ethical rigor)

in the same way as they fine-tune the sound level with a volume 'potentiometer'. The arrow shown in Figure 13.1 tries to evoke a sense that the nature and level of ethical behaviour can be *varied*, not that it can be *measured*. In addition, we note that by rotating the arrow clockwise, ethical rigour will diminish.

As instances of *CEi*, the 'degrees' of a five-positions ethical scale, represented metaphorically in Figure 13.1 are:

1. Subliminal messages are forbidden;
2. Subliminal messages are allowed, but the patient can see them in advance and is able to stop them;
3. The patient can see the subliminal messages in advance but cannot turn them off;
4. When the actual topic needs to be hidden from the patient for the therapy to work, the patient is warned that subliminal messages are used but can neither see them nor turn them off;
5. Subliminal messages are used without notifying the patients (for example, for patients with severe drinking or drug problems).

An example of how a subliminal message might look is shown in the snapshot, where the image of the 'human' flashes up very quickly (Figure 13.2).[14]

---

strict ethics need not be eliminated explicitly because their potential ethical impact is already controlled through this gradual feedback mechanism. For instance, if approval works as a carrot and tends to become flattery it will still not be a problem because the ethically arguable strategy of 'overdone' flattery is avoided through the very fact that feedback is gradual. Likewise, if warnings are enough of a stick to bring about prudent patient behaviour (for example following unpleasant medical prescriptions) then we will never reach the stage of causing the ethically problematic state where the patient experiences exaggerated fear.

14 This image was never actually used as subliminal message – not even when testing its optimal exposure time on screen.

Generic Architectural Features as Benchmarks for Ethics

Human-agent interaction is fundamentally unlike that between humans and conventional software because of the illusion-creating features of agents as entities mimicking biological organisms. Therefore, most architectural features related to agents could exhibit ethical side-effects. In this chapter we discuss only those having direct links to ethics.

The large palette of potentially ethical behaviour (covering categories of ethics, strategies and methods, awareness, intensity and form of expression) means that we require versatility in choosing and priorities in applying suitable mechanisms for addressing these ethical issues. This implies that many ethical variables have to be handled in real time, including transparency, forgiveness, deontological intransigence, confidentiality, decency, etc. On the other hand, in therapy the fine-tuning of ethical features becomes essential.[15] Hence, since the example discussed above concerns the technology infrastructure relating to the ethics of medical acts, any software mechanism involved should promote as much as possible continuity and flexibility in varying those ethics as a blend. In other words, these mechanisms should reflect first and foremost the qualities shared by most ethical features: a well-

Figure 13.2   Snapshot with subliminal messages

---

15 For example, it is sometimes difficult to separate, categorically, transparency from confidentiality or even from decency

balanced trade-off between evenness and flexibility. In this respect the previous example with subliminal messages was not challenging enough since the mechanism we outlined was confined to only five positions on the 'potentiometer'.

Based on this general framework, characterising the generic architecture for individual agents becomes straightforward. The agent is seen as an entity situated in an environment, with goals, actions and knowledge within a given domain. It integrates three basic qualities implied by the very agent metaphor. Thus, when clients hire agents (in any domain, for example banking, real-estate, travel) they expect:

1. personalisation (agents act considering the specific momentary needs of their clients);
2. authorisation (agents act on behalf of their clients, within the limits stipulated by the hiring agreement);
3. competence.

In short, the agent metaphor suggests that I hire an agent when I do not have enough time or lack competence to handle the problem myself. Now the agent could also have (a limited kind of) self-awareness (here, being aware of its own 'ethical level'). Judged from the ethical standpoint, personalisation can be user-driven, but authorisation and self-awareness stem from the application developer. Apart from these extra restrictions, the essential agency characteristics (i.e. autonomy, reactivity, pro-activeness, communication ability and longevity) are carried out as usual. Regarding the optional characteristics of agents, only three of them are subject to both ethical and medically specific requirements:

– *Benevolence* and *rationality*. Although still unclear, such concepts have to be considered, because of the 'primum non nocere' principle. Thus, agents shall act so as to accomplish their tasks, at least insofar as those do not challenge their 'beliefs'. For instance, a benevolent virtual therapist can have in its ontology[16] a rule stating that when the patient asks for a break during a normal therapy session, it should be granted. But if the case-specific information shows that the patient is under intensive care, other rules in its ontology (regarding medical urgency) might lead the agent to the belief that it should deny the request. Fortunately, this problem is not very important.[17]

– *Trustworthiness*. Interface agents in particular, especially when their task is to persuade, have to be *credible* in order to be effective. Agent credibility itself has two components: *expertise* (outside the scope of this chapter) and *trustworthiness* (in short, the agent's 'ethos'). Credibility, viewed in medical contexts almost as commitment (patients recover faster and better when they rely on their – virtual or human – therapists), can be enhanced through *cooperation* between the therapist

---

16 A kind of knowledge-base including the agent's general culture and expertise composed of domain-related concepts and rules to use them in its actions.

17 Since, in practice, there are not yet agents with many strong beliefs, this aspect was not considered in the model.

and patient. For instance, the agent becomes more credible when it tolerates some flexibility or even minor patient faults as regards the prescribed therapy and can set up a partnership with the patient. However, that depends on the ethics applied (when ethical rigour is extreme, forgiveness is out of the question and even fault tolerance is very limited).

– *Self-awareness*. This elusive and debated feature is rooted in two ideas of Hofstadter (1999): a) 'consciousness is not an on/off phenomenon, but admits of degrees, grades, shades'; b) the first step is self-reference.[18] However, self-reference is applied in an unusual way: when the agent decides to switch to more rigorous ethical behaviour, it clones itself into a 'more principled' agent.

Other (not agent specific) features can also have a significant impact upon ethical behaviour:

– *Privacy*. Because various stakeholders (for example, patients, nurses, physicians, parents) have different ethical stances, in order to avoid misuse of confidential information a multi-level scheme of privilege, rights and/or restriction filters should limit access to data and to some facilities.

– *Openness to inspection*. To enable the patient to check their earnestness, all agents can be interrupted during their discourse, by clicking the 'Explain' icon to require an explanation (where the label 'explanation' has both connotations: to *give details* and to *justify*).

– *The dynamic priorities of agents*. In the case of some persuasive strategies (for example 'carrot and stick') the ethical behaviour may be modified over time (either through a pre-existent script built into the agent's design or through the patient's choice). Since such a mechanism is usually not implemented directly in common operating systems, it has to be simulated. For instance, in an application of higher complexity, involving several agents representing different levels of ethical rigour, an intransigent agent has its intransigence – or the intensity of any other ethical attitude – could be decreased (by itself or by another agent) by 'sliding down' over time (like simulated emotions do in affective computing: they appear suddenly but disappear slowly).

As regards the software tools employed, the current implementation of the 'potentiometer' (albeit technologically unchallenging) represents the first productive attempt of the design team to program using Python and Spyse.

Finally we have some speculative remarks about the artificial intelligence paradigms suitable to implement ethical agent behaviour. To prevent unintended conduct, or conduct that one could not reasonably predict, in open, dynamic and

---

18 Self-reference is implied from the beginning by any kind of self-awareness (the very use of the word 'I'). A child shows self-awareness when it refers to its 'self' using 'I' (at the age of about two years, when it begins to recognise itself in the mirror). For instance, when it desires a cake it says: 'I want a cake' and no longer 'Give a cake to Johnny'. (Only a few animal species pass the mirror test: dolphins, elephants and some monkeys but not dogs or cats!)

uncertain environments, agent (inter)actions having potential ethical implications should be more strictly controlled.

Conclusions

Conclusions (1) – (5) pertain to the research per se as regards controlling ethics in agent-based applications, whereas (6) – (8) pertain to the actual experimental model given as an example (subliminal messages in e-therapy).

1. Despite being 'ethically neutral', broadband technology amplifies the risks of ethical problems, above all in modern applications, where humans and agents interact in open and uncertain environments.
2. Management of such risks can be effective and affordable even if ethically divisive issues are involved.
3. Users should control the ethical behaviour of interface agents according to 'human ethics', ignoring suspicious concepts like 'digital ethics'.
4. The easily implemented 'ethical potentiometer' supports the first three conclusions, since it is able to model suitably a wide range of ethics and to control agent behaviour from the perspective of the chosen level of ethical rigor.
5. Neither research nor application development can advance without extensive transdisciplinary research (involving not only domain theory and ethics themselves, but connecting them to psychology, sociology, application domains, etc.).
6. Due to the impact of ethics in any medical act, in agent-based medical applications virtual therapists showing ethical behaviour can contribute to both the therapy's effectiveness and patient acceptance.
7. Agent-oriented approaches based on design-space dimensions (here, including an ethics dimension) are shown to be useful within medical informatics, both for research purposes and for the development of applications (initially, in therapy).
8. Modelling the ethical behaviour of e-therapists via self-cloning (self-aware) agents indicates that the feature of agent self-awareness is appealing not just for agent-oriented research but for application design too.

Looking forward to future directions[19] of research in this field we would propose further investigation of the impact of uncertainty upon ethical behaviour and the way it is perceived. In other words, what are the implications for ethics when interacting in uncertain environments?

---

19 The cautious term 'directions' instead of the usual 'plans' underlines an often neglected fact: it is unthinkable to consider that such research could succeed that is not transdisciplinary in nature.

References

AgentLink III (2005), *Agent-based computing. AgentLink Roadmap: Overview and Consultation Report*, University of Southampton, September 2005. Available at: <http://www.agentlink.org/roadmap/al3rm.pdf>.

Andersen, K. (1971), *Persuasion Theory and Practice* (Boston: Allyn and Bacon).

Bărbat, B.E. (2005), 'Communicating in the world of humans and ICTs', in Fortunati, L. (ed.), *COST Action 269. e-Citizens in the Arena of Social and Political Communication*, EUR21803, Office for Official Publications of the European Communities, Luxembourg.

Bărbat, B.E. and Crețulescu, R. (2003), 'Digital Ethics. Agents, Between Machiavelli and Hippocrates' *The Good, the Bad, the Irrelevant: The User and the Future of Information and Communication Technologies*, Conference proceedings, COST Action 269, Helsinki, 3–5 September 2003. Available at: <http//goodbad.uiah.fi>.

Bărbat, B.E. and Moiceanu, A. (2007), 'I Agent' *The Good, the Bad, the Unexpected: The User and the Future of Information and Communication Technologies*, Conference proceedings, COST Action 298, Moscow, 23–25 May 2007.

Berdichevsky, D. and Neunschwander, E. (1999), 'Toward an Ethics of Persuasive Technologies', *Communications of the ACM* 42 (5), 51–8.

Dennett, D. (1987), *The Intentional Stance* (Cambridge: MIT Press).

Dobson, J. (2006), 'Applying virtue ethics to business: The agent-based approach', *Electronic Journal of Business Ethics and Organization Studies* 11 (2). Available at: <http://ejbo.jyu.fi/index.cgi?page=articles/0901_3>.

Fogg, B.J. (1999), 'Persuasive Technologies', *Communications of the ACM* 42 (5), 27–29.

Heckman C.E. and Wobbrock, J.O. (2000), 'Put your best face forward: anthropomorphic agents, e-commerce consumers, and the law', *Procedures 4th International Conference on Autonomous agents*, ACM Press, 435–42, Barcelona, 2000.

Hofstadter, D.R. (1999), *GÖDEL, ESCHER, BACH: An Eternal Golden Braid* (New York: Basic Books).

King, P. and Tester, J. (1999), 'The Landscape of Persuasive Technologies', *Communications of the ACM* 42 (5), 31–38, 1999.

McDonald, J. and McDonald, M.A. (2004), 'Digital Ethics? Can digital manipulation produce a benign shooting environment?', *Wildlife Photography. May 2004. Question of the Month*. Available at: <www.hoothollow.com/Question-May%202004.html>.

Moiceanu, A. and Bărbat, B.E. (2007) 'Ethical Behaviour of Self-aware Agents' *The Good, the Bad, the Unexpected: The User and the Future of Information and Communication Technologies*. Conference proceedings, COST Action 298, Moscow, 23–25 May 2007.

Chapter 14

Challenging Sensory Impairment[1]

Keith Gladstone

Introduction

There is no doubt that the rapid growth of ICTs over the last 20 to 30 years has had a major positive impact on the lives of many disabled people. For visually impaired (VI) people, some of the earliest uses of computer technology enhanced access to information both by facilitating the production of large print and by enhancing the rapid transcription from text to braille. Developments such as suck-blow keys for paraplegic people and text-to-speech systems for blind people enable disabled people to use computers directly. The growth of the Internet and the more general use of the World Wide Web since 1993, though causing many problems along the way, now provide disabled people not just with a window on the information world but one that they can use without acknowledging their impairment to anyone else. As each new technology is introduced, projects are initiated that seek to find uses to address disabled people's needs. The nagging question is why, with all of this technology available, do surveys of disabled people still show many of them living in poverty, isolated from their social communities?

This chapter, while acknowledging the benefits of ICT, focuses on the limitations of technology in terms of addressing the deep-seated needs of disabled people, particularly those with a sensory impairment. Whereas part of the cause is the inherent human qualities of our five senses that are outside the scope of technology, another major element is the lack of an holistic approach in many developments. Although the discussion focuses on disabled people, it also throws into sharper relief effects that can be traced in the wider community.

The Reality of Sensory Impairment

As sentient beings, knowledge of the world is entirely dependent on what humans perceive through their senses. In its primitive form, such knowledge is gained through direct observation of the environment as it is seen, heard, touched, smelt and

1 Much of the background work was part funded by the EU Commission TIDE & IST programmes and by the Royal National Institute of Blind People (RNIB) through a variety of projects. The views expressed within this paper are the author's own and should be assumed neither to reflect nor to predict RNIB policy in these areas.

tasted. Any study of the workings of the brain to interpret this mass of sensory input shows not only the complexity of the task but also how often the brain can become confused (Ramachandran, 2003), as in the case of optical illusions. MRI scans of the brain also demonstrate how any specific sensory input rapidly energises seemingly unconnected areas of the brain as the initial trigger is characterised, analysed, combined with earlier memories and, if necessary, processed by the conscious intellect. As I write, the particular photons hitting my retina are progressively combined to what I recognise as bright orange in a flower shape. Learnt information tells me that I am seeing a nasturtium flower while my higher intellect places this in context with the garden, the time of year, the fact that the sun is shining and a host of other reflections that seem to have little to do with those initial photons. Whereas everyone understands the power of our senses to evoke feelings and memories, no one really understands how that occurs nor can they, in scientific terms, define what a feeling is (Greenfield, 2002).

The use of the intellect has allowed humans to take one giant leap that is generally assumed to be beyond the capability of any other animal: the use of language. Here, 'language' is used in its widest sense as being any method of coding that allows humans to communicate with one another or to collect, store and retrieve thoughts. Clearly, this includes spoken and written material but it also encompasses the visual and aural arts as well as the world of touch. In time, ways may also be devised to communicate through taste and smell, though even now the judicious use of perfume, for instance, can recall some treasured memory. Stephen Pinker (Pinker, 1995) argues that a great part of the mechanism of language is innate, which explains why even young children can master many of its intricacies without undue effort. Even he concedes that what needs to be learnt is vocabulary, which in a spoken or written sense defines the link between words and what they represent. Both the mechanism and the coding of language lie at the heart of the use of ICT. Any impairment in the link between the intention of the originator and the intellect of the recipient will cause a poorer quality of communication.

Those who suffer a sensory or cognitive impairment will find that at times they do not perceive the same level of richness in the environment as their unimpaired peers. The deaf person will not hear the tinkling of the fountain, the blind person will not see the delicate gradation of colour in the flower of the foxglove and the person suffering from dementia may not recall particular memories. It is often said that beauty is in the eye of the beholder. If the eye does not see then, for the would-be viewer, the beauty does not exist. Even leaving such philosophical thoughts aside, it has to be acknowledged that any sensory impairment, by definition, will reduce the potential information flow. Although some detail may be missed, visually people assess their surroundings literally in the twinkling of an eye. That is not to denigrate hearing. One may well hear the speeding car, and react defensively, well before it comes into view. A typical approach to mitigate the effects of impairment to vision or hearing is to move some information to another modality, for instance, by describing a picture or using subtitles. However, any shift from one modality to another inevitably restricts the target modality's ability to perform its original function.

An analysis of a great many ICT developments shows that they concentrate on tangible elements such as text, graphics and sounds. This is not surprising since these are the ones most amenable to computer processing. On the other hand, people, i.e. the users of ICT, operate primarily on the level of thoughts, concepts and feelings. The human-computer-human interface works when it enhances the quality and effectiveness of the communication of those intangible elements. Where the computer simply acts as a carrier, such as transferring an image over time or space, then the communication is generally effective. When impairment in the user's access necessitates a change in modality then the quality of communication can suffer markedly. Although impairments are normally thought of in terms of disability, they also occur where there is a hostile environment, for example trying to hear in a noisy machine shop, or when involved in particular activities, such as wanting to read while driving.

The ubiquitous nature of the computer has tended to mean that information is usually taken to refer generally to that which would traditionally have been printed in books and other publications. There is also some interesting work around environmental information, for instance the use of global positioning and localised information to tell a hungry user where the nearest restaurant is to be found. Whereas such information fulfils an important segment of human needs, the primary and essential use of information is far wider and is often taken for granted. Maybe the need is best illustrated by the elderly lady who said to an evaluator '*I am sure that all that technology is very useful but my problem is that I won't see my granddaughter grow up.*' The narrow view of information has meant that many proposed 'solutions' fail to address users' needs sufficiently to be practically worthwhile.

The UK Government estimate that more than 10 per cent of the population are disabled (Office of National Statistics, 2001), while the Royal National Institute for Deaf People (RNID) claim that 9 million people in the UK (15 per cent of the population) are deaf or hard of hearing (RNID, 2004) and the Royal National Institute of Blind People (RNIB) estimate that 2 million people in the UK (3.5 per cent of the population) suffer serious sight loss (RNIB, 2004). Analysis of the figures shows a very clear correlation between disability and age, with its attendant problems of ill health and growing isolation. Whereas coping with the disabling effects of failing faculties is hard, far harder is the emotional trauma when the future looks so bleak and full of pain. Clearly, this is not and will not be everyone's experience but the usual factor that lifts the gloom is human rather than technological. Again, this is illustrated by another elderly client who said, '*All I want to do is to reminisce about the old times with my friends, and as the years go by there are less of those.*'

There is no doubt that ICT has addressed some very important issues within the lower levels of Maslow's hierarchy of needs (Maslow, 1970) (see Figure 14.1). For instance, the increasing deployment of health and safety monitoring is enabling many people to retain their independence without putting themselves at undue risk. Email and mobile phones have enabled people to stay in far closer touch with their loved ones. There is still a tendency, however, for technology to lead the way, encouraging people to 'discover' needs of which they were hitherto unaware, or put another way, technology increasingly represents a solution that is looking for a problem.

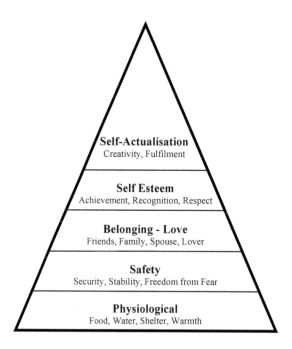

Figure 14.1   Maslow's hierarchy of needs

The Place of Assistive Technology

As has been noted, any sensory impairment means that a particular modality is hard or impossible to use. If that mode is used by an ICT system then information needs to be shifted to an alternative mode. For many people with partial loss of vision or hearing, the alternative information channel is used to support rather than replace their residual sense. A good example is the use of television subtitles where someone with limited hearing may only read the subtitles to provide clues as to what they heard imperfectly. For people who have almost no useful residual sight or hearing, the alternative presentation becomes the only means of access to the information source. If the shift in modality is to be successful then the transformation must retain the integrity of the original and the target modality must have sufficient slack.

Subtitles are usually successful because they take up a limited portion of the television screen that often contains relatively redundant material. However, if the television producer wishes to use that area, for instance to identify an interviewee, then that slack is no longer available and contention arises. In many cases, there is no slack in the target modality. There have been many proposals aimed at helping a blind person to be more aware of their environment. These involve a number of potential data sources including 'talking signs', proximity detectors, GPS based information or interpretation of images from a digital camera. The output to the user is usually envisaged in the form of an audio stream, both speech and non-speech, that relays useful information. One of the problems with such systems is that the user is already fully utilising hearing both for orientation and as a warning of potential danger. The extra input is likely to interfere with this primary function and, hence, such systems prove to be far less useful than might initially appear.

Each modality has its own characteristics. People are able to take in vast amounts of information visually, though they generally only consciously process a small minority of it. This ability allows them to scan whole pages of print and gather a surprising amount of the information before starting to read in detail. Print, per se, holds no clue to the emotive content of the text. Speech, however, cannot escape placing text within an emotive context. The climax to an amorous encounter will leave a quite different impression on the listener if it is read with sympathy, empathy, enmity or just blandly. Speech is also unidirectional, which means that the listener has to carry out a complex cue and review function in order to emulate the print reader's ability to reread an earlier sentence or paragraph. On the other hand, speech will support simultaneous information tracks, such as in conversations, that are difficult to represent adequately in print. Tactile codes, such as braille, are read very slowly, which restricts their utility for dealing with long documents. This diversity of characteristics means that successful mapping between modalities can be very complex.

The prime information standards that form the basis of electronic publishing, such as XML and HTML, have an inbuilt assumption about the independence of text, structure and presentation. For instance, sections of text can be designated as headings or specific types of paragraph with decisions about how they will be rendered being dependent on the output device and the recipient's whim. Whereas this may be suitable for professional publications, such as this book, it manifestly does not hold for promotional material or 'glossy' publications where significant parts of the message are contained within the graphical elements and presentation. Any transformation of such material to another modality must respect not just the content but also the way in which it was used and the part it played within the whole presentation. For instance, a picture in a child's reading book that shows children from many nationalities playing would be far better represented in audio by a babble of voices than by a verbal description. This not only performs the same function as the picture in the book but also coincides with a blind child's actual experience of the playground.

There has been a great deal of effort to establish standards and methods whereby major computer applicators, including the World Wide Web, can be accessed by visually impaired people using devices that perform dynamic transformations to speech or braille. For many people these are very effective, though they are not necessarily easy to learn or to use. Whereas such systems do allow VI people to have independent access to these types of applications, their usability is more questionable. The differentiation of accessibility and usability is being explored by many researchers in the field and hinges on fitness for purpose. As an example, all parts of an e-learning course may be accessible to a VI user, but if the system does not include an environment that is conducive to learning then it is less usable.

Holistic Design

It is a truism that people live whole lives. However, ICT developments seem frequently to ignore the context and environment in which they might be used. For instance, there have been a number of projects that have looked at how a blind shopper might use a hand-held scanner to read the barcode on a product in order to pull all the relevant information from the shop's product database. As a technique, it has been shown to be reasonably successful even though barcodes do not have a consistent position on the packaging. However, looking at the context in which it would be used, say, the supermarket, such a development looks far less attractive. Some problems in this supermarket example were solvable. At the moment the data held in most product databases is far too abbreviated to be of practical help and does not include more general information about ingredients, nutrition, cooking hints or special offers. But this extra data can be supplied. However, there is a far more intractable problem with the use of the scanner. Presuming that the VI user has found their way to the right part of the shop, which is rarely easy in modern shops, and has discovered that the product that he took from the shelf is not the one he wants, what does he do next? He has to put it back, which could be difficult, and then decide whether to try the adjacent product, which may be identical, or move further down the shelf, with the probability of missing what he wants. Such a trial and error strategy will never meet the user's shopping requirements and, without finding a suitable solution to this issue, there is little point in refining the scanner technology. One participant evaluating the scanner technology identified a more general objection. He said that shopping in the local supermarket was one of the few opportunities when he met anyone else, so going around the shop with an assistant was also an important time of social contact. Although he undoubtedly needed to buy food, the approach was incorrectly assuming that this was his sole need when shopping.

Holistic design means considering all aspects of design from the users' point of view. Who are the users? Obviously, they are those who directly benefit from the system or device. But they also include the people involved in installation and support. For each user, there is an interface that has to be learnt and used but any assessment of usability must take into account such characteristics as frequency of use, motivation and user competence. The concept of cost-benefit analysis can be useful both in a financial and non-financial sense. One system purported to give users tactual access to map information. However, it was so large and expensive that it would have had to be located in a library or other central place, so users would have to travel. The user's access to the map information was slow and non-intuitive, meaning that they had to learn and memorise how to use the system. For many people, the cognitive conversion from limited tactual input to useful mental image is a difficult, and often unsuccessful, process. Hence, for the end user there were a large number of 'costs'. For intermediaries supporting the use of this device, the size and complexity of the system meant that it both used a lot of space and needed the availability of a trained operator. Meanwhile, the benefits were less easy to enumerate, leaving the whole development looking decidedly unattractive. This is an extreme example but it serves to illustrate how developers can become too closely immured in their detailed design to consider how it will be practically used.

The holistic approach also requires developers to ensure that their designs are maintainable. Many projects concentrate on the mechanism for processing source data such that it fulfils an identified need. Frequently, the reason a project falters is not the inadequacy of the process but because the data source was either non-existent or could not be maintained. Good examples are web sites where information maintenance is so labour intensive that they are constantly out-of-date. Another example is a mapping project based in Dublin that could provide the user with information about local shops. This foundered because it was necessary for someone to walk regularly through the whole area in order to gather the data about changes to shop types and names.

Design for All?

The objective of designing products, services and systems such they are equally useful for all potential users is one that should be included in every design brief. Unfortunately, it has to be recognised that it is not always achievable and that some users' requirements are in direct conflict with others. Anyone who has impaired manual dexterity finds the tiny keyboards of most mobile phones virtually unusable but that small size is dictated by the desires of the wider population. The need of partially sighted people for high contrast and large text on the controls of domestic appliances is less than acceptable to people who prefer low impact pastel shades. RNIB has worked with many manufacturers to instigate good design practice such that the needs of VI people are addressed where possible. In some cases, the outcomes have been unexpected. RNIB now sells a range of coloured braille paper not because the colour offers any direct advantage to a blind child but because all the other children in an integrated class have their work displayed on coloured paper.

Conflicts of purpose arise in many other areas of ICT design, often to the frustration of those affected. For instance, many e-commerce sites have introduced a novel way of preventing access by automatic systems through asking the user to input a number hidden in an image. This works well unless you cannot see the actual number because then such a device acts as a complete barrier. Similar issues have arisen around other security measures, including digital rights management, since the way in which they work inherently prevents access by assistive technology devices. The use of automatic teller machines (ATMs) by VI people raises related issues since large, high contrast text on ATM screens or the addition of speech technology immediately reduces the privacy on which much of their security is dependent.

In information systems, 'design for all' has come to mean ensuring that exactly the same 'content' is available to all users regardless of their method of access. The extent to which this is effective hinges upon our understanding of content and the degree to which it is invariant in different contexts. Too often, content is understood to be only the textual elements with little thought about how that is only meaningful within its context. Giving directions to a blind person such as 'near the church with a steeple' is clearly not very useful, whereas reference to kerbs and railings could be far more relevant. As shown above, change of modality can challenge the notion of content. For instance, what is the 'content' of a painting and to what extent is that caught in a text description? Even with pure text, however, the situation is not straightforward since the ability of a sighted person to scan large documents and select specific parts of interest is not available to anyone dependent on assistive technology. This led one senior VI member of RNIB to ask, '*Now so much material is available to me in audio, how do I find time to live the rest of my life?*'

Some very interesting developments are seeking to provide automated document summaries as one approach to the problem but they usually need access to large numbers of related documents and some very powerful processing in order to be effective.

The Human Touch

It is important to stress that none of these problems are caused by the technologies per se but rather by their application, often driven by cost. Most organisations, whether formal or informal, are seeking to reduce costs and, in general, people are seen as more costly than machines. The question that is rarely asked, but is an implicit thread running throughout this chapter, is whether the machine does or even can perform as well as a person. Again, it must be acknowledged that machines are usually very effective at what they are designed to do but, as noted above, they are often not designed to holistically address people's needs.

The relationships between the external stimuli that are perceived, such as light and sound, and the interpretations that people make, consciously or unconsciously, are very complex. As a result, impairment of any portion of the information paths tends to be far reaching in influencing people's interaction with the environment around them. For example, someone who has minimal sight will not only have problems in finding their way to the local shops but could also walk straight past their closest friend without ever realising it. Having someone, whether they are a social worker, a friend or a family member, to act as a companion provides a richness that goes far beyond what might considered to be mobility. This means that the human agents must be prepared to be open in the way that they interact. It may be preferable to phone an impersonal interactive system than to be answered by someone who is clearly bored with the job. However, an open and friendly voice on the other end of the telephone can entirely change one's day.

It is in the personal touch that so many deep needs can be met. Encroaching sensory impairment, with the growing loss of the world of vision or sound, is a very traumatic experience for many people. Society likes to deal with this by registering people with labels such as blind or deaf before opening up a range of support mechanisms. The reluctance by many, especially elderly, people to seek registration is often seen as an attempt to avoid the stigma of such labels. However, it may have far more to do with people not wanting to admit what is happening to them. Many people have aging relatives who will say things like, '*I am not blind – I just don't see so well*' or '*Young people talk so quietly nowadays.*'

As the world closes in then the opportunity to live life through memories and the eyes and ears of other people becomes increasingly important. So, the pleasure of receiving a letter from cousin Stephanie can be greatly enhanced when it is read by a close family member who can recall some of the happy events of the past. The automatic scanner may do the same job of reading the text but could never provide the emotional context.

As discussed above, the effective transformation of information content between modalities is not a simple mapping exercise. This is well known in the world of advertising where no one would dream of simply describing a magazine advertisement for use on the radio. The mechanical transform usually works well where the user has the prime motivation to pull out the information, as is the case with scientific papers, minutes of meetings or fiction. The approach is far less successful where the provider has the prime motivation to push the information, as in promotional literature, junior education or many leisure books. In the world of print, this difference is clearly seen in the quality of presentational design with 'pull' information generally being remarkably bland. Due to its inherent nature, there are only a very limited number of design options possible with braille apart from substantially modifying the text to better suit a slow reading speed. For audio, however, there are limitless possibilities to bring the rich and diverse world of sound to bear but they can only be effectively used through substantial design effort. Where the textual content contains all or the great majority of the information, such as in a novel, the presentation has little affect on access. This allows a relatively simple transform between modalities such as text to braille or audio. For fiction, many recipients prefer the rendition to be as plain as possible in order to facilitate their direct interaction with the text. When presentation becomes more task orientated, such as creating a learning environment, then the strategies used for visual, audio or multi-modal interaction differ significantly. Although there are attempts to develop mechanisms to automate the transformation process between, for instance, print and audio, there is little evidence that they produce quality outcomes for the user.

Moving back through the information chain from the user interface and through the transformation process, we arrive at data collection and collation. This tends to demand a high level of human resources and, as noted earlier, is often the point at which otherwise excellent developments falter. Often the issue can be viewed primarily as who pays. The UK mapmakers, Ordnance Survey, can afford to spend vast sums on surveying to maintain their truly excellent databases because of the massive market that they serve. As they identify new potential markets, so they modify their data collection. However, even Ordnance Survey cannot record or keep track of a great deal of the detail that affects the mobility of a VI person, such as where the number 7 bus stops or the advent of a pavement café. This sort of information can only be provided locally and has to be fine tuned to the user's sphere of interest.

The Wider Community

Although this discussion has centred on the needs of people who have a sensory impairment, many of the arguments can also be applied more generally. There are plenty of instances, for example, where people's use of vision or hearing is impaired either by the environment or by what they are doing. For example, voice access to information services may be desirable for many people who are on the move and have no access to a networked computer. Although such people do not suffer the wider disabling effects of impairment, they still experience the relatively slow information channels and the cognitive load of working with voice access as a sequential medium.

Many of the issues discussed about information presentation are also relevant where information is displayed on a small screen device, such as a PDA. Physically, such a device is able to display full standard web pages but it is not possible for anyone to use them effectively. Again, the transformation, in this case of web pages to a small screen, is not straightforward and needs significant design input for a quality outcome.

People tend to take much of the world for granted, not least because they have amazing brains that allow them to deal unconsciously with most of what they sense. The degree of complexity and redundancy means that a better understanding of the processes we all invoke can be achieved by studying situations in which the number of cognitive strategies is limited. Thus, studies with people who have sensory impairments are an inherently excellent basis for improving insight into the experience of the wider population. By viewing the relationship between humans and their environment from this stance, there is a far better chance of developing technological solutions that are in tune with users rather than trying to impose unrealistic strictures.

Conclusions

There is no doubt that ICT solutions have transformed the lives of many people who have impaired vision or hearing loss by giving increased access to information. Assistive technology makes it possible for deaf people to use telephones and for blind people to navigate the Internet. Global Positioning Systems, now accurate to a few metres, could form the basis of many location systems, which could be a major boon for people who cannot see. As technology takes advantage of increased power and speed of processing then all sorts of wonders seem to hover on the horizon. Advances in natural language, speech recognition and optical systems are presumed to offer a future where the computer system will largely overcome sensory impairment.

For many visually impaired people, the promised potential seems to be always beyond their grasp. This chapter has shown that some ICT 'solutions' only address peripheral needs or presume an undue technical competence. More often, they ignore the user's context, particularly factors such as poor mobility or limited finance. The greatest problem, though, is the technological leap, usually seen in the assumption that the carefully controlled lab model operated by technicians will work just as well when used by the non-specialist in a real environment. The major discrepancy between, on the one hand, user needs and technological potential and, on the other hand, actual take up is often put down to fundamental demographic correlation between sensory disability and age. It is also presumed that this effect will diminish with time, as increasing numbers of elderly people will have been technology users during their earlier life.

Until technology is able to correct a sensory impairment entirely, any technical aid can only offer a partial solution. However, for most people the physical effects of impairment are only part of the story. The tendency to replace human based services by technical systems in the name of independence for the user and economy for the supplier addresses neither the real implications for the user nor the complexity of the world in which people live. The human element in collection, presentation and delivery of ICT services is, and remains, vital.

References

Greenfield, S. (2002), *The Private Life of the Brain* (London: Penguin).

Maslow, A. (1970), *Motivation and Personality*, 2nd Edn. (New York Harper & Row).

Office of National Statistics (2001), *Economic activity status of disabled people: by gender, Spring 2001: Social Trends 32*. Available at http://www.statistics.gov. uk/STATBASE/ ssdataset.asp?vlnk=5094.

Pinker, S. (1995), *The Language Instinct* (London: Penguin).

Ramachandran, V. (2003), *The Emerging Mind: The BBC Reith Lectures 2003* (London: Pro-file Books).

RNIB (2004), *Research Library statistics on sight problems*. Available at <http://www. rnib. org.uk/xpedio/groups/public/documents/publicwebsite/public_researchstats. hcsp>.

RNID (2004), *Facts and figures on deafness and tinnitus*. Available at <http://www. rnid.org. uk/html/factsheets/general_statistics_on_deafness.htm>.

Conclusion

Enid Mante-Meijer, Leslie Haddon and Eugène Loos

This book clearly covers very diverse fields and approaches to the study of ICTs, but there are some themes that cut across both the individual chapters and the sections. Some of these key themes, which are recurrent in the study of ICTs, will be outlined briefly below. These are disciplinary contributions, the symbolic nature of technologies, the influence of design on the experience of ICTs and the role of users in shaping design, the social constraints influencing usage and strategies in evaluating the social consequences of innovations.

Disciplinary Contributions

At the heart of the Helsinki conference, and the wider COST project, from which these chapters were drawn (see also Origins and questions in the Introduction) is the principle that we benefit from looking beyond our own specialism to appreciate the contributions that different disciplines, themselves containing multiple approaches, have to make (Haddon et al., 2005). In the first part of this book we highlighted this with examples from psychology (Beckers et al., Contarello et al.), economics (Turk et al.) and design (Jensen at al.). But different disciplines continued to be reflected in the rest of the book, including law (Gies), informatics (Bărbat et al.) and various different types of contribution from sociology (for example Pierson, De Jong and Mante-Meijer, Sourbati, Loos, Carmagnet et al.). This stresses the fact that the adoption and domestication of ICTs is a far reaching phenomenon that permeates all aspects of human life.

ICTs' Symbolic Meaning

The adoption and domestication of ICTs is a profoundly social phenomenon driven by the ways in which people make sense of their environment:

> Rather than talking about adapting to an external environment, it may be more correct to argue that organizing consists of adapting to an enacted environment, an environment which is *constituted by* the actions of interdependent human actors. (...) The phrase "enacted environment" preserves the crucial distinction that we wish to make, the most important being that the human *creates* the environment to which the system then adapts. The human actor does not *react* to an environment, he *enacts* it. (Weick, 1969: 27, 64)

Apart from users evaluating the functionality of various ICTs, part of the way in which they make sense of that environment, and part of this process of enacting it, is through the symbolic meaning of ICTs and of the practices that involve their use. For example, the chapter on the social representations of ICTs (and of the body) looks at the more general social meaning of certain technologies in order to evaluate how acceptable they are (Contarello et al.). The chapter on divorce self-help sites argued for the gendered nature of this particular innovation (Gies). We saw how there were different meanings of telework for different types of teleworkers (De Jong and Mante-Meijer). Within organisations we had an example of how social workers symbolically understood their work and their relationship to clients and organisation (Loos) and in the study of the elderly in sheltered accommodation we had a discussion of images of elderly people's relation to technology in general and also what electronic delivery of services meant for this particular group of elderly people (Sourbati). This broad range shows just how we can investigate the symbolism associated with both ICTs and users in multiple, and very different, ways.

Designing ICTs: A Social Shaping Perspective

Several of the chapters illustrate the different ways in which we can reflect upon the design of ICTs, of interest, given the social shaping perspective that informs this volume more generally. We have insights into the approach to design of design teams themselves (Jensen et al). There are recommendations relating to design for non-exclusion by taking disabilities into account (Gladstone) and a focus on the very ethics of design (Bărbat et al.) The family web-site chapter showed how design has a bearing upon the very content that appeared online (Carmagnat et al.). We saw how divorce self-help websites in some senses offered a package that entailed far more than the face-to-face professional advice (Gies). Meanwhile, the workings of a new organisational systems affected how its users felt, causing decreased social interaction amongst media staff in one study (Rintala). Quite often the outcomes of the design give way to unexpected, not always desired, results and consequences which ask for new solutions and new ways of working. Technology is perceived and shaped in interaction with the user. One thing that is clear from these design studies is the importance not only of looking into the apparent advantages of the new technology, but also into the possible alienating, undesirable side effects, as a consequence of the social structure of which the user forms a part.

Many of those same chapters had some comments about the input (or lack of input) of potential users in design, the focus of numerous other papers published from the same conference (Haddon et al., 2005). Once again, this came in diverse forms, such as using feedback from particular users as a starting point for design (Jensen et al.), management seeking feedback about workers' potential responses to design innovations (Loos, Halonen), and utilising aggregated data about users as inputs into microsimulations (Turk et al.). Meanwhile, a discussion of inclusive cases could draw upon the accumulated studies of the experience of disabled users as a basis for making general design recommendations (Gladstone). One important lesson of Gladstone's study is that even if users are involved in the design of technology, we still have to be aware of the technological leap between laboratory and real life. The world in which people live is far more complex than we can simulate in a lab situation.

The Role of Social Constraints

Since social constraints can have a bearing upon adoption and use, the implication is that we need to appreciate such constraints if we are to understand the experience of ICTs. For example, Pierson shows the diverse considerations that shaped ICT take-up by SMEs and in some cases, indeed in some industry sections, such constraints led to a lack of take up. We saw how carers could be potential gatekeepers to elderly people's interest in and use of the Internet (Sourbati). But in this case study one constraint was that these carers did nothing to support that use. The 'option' to telework, and hence the constraints on such telework, depended on the very relationship between worker and the employing organisation (De Jong and Mante-Meijer). And in the case of the cable manufacturing company, the workers' lack of familiarity with computers in general and their questioning of the need for a new information system in particular created resistance to this particular innovation (Halonen). The adoption of an innovation is related to the people's points of view, their visions of the world (Malinowski, 1922: 25). Their reactions to ICTs are coloured by their perceptions of their goals, or how the technologies might fit into their lives and their capabilities to use them as well as anticipated (and real) reactions from their wider social environment. This means that the same innovation will evoke totally different reactions from different people and in different cultural environments. There is not one option as regards whether and how to use ICTs – the options are as manifold as are people.

Potential Social Consequences of the Adoption of ICTs

Finally, various contributors to this book draw attention to potential social consequences of the adoption of ICTs. Thus some chapter authors ask whether the availability and adoption of various ICTs lead to a 'digital divide', be that in terms of producing second class legal option support in the case of divorce self-help websites (Gies), disparities between the options open to disabled and more able-bodied users (Gladstone) or between those of SMEs and larger companies (Pierson). But in some other cases evaluations of any consequences are mixed, the self-help websites cited above being one example of this. To give another example, the ICTs introduced in the media company had mixed results both for different staff and for the very same staff, where in some cases a richer job content was traded off against less interaction with colleagues (Rintala). And in the case of social workers it was the potential for increased information sharing between these professionals that was counterposed to the potential loss of control by management (Loos). Most technical innovations are, at least in the beginning, a mixed blessing. Their adoption and domestication of ICTs is part of the socially dynamic forces that govern the lives of individuals and societies. Precisely for this reason it is very difficult to evaluate beforehand in which way particular ICTs will be beneficial or not and for whom. At least it is important to be aware of their mixed potentiality.

Challenging the Guiding Models and Principles Underlying the Technology Dream

In the introductory chapter we argued that in the information society as envisaged by the politicians and technologists technology must somehow be unconsciously integrated into people's lives (just as the car is for most car owners). But this process is also dynamic as the on-going development of ICT asks us to adapt our ways of communicating continuously and to maintain a positive attitude towards the ever-changing content of technology. In reality, as has been illustrated in various chapters in this book, there is still a good deal of reluctance to make use of ICTs, which makes the adoption of new devices and services unpredictable (Frissen and Pierson, 2004). In fact, the adoption process is, according to Fischer (1992), both continuously advancing and retreating as people develop their experience with technology or else they have to decide about the adoption anew if their circumstances change over their own life course (Haddon, 2004). For some, indeed, non-adoption and non-use might not be a temporary phenomenon, but rather a deliberate choice (Wyatt et al., 2002). And perhaps some of this is understandable given both the symbolic meanings discussed above and the very design of the ICTs that they encounter.

By counterpoising the utopian ideas of technologists and policy makers to the actual experience of users, we can challenge the guiding models and principles that underlie technology dreams. We have to think more carefully and critically, for example, about visions of ICT as solutions for re-structuring work and private time or for loosening the boundaries between the workplace and home. More generally we have to re-think any assumptions about the empowering role of ICT, as solutions for all the problems in society. Are ICTs as beneficial as assumed? What are the dangers and the elements of which we need to be cautious? Through examining and illustrating very specific experiences of particular ICTs, and through developing some general considerations outlined in this conclusion, this book has aimed to make a contribution to those types of discussions.

References

Fischer, C. (1992), *America Calling: A Social History of the Telephone to 1940* (Berkeley: University of California Press).

Frissen, V. and Pierson, J. (2004), *ISTs and User Behaviour*, Delft TNO STB 9.

Haddon, L. (2004), *Information and Communication Technologies in Everyday Life: A Concise Introduction and Research Guide* (Oxford: Berg).

Haddon, L., Mante, E.A., Sapio, B., Kommonen, K.-H., Fortunati, L. and Kant, A. (eds) (2005), *Everyday Innovators: Researching the Role of Users in Shaping ICTs* (Dordrecht: Springer).

Malinowski, B. (1922) *Argonauts of the Western Pacific* (London: Routledge & Kegan).

Weick, K.E (1969), *The Social Psychology of Organizing* (Reading: Blackwell).

Wyatt, S., Thomas, G. and Terranova, T. (2002), 'They Came, they Surfed, they went back to the Beach: Conceptualising Use and Non-Use of the Internet', in Woolgar, S. (ed.), *Virtual Society? Get Real* (Oxford: Oxford University Press).

Index